# The Books of
# PSALMS
— & —
# PROVERBS

This Book Is Presented to

_____

_____

By

_____

On

_____

*Your word is a lamp for my feet and a light for my path.*
Psalm 119:105

# The Books of
# PSALMS
— & —
# PROVERBS

**THE BIBLE FOR A LIFETIME™**

© 1995, 2003, 2013, 2014, 2019, 2020 by God's Word to the Nations Mission Society.
All rights reserved.

No part of this publication may be reproduced, stored in a retrieval system, or transmitted in any form or by any means—for example, electronic, photocopy, recording—without prior written permission of God's Word to the Nations Mission Society. The only exception is brief quotations in printed reviews.

Up to 250 Scripture verses may be quoted in any form (printed, written, visual, electronic, or audio) without written permission, provided that no more than half of any one book of the Bible is quoted, and the verses quoted do not amount to 25 percent of the text of the product in which they are quoted.

If the quotation is used in a product that uses GOD'S WORD® exclusively, the following copyright notice must be used:

Scripture is taken from GOD'S WORD.®
© 1995, 2003, 2013, 2014, 2019, 2020 by God's Word to the Nations Mission Society.
Used by permission.

However, if the product contains quotations from other translations, the following copyright notice must be used:

All Scripture marked with the designation "GW" is taken from GOD'S WORD.®
© 1995, 2003, 2013, 2014, 2019, 2020 by God's Word to the Nations Mission Society.
Used by permission.

For quotations over 250 verses and/or questions about these policies, please write to God's Word to the Nations Mission Society, P.O. Box 400, Orange Park, FL 32067-0400. You may also contact us through our web site: godsword.org.

Cover and interior design by Aespire® {aespire.com}.

GOD'S WORD® Bibles are available in:
- Deluxe Wide-Margin, ISBN-13: 978-0-9984477-4-2
- Deluxe Large-Print, ISBN-13: 978-0-9984477-3-5
- Large-Print Hardcover, ISBN-13: 978-0-9984477-2-8
- Large-Print Paperback, ISBN-13: 978-0-9984477-1-1
- eBook, ISBN-13: 978-0-9984477-5-9
- The Books of Psalms & Proverbs, 978-0-9984477-6-6

Visit godsword.org to obtain more information or purchase GOD'S WORD® products.

# CONTENTS

**Life Applications** .................................................... vi
Psalms.................................................................. 1
Proverbs ............................................................ 165
**The Translation Process of God's Word** ............................. 220
**About God's Word to the Nations** ...................................224

# LIFE APPLICATIONS

**Achievement,
Prosperity,
and Success**
Psalm 1:1–3
Proverbs 3:3–4
Proverbs 16:3, 20
Proverbs 21:5
Proverbs 22:4
Proverbs 28:13, 25

**Anger, Hatred,
and Revenge**
Psalm 37:8
Proverbs 10:12
Proverbs 15:18
Proverbs 16:32
Proverbs 22:24–25
Proverbs 29:22

**Arrogance
and Humility**
Psalm 138:6
Proverbs 11:2
Proverbs 15:33
Proverbs 16:18–19
Proverbs 18:12
Proverbs 21:4
Proverbs 27:2
Proverbs 29:23

**Attitude**
Proverbs 15:7

**Compassion,
Giving to Others,
and Serving Others**
Psalm 41:1–2
Psalm 112:5–9
Proverbs 12:10
Proverbs 18:16
Proverbs 19:17
Proverbs 28:27

**Confidence**
Psalm 71:5
Proverbs 3:26
Proverbs 14:26

**Contentment**
Psalm 131

**Criticism**
*How to handle it*
Proverbs 13:18
Proverbs 25:12

**Death**
Psalm 23
Psalm 48:14
Psalm 49:15
Psalm 68:20
Proverbs 12:28

**Decisions and
Guidance**
Psalm 25:4–12
Psalm 31:3
Psalm 43:3
Proverbs 1:1–5
Proverbs 11:3, 14
Proverbs 12:26
Proverbs 13:14
Proverbs 14:8

**Difficult Times**
Psalm 18:1–3
Psalm 23
Psalm 27
Psalm 34:15, 17–20, 22
Psalm 37:39
Psalm 42:1–3, 5
Psalm 46
Psalm 50:15
Psalm 57:1–3
Psalm 61:1–4
Psalm 62:8
Psalm 73:25–26
Psalm 138:7

**Discouragement**
Psalm 42
Psalm 55:22

**Duties of Children**
Proverbs 1:8–9
Proverbs 6:20–23
Proverbs 10:1
Proverbs 13:1
Proverbs 15:5
Proverbs 23:22

**Duties of Parents**
Psalm 78:4–7
Proverbs 13:24
Proverbs 23:13–14

**Encouragement**
*When lonely*
Psalm 23

*When fearful*
Psalm 23
Psalm 27:1–3
Psalm 46:1–2
Psalm 91
Psalm 121:1–8
Proverbs 3:25–26

*When afraid of death*
Psalm 23
Psalm 48:14
Psalm 49:15
Psalm 68:20
Proverbs 12:28

*When discouraged*
Psalm 42
Psalm 55:22

# Life Applications

*When facing difficult times*
Psalm 23
Psalm 27
Psalm 34:15, 17–20, 22
Psalm 42:1–3, 5
Psalm 46
Psalm 50:15
Psalm 57:1–3
Psalm 61:1–4
Psalm 62:8

*When sick or suffering*
Psalm 30:2
Psalm 41:3
Psalm 103:1–5
Psalm 147:3

*When tempted*
Proverbs 7:1–5

## Fear
Psalm 23:4
Psalm 27:1–3
Psalm 46:1–2
Psalm 91
Psalm 121:1–8
Proverbs 3:25–26
Proverbs 29:25

## God's Forgiveness
Psalm 19:12–14
Psalm 32
Psalm 103:11–14
Psalm 130

## Gossip
Psalm 34:13
Proverbs 11:13
Proverbs 26:20–22

## Guilt
Psalm 19:12–14
Psalm 25:4–18
Psalm 51:1–17
Psalm 103:12

## Honesty and Integrity
Psalm 1
Psalm 24:1–6

Psalm 37:21
Psalm 101:3–8
Psalm 119:113–117
Proverbs 8:13
Proverbs 11:1–3
Proverbs 12:17, 19
Proverbs 16:8
Proverbs 19:1

## Hope
Psalm 31:24
Psalm 42:11
Psalm 71:5

## Jealousy and Envy
Proverbs 27:4

## Joy and Happiness
Psalm 16:11
Psalm 112:1
Psalm 126:2–3

## Laziness
Proverbs 10:4–5
Proverbs 12:24
Proverbs 13:4
Proverbs 15:19
Proverbs 24:30–34

## Loneliness
Psalm 23:4

## Lying
Proverbs 6:12–19
Proverbs 19:5, 9
Proverbs 25:18

## Marriage
Proverbs 5:18–20

## Praying to God
*Why and how*
Psalm 34:17
Psalm 50:14–15
Psalm 55:17
Psalm 102:17
Psalm 145:18–19
Proverbs 15:29

## Sexual Sin
*How to avoid it*
Proverbs 5:1–21
Proverbs 6:32–35

## Sickness and Suffering
Psalm 30:2
Psalm 41:3
Psalm 103:1–5
Psalm 147:3

## Temptation to Sin
*How to overcome it*
Proverbs 7:1–5

## Thanking and Praising God
Psalm 9:1
Psalm 67
Psalm 96
Psalm 100
Psalm 105:1–3
Psalm 106:1–2
Psalm 111
Psalm 145
Psalm 150

## Wealth, Greed, and Materialism
Psalm 24:1
Psalm 49:16–17
Psalm 62:10
Proverbs 3:9–10, 27
Proverbs 11:24–26
Proverbs 13:22
Proverbs 19:17
Proverbs 21:17

## Wisdom
Proverbs 1:7
Proverbs 2:1–22
Proverbs 4:6–10
Proverbs 8:1–36
Proverbs 13:10
Proverbs 24:13–14

## AUTHOR
*The book of Psalms is a collection of songs and praises written by various authors. Included are David (73 Psalms), Solomon (2), the sons of Korah (12), Asaph (12), Ethan (1), Moses (1), and Heman (1). The authorship of the rest of the Psalms cannot be conclusively determined.*

## DATE
*The Psalms were collected over a long period of time. The form and design of the book today was most likely assembled over the years by temple personnel so the psalms could be used in worship. It was probably completed by the third century B.C.*

## BACKGROUND & PURPOSE
*The title of the book means "praises." But the term* psalms *is a more general word meaning all lyrical compositions that can be sung. The content of the various psalms may be historical, doctrinal, songs of petition, or songs of praise. The intention of these psalms is more than for singing; they may be used to express sorrow as well as joy. The priests had mournful tunes as well as joyful ones. The intent of the Psalms is to kindle in the souls of men and women a devotion and affection for God, the Creator and Lord.*

## MAJOR THEME
*The Psalms tell us much about God—his character, his love, his righteous dealings with men and women, his patient care, and his concern for those who call him Lord. Our response is to offer praise and thanksgiving to him.*

## OUTLINE
I. Book 1   1:1–41:13
II. Book 2   42:1–72:20
III. Book 3   73:1–89:52
IV. Book 4   90:1–106:48
V. Book 5   107:1–150:6

# PSALMS

## BOOK ONE
(Psalms 1–41)

### Psalm 1

1 Blessed is the person who does not
    follow the advice of wicked people,
        take the path of sinners,
        or join the company of mockers.
2 Rather, he delights in the teachings of the Lord
    and reflects on his teachings day and night.
3 He is like a tree planted beside streams—
    a tree that produces fruit in season
    and whose leaves do not wither.
He succeeds in everything he does.[a]

4 Wicked people are not like that.
    Instead, they are like husks that the wind blows away.
5     That is why wicked people will not be able to stand
            in the judgment
        and sinners will not be able to stand where righteous
                people gather.

6 The Lord knows the way of righteous people,
    but the way of wicked people will end.

### Psalm 2

1 Why do the nations gather together?
    Why do their people devise useless plots?
2     Kings take their stands.
        Rulers make plans together
            against the Lord and against his Messiah[b] by saying,
3         "Let's break apart their chains
                and shake off their ropes."

4 The one enthroned in heaven laughs.
    The Lord makes fun of them.

---

[a] 1:3 Or "and its leaves do not wither, and whatever it produces thrives."
[b] 2:2 Or "anointed one."

⁵ Then he speaks to them in his anger.
　　In his burning anger he terrifies them by saying,
⁶ 　"I have installed my own king on Zion, my holy mountain."

⁷ I will announce the Lord's decree.
　He said to me:
　　"You are my Son.
　　　Today I have become your Father.
⁸ 　　　Ask me, and I will give you the nations
　　　　as your inheritance
　　　　and the ends of the earth as your own possession.
⁹ 　　　　You will break them with an iron scepter.
　　　　You will smash them to pieces like pottery."

¹⁰ Now, you kings, act wisely.
　Be warned, you rulers of the earth!
¹¹ 　Serve the Lord with fear, and rejoice with trembling.
¹² 　Kiss the Son, or he will become angry
　　and you will die on your way
　　　because his anger will burst into flames.
　Blessed is everyone who takes refuge in him.

## Psalm 3

*A psalm by David when he fled from his son Absalom.*

¹ O Lord, look how my enemies have increased!
　　Many are attacking me.
² 　Many are saying about me,
　　　"Even with God ⌐on his side⌐,
　　　he won't be victorious."　　　　　　　　　　*Selah*

³ But you, O Lord, are a shield that surrounds me.
　　You are my glory.
　　You hold my head high.

⁴ I call aloud to the Lord,
　　and he answers me from his holy mountain.　　*Selah*
⁵ I lie down and sleep.
　I wake up again because the Lord continues to
　　　support me.
⁶ I am not afraid of the tens of thousands
　　who have taken positions against me on all sides.

⁷ Arise, O Lord!

Save me, O my God!
   You have slapped all my enemies in the face.
   You have smashed the teeth of wicked people.
⁸   Victory belongs to the LORD!
      May your blessing rest on your people.              *Selah*

## Psalm 4
*For the choir director; with stringed instruments;*
*a psalm by David.*

¹ Answer me when I call, O God of my righteousness.
    You have freed me from my troubles.
  Have pity on me, and hear my prayer!

² You important people,
    how long are you going to insult my honor?
    How long are you going to love what is empty
      and seek what is a lie?                             *Selah*
³   Know that the LORD singles out godly people for himself.
      The LORD hears me when I call to him.
⁴   Tremble and do not sin.
      Think about this on your bed and remain quiet.     *Selah*
⁵   Offer the sacrifices of righteousness
      by trusting the LORD.

⁶ Many are saying, "Who can show us anything good?"
    Let the light of your presence shine on us, O LORD.
⁷   You put more joy in my heart
      than when their grain and new wine increase.
⁸ I fall asleep in peace the moment I lie down
    because you alone, O LORD, enable me to live securely.

## Psalm 5
*For the choir director; for flutes; a psalm by David.*

¹ Open your ears to my words, O LORD.
  Consider my innermost thoughts.
² Pay attention to my cry for help, my king and my God,
    because I pray only to you.
³   In the morning, O LORD, hear my voice.
      In the morning I lay my needs in front of you,
        and I wait.

⁴ You are not a God who takes pleasure in wickedness.
    Evil will never be your guest.

⁵ Those who brag cannot stand in your sight.
 You hate all troublemakers.
⁶ You destroy those who tell lies.
  The Lord is disgusted with bloodthirsty and
    deceitful people.

⁷ But I will enter your house because of your great mercy.
  Out of reverence for you, I will bow toward your
    holy temple.
⁸ O Lord, lead me in your righteousness because of those
   who spy on me.
 Make your way in front of me smooth.

⁹ Nothing in their mouths is truthful.
   Destruction comes from their hearts.
    Their throats are open graves.
     They flatter with their tongues.

¹⁰ Condemn them, O God.
   Let their own schemes be their downfall.
   Throw them out for their many crimes
     because they have rebelled against you.
¹¹ But let all who take refuge in you rejoice.
   Let them sing with joy forever.
   Protect them, and let those who love your name
     triumph in you.
¹²   You bless righteous people, O Lord.
    Like a large shield, you surround them with
      your favor.

## Psalm 6

*For the choir director; with stringed instruments, on the sheminith;*<sup>a</sup> *a psalm by David.*

¹ O Lord, do not punish me in your anger
   or discipline me in your rage.
² Have pity on me, O Lord, because I am weak.
  Heal me, O Lord, because my bones shake with terror.
³   My soul has been deeply shaken with terror.
  But you, O Lord, how long … ?

⁴ Come back, O Lord.
  Rescue me.

---

*a* 6:1 Unknown musical term.

Save me because of your mercy!
5    In death, no one remembers you.
     In the grave, who praises you?

6  I am worn out from my groaning.
   My eyes flood my bed every night.
   I soak my couch with tears.
7  My eyes blur from grief.
       They fail because of my enemies.

8  Get away from me, all you troublemakers,
       because the LORD has heard the sound of my crying.
9      The LORD has heard my plea for mercy.
       The LORD accepts my prayer.
10 All my enemies will be put to shame and deeply shaken
       with terror.
   In a moment they will retreat and be put to shame.

## Psalm 7

*A shiggaion<sup>a</sup> by David; he sang it to the LORD about the ⌊slanderous⌋ words of Cush, a descendant of Benjamin.*

1  O LORD my God, I have taken refuge in you.
       Save me, and rescue me from all who are pursuing me.
2      Like a lion they will tear me to pieces
           and drag me off with no one to rescue me.

3  O LORD my God,
       if I have done this—
           if my hands are stained with injustice,
4      if I have paid back my friend with evil
           or rescued someone who has no reason
               to attack me—

5  then let the enemy chase me and catch me.
       Let him trample my life into the ground.
       Let him lay my honor in the dust.              *Selah*

6  Arise in anger, O LORD.
   Stand up against the fury of my attackers.
   Wake up, my God.<sup>b</sup>
       You have already pronounced judgment.

---
<sup>a</sup>7:1 Unknown musical term.
<sup>b</sup>7:6 Greek; Masoretic Text "Wake up to me."

⁷ Let an assembly of people gather around you.
   Take your seat high above them.
⁸ The Lord judges the people of the world.
  Judge me, O Lord,
     according to my righteousness,
     according to my integrity.

⁹ Let the evil within wicked people come to an end,
     but make the righteous person secure,
        O righteous God who examines thoughts and emotions.
¹⁰ My shield is God above,
     who saves those whose motives are decent.

¹¹ God is a fair judge,
     a God who is angered by injustice every day.
¹²    If a person does not change, God sharpens his sword.
         By bending his bow, he makes it ready ⌊to shoot⌋.
¹³    He prepares his deadly weapons
         and turns them into flaming arrows.
¹⁴ See how that person conceives evil,
     is pregnant with harm,
        and gives birth to lies.
¹⁵ He digs a pit and shovels it out.
     Then he falls into the hole that he made ⌊for others⌋.
¹⁶ His mischief lands back on his own head.
   His violence comes down on top of him.

¹⁷ I will give thanks to the Lord for his righteousness.
   I will make music to praise the name of the
        Lord Most High.

## Psalm 8
*For the choir director; on the* gittith;*ᵃ a psalm by David.*

¹ O Lord, our Lord, how majestic is your name throughout
     the earth!

Your glory is sung above the heavens.
² From the mouths of little children and infants,
     you have built a fortress against your opponents
        to silence the enemy and the avenger.

---
ᵃ 8:1 Unknown musical term.

³ When I look at your heavens,
  the creation of your fingers,
  the moon and the stars that you have set in place—
⁴   what is a mortal that you remember him
    or the Son of Man that you take care of him?
⁵   You have made him a little lower than yourself.
    You have crowned him with glory and honor.
⁶   You have made him rule what your hands created.
    You have put everything under his control:
⁷    all the sheep and cattle, the wild animals,
⁸    the birds, the fish,
    whatever swims in the currents of the seas.

⁹ O Lord, our Lord, how majestic is your name throughout
  the earth!

## Psalm 9

*For the choir director; according to* muth labben;*ᵃ*
*a psalm by David.ᵇ*

¹ I will give ⌞you⌟ thanks, O Lord, with all my heart.
  I will tell about all the miracles you have done.
² I will find joy and be glad about you.
  I will make music to praise your name, O Most High.

³ When my enemies retreat, they will stumble and
    die in your presence.
⁴   You have defended my just cause:
    You sat down on your throne as a fair judge.
⁵   You condemned nations.
    You destroyed wicked people.
    You wiped out their names forever and ever.
⁶ The enemy is finished—in ruins forever.
  You have uprooted their cities.
    Even the memory of them has faded.

⁷ Yet, the Lord is enthroned forever.
  He has set up his throne for judgment.
⁸   He alone judges the world with righteousness.
    He judges ⌞its⌟ people fairly.
⁹ The Lord is a stronghold for the oppressed,
  a stronghold in times of trouble.

---
ᵃ9:1 Or "*almuth labben*"; unknown musical term.
ᵇ9:1 Some Hebrew manuscripts, Greek, and Latin treat Psalms 9 and 10 as one psalm.

¹⁰ Those who know your name trust you, O Lord,
  because you have never deserted those who
    seek your help.

¹¹ Make music to praise the Lord, who is enthroned in
    Zion.
  Announce to the nations what he has done.
¹²   The one who avenges murder has remembered
      oppressed people.
  He has never forgotten their cries.
¹³ Have pity on me, O Lord.
  Look at what I suffer because of those who hate me.
  You take me away from the gates of death
¹⁴   so that I may recite your praises one by one
    in the gates of Zion
      and find joy in your salvation.

¹⁵ The nations have sunk into the pit they have made.
    Their feet are caught in the net they have hidden
      ⌊to trap others⌋.
¹⁶ The Lord is known by the judgment he has carried out.
    The wicked person is trapped
      by the work of his own hands.          *Higgaion Selah*
¹⁷ Wicked people, all the nations who forget God,
    will return to the grave.
¹⁸ Needy people will not always be forgotten.
    Nor will the hope of oppressed people be lost forever.
¹⁹ Arise, O Lord.
    Do not let mortals gain any power.
    Let the nations be judged in your presence.
²⁰   Strike them with terror, O Lord.
    Let the nations know that they are ⌊only⌋ mortal.  *Selah*

## Psalm 10

¹ Why are you so distant, Lord?
  Why do you hide yourself in times of trouble?

² The wicked person arrogantly pursues oppressed people.
    He will be caught in the schemes that he planned.
³ The wicked person boasts about his selfish desires.
    He blesses robbers, but he curses the Lord.
⁴ He turns up his nose ⌊and says⌋, "God doesn't care."
    His every thought ⌊concludes⌋, "There is no God."
⁵   He always seems to succeed.
    Your judgments are beyond his understanding.

He spits at all his opponents.
6 He says to himself, "Nothing can shake me.
  I'll never face any trouble."
7 His mouth is full of cursing, deception, and oppression.
  Trouble and wrongdoing are on the tip of his tongue.
8 He waits in ambush in the villages.
  From his hiding places he kills innocent people.
  His eyes are on the lookout for victims.
9 He lies in his hiding place like a lion in his den.
  He hides there to catch oppressed people.
  He catches oppressed people when he draws them
      into his net.
10 ⌊His⌋ victims are crushed.
  They collapse,
      and they fall under ⌊the weight of⌋ his power.
11 He says to himself,
  "God has forgotten.
      He has hidden his face.
      He will never see it!"

12 Arise, O Lord!
  Lift your hand, O God.
  Do not forget oppressed people!
13    Why does the wicked person despise God?
      Why does he say to himself, "God doesn't care"?
14 You have seen ⌊it⌋; yes, you have taken note of
      trouble and grief
  and placed them under your control.
      The victim entrusts himself to you.
  You alone have been the helper of orphans.
15   Break the arm of the wicked and evil person.
      Punish his wickedness until you find no more.

16 The Lord is king forever and ever.
      The nations have vanished from his land.
17 You have heard the desire of oppressed people, O Lord.
  You encourage them.
  You pay close attention to them
18   in order to provide justice for orphans and
          oppressed people
      so that no mere mortal will terrify them again.

## Psalm 11
*For the choir director; by David.*

¹ I have taken refuge in the L&#xf024;ord.
　　How can you say to me:
　　　"Flee to your mountain like a bird?
² 　　Wicked people bend their bows.
　　　　They set their arrows against the strings
　　　　　to shoot in the dark at people whose motives
　　　　　　are decent.
³ 　　When the foundations ⌊of life⌋ are undermined,
　　　what can a righteous person do?"

⁴ The Lord is in his holy temple.
　The Lord's throne is in heaven.
　　His eyes see.
　　　They examine Adam's descendants.
⁵ The Lord tests righteous people,
　　but he hates wicked people and the ones who
　　　　love violence.
⁶ 　He rains down fire and burning sulfur upon
　　　wicked people.
　　He makes them drink from a cup filled with
　　　scorching wind.
⁷ The Lord is righteous.
　　He loves a righteous way of life.
　　　Decent people will see his face.

## Psalm 12
*For the choir director; on the* sheminith; *a psalm by David.*

¹ Help, O Lord.
　　No godly person is left.
　　Faithful people have vanished from among Adam's
　　　descendants!
² All people speak foolishly.
　　They speak with flattering lips. They say one thing
　　　but mean another.
³ 　May the Lord cut off every flattering lip
　　　and every bragging tongue
⁴ 　　that has said,
　　　　"We will overcome with our tongues.
　　　　　With lips such as ours, who can be our master?"

⁵ "Because oppressed people are robbed and needy
    people groan,
  I will now arise," says the LORD.
  "I will provide safety for those who long for it."
⁶ The promises of the LORD are pure,
    like silver refined in a furnace and purified seven times.
⁷ O LORD, you will protect them.
  You will keep each one safe from those people forever.
⁸   Wicked people parade around
        when immorality increases among Adam's
            descendants.

## Psalm 13

*For the choir director; a psalm by David.*

¹ How long, O LORD? Will you forget me forever?
  How long will you hide your face from me?
² How long must I make decisions alone
    with sorrow in my heart day after day?
  How long will my enemy triumph over me?

³ Look at me! Answer me, O LORD my God!
  Light up my eyes,
    or else I will die
⁴     and my enemy will say, "I have overpowered him."
        My opponents will rejoice because I have
            been shaken.

⁵ But I trust your mercy.
  My heart finds joy in your salvation.
⁶ I will sing to the LORD because he has been good to me.

## Psalm 14[a]

*For the choir director; by David.*

¹ Godless fools say in their hearts,
    "There is no God."
  They are corrupt.
  They do disgusting things.
    There is no one who does good things.
² The LORD looks down from heaven on Adam's
        descendants

---

[a] 14:1 Psalm 14 is virtually identical in wording to Psalm 53.

to see if there is anyone who acts wisely,
    if there is anyone who seeks help from God.
³ Everyone has turned away.
    Together they have become rotten to the core.
        No one, not even one person, does good things.
⁴ Are all those troublemakers,
    those who devour my people as if they were devouring food,
        so ignorant that they do not call on the LORD?
⁵ There they are—panic-stricken
    because God is with the person who is righteous.
⁶ They put the advice of oppressed people to shame
    because the LORD is their refuge.

⁷ If only salvation for Israel would come from Zion!
    When the LORD restores the fortunes of his people,
        Jacob will rejoice.
        Israel will be glad.

## Psalm 15
*A psalm by David.*

¹ O LORD, who may stay in your tent?
  Who may live on your holy mountain?

² The one who walks with integrity,
       does what is righteous,
       and speaks the truth within his heart.

³ The one who does not slander with his tongue,
       do evil to a friend,
       or bring disgrace on his neighbor.

⁴ The one who despises those rejected by God
       but honors those who fear the LORD.

   The one who makes a promise and does not break it,
       even though he is hurt by it.

⁵ The one who does not collect interest on a loan
       or take a bribe against an innocent person.

   Whoever does these things will never be shaken.

## Psalm 16
*A miktam<sup>a</sup> by David.*

1 Protect me, O God, because I take refuge in you.
2   I said to the LORD,
      "You are my Lord. Without you, I have nothing good."
3 Those who lead holy lives on earth
      are the noble ones who fill me with joy.
4 Those who quickly chase after other gods multiply
      their sorrows.
   I will not pour out their sacrificial offerings of blood
      or use my lips to speak their names.

5 The LORD is my inheritance and my cup.
      You are the one who determines my destiny.
6   Your boundary lines mark out pleasant places for me.
   Indeed, my inheritance is something beautiful.

7 I will praise the LORD, who advises me.
      My conscience warns me at night.
8 I always keep the LORD in front of me.
      When he is by my side, I cannot be moved.
9      That is why my heart is glad and my soul rejoices.
         My body rests securely
10         because you do not abandon my soul to the grave
            or allow your holy one to decay.
11 You make the path of life known to me.
      Complete joy is in your presence.
         Pleasures are by your side forever.

## Psalm 17
*A prayer by David.*

1 Hear my plea for justice, O LORD.
   Pay attention to my cry.
   Open your ears to my prayer,
      ⌊which comes⌋ from lips free from deceit.
2 Let the verdict of my innocence come directly from you.
   Let your eyes observe what is fair.

---

<sup>a</sup>16:1 Unknown musical term.

³ You have probed my heart.
You have confronted me at night.
You have tested me like silver,
   but you found nothing wrong.
I have determined that my mouth will not sin.
⁴ I have avoided cruelty because of your word.
   In spite of what others have done,
⁵    my steps have remained firmly in your paths.
   My feet have not slipped.
⁶ I have called on you because you answer me, O God.
   Turn your ear toward me.
   Hear what I have to say.
⁷    Reveal your miraculous deeds of mercy,
     O Savior of those who find refuge by your side
      from those who attack them.
⁸    Guard me as if I were the pupil in your eye.
   Hide me in the shadow of your wings.
⁹    Hide me from wicked people who violently attack me,
     from my deadly enemies who surround me.

¹⁰ They have shut out all feeling.
Their mouths have spoken arrogantly.
¹¹ They have tracked me down.
They have surrounded me.
They have focused their attention on throwing me
   to the ground.
¹²    Each one of them is like a lion eager to tear ⌊its prey⌋
     apart
   and like a young lion crouching in hiding places.

¹³ Arise, O Lord; confront them!
Bring them to their knees!
   With your sword rescue my life from wicked people.
¹⁴    With your power rescue me from mortals, O Lord,
     from mortals who enjoy their inheritance only
      in this life.
     You fill their bellies with your treasure.
     Their children are satisfied ⌊with it⌋,
      and they leave what remains to their children.

¹⁵ I will see your face when I am declared innocent.
   When I wake up, I will be satisfied ⌊with seeing⌋ you.

# Psalm 18[a]

*For the choir director; by David, the servant of the Lord. He sang this song to the Lord when the Lord rescued him from all his enemies, especially from Saul. He said,*

1 I love you, O Lord, my strength.
2 The Lord is my rock and my fortress and my Savior,
    my God, my rock in whom I take refuge,
        my shield, and the strength of my salvation,
            my stronghold.
3 The Lord should be praised.
    I called on him, and I was saved from my enemies.

4 The ropes of death had become tangled around me.
    The torrents of destruction had overwhelmed me.
5     The ropes of the grave had surrounded me.
    The clutches of death had confronted me.

6 I called on the Lord in my distress.
    I cried to my God for help.
        He heard my voice from his temple,
            and my cry for help reached his ears.

7 Then the earth shook and quaked.
    Even the foundations of the mountains trembled.
        They shook violently because he was angry.
8 Smoke went up from his nostrils,
    and a raging fire came out of his mouth.
        Glowing coals flared up from it.
9 He spread apart the heavens
    and came down with a dark cloud under his feet.
10 He rode on one of the angels[b] as he flew,
    and he soared on the wings of the wind.
11 He made the darkness his hiding place,
    the dark rain clouds his covering.
12 Out of the brightness in front of him,
    those rain clouds passed by with hailstones
        and lightning.
13 The Lord thundered in the heavens.
    The Most High made his voice heard with hailstones
        and lightning.
14 He shot his arrows and scattered them.

---

[a] 18:1 Psalm 18 is virtually identical in wording to 2 Samuel 22.
[b] 18:10 Or "cherubim."

>       He flashed streaks of lightning and threw them
>           into confusion.
> ¹⁵   Then the ocean floor could be seen.
>       The foundations of the earth were laid bare
>           at your stern warning, O Lord,
>               at the blast of the breath from your nostrils.

¹⁶ He reached down from high above and took hold of me.
   He pulled me out of the raging water.
¹⁷ He rescued me from my strong enemy
     and from those who hated me,
       because they were too strong for me.
¹⁸ On the day when I faced disaster, they confronted me,
     but the Lord came to my defense.
¹⁹     He brought me out to a wide-open place.
       He rescued me because he was pleased with me.

²⁰ The Lord rewarded me
     because of my righteousness,
     because my hands are clean.
   He paid me back
²¹   because I have kept the ways of the Lord
       and I have not wickedly turned away from my God,
²²   because all his judgments are in front of me
       and I have not turned away from his laws.
²³       I was innocent as far as he was concerned.
         I have kept myself from guilt.
²⁴ The Lord paid me back
     because of my righteousness,
     because he can see that my hands are clean.

²⁵ ⌊In dealing⌋ with faithful people you are faithful,
     with innocent people you are innocent,
²⁶   with pure people you are pure.
   ⌊In dealing⌋ with devious people you are clever.

²⁷ You save humble people,
     but you bring down a conceited look.
²⁸ O Lord, you light my lamp.
     My God turns my darkness into light.
²⁹     With you I can attack a line of soldiers.
       With my God I can break through barricades.

³⁰ God's way is perfect!
     The promise of the Lord has proven to be true.

He is a shield to all those who take refuge in him.
³¹ Who is God but the LORD?
  Who is a rock except our God?
³² God arms me with strength
  and makes my way perfect.
³³ He makes my feet like those of a deer
  and gives me sure footing on high places.
³⁴ He trains my hands for battle
  so that my arms can bend an ⌞archer's⌟ bow
    of bronze.
³⁵ You have given me the shield of your salvation.
Your right hand supports me.
Your gentleness makes me great.
³⁶ You make a wide path for me to walk on
  so that my feet do not slip.
³⁷ I chased my enemies and caught up with them.
I did not return until I had ended their lives.
³⁸ I wounded them so badly that they were unable to get up.
  They fell under my feet.
³⁹ You armed me with strength for battle.
You made my opponents bow at my feet.
⁴⁰ You made my enemies turn their backs to me,
  and I destroyed those who hated me.
⁴¹ They cried out for help, but there was no one to save them.
They cried out to the LORD, but he did not answer them.
⁴² I beat them into a powder as fine as the dust blown
    by the wind.
I threw them out as though they were dirt on the streets.
⁴³ You rescued me from my conflicts with the people.
You made me the leader of nations.
  A people I did not know will serve me:
⁴⁴ As soon as they hear of me, they will obey me.
  Foreigners will cringe in front of me.
⁴⁵ Foreigners will lose heart,
    and they will tremble when they come out
      of their fortifications.

⁴⁶ The LORD lives!
  Thanks be to my rock!
    May God my Savior be honored.
⁴⁷ God gives me vengeance!
  He brings people under my authority.
⁴⁸ He saves me from my enemies.
    You lift me up above my opponents.
    You rescue me from violent people.

⁴⁹ That is why I will give thanks to you, O Lord, among
      the nations
   and make music to praise your name.
⁵⁰ He gives great victories to his king.
   He shows mercy to his anointed,
      to David, and to his descendant*ᵃ* forever.

## Psalm 19

*For the choir director; a psalm by David.*

¹ The heavens declare the glory of God,
      and the sky displays what his hands have made.
² One day tells a story to the next.
   One night shares knowledge with the next
³    without talking,
      without words,
      without their voices being heard.
⁴ ⌊Yet,⌋ their sound has gone out into the entire world,
      their message to the ends of the earth.
   He has set up a tent in the heavens for the sun,
⁵    which comes out of its chamber like a bridegroom.
         Like a champion, it is eager to run its course.
⁶       It rises from one end of the heavens.
         It circles around to the other.
            Nothing is hidden from its heat.

⁷ The teachings of the Lord are perfect.
      They renew the soul.
   The testimony of the Lord is dependable.
      It makes gullible people wise.
⁸ The instructions of the Lord are correct.
      They make the heart rejoice.
   The command of the Lord is radiant.
      It makes the eyes shine.
⁹ The fear of the Lord is pure.
      It endures forever.
   The decisions of the Lord are true.
      They are completely fair.
¹⁰   They are more desirable than gold, even the finest gold.
      They are sweeter than honey, even the drippings
         from a honeycomb.
¹¹      As your servant I am warned by them.
         There is a great reward in following them.

---

*ᵃ*18:50 Or "to his descendants."

¹² Who can notice every mistake?
   Forgive my hidden faults.
¹³ Keep me from sinning.
   Do not let anyone gain control over me.
      Then I will be blameless,
         and I will be free from any great offense.

¹⁴ May the words from my mouth and the thoughts
      from my heart
   be acceptable to you, O LORD, my rock and
      my defender.

## Psalm 20
*For the choir director; a psalm by David.*

¹ The LORD will answer you in times of trouble.
   The name of the God of Jacob will protect you.
² He will send you help from his holy place
   and support you from Zion.
³ He will remember all your grain offerings
   and look with favor on your burnt offerings.     *Selah*
⁴ He will give you your heart's desire
   and carry out all your plans.

⁵ We will joyfully sing about your victory.
   We will wave our flags in the name of our God.
   The LORD will fulfill all your requests.

⁶ Now I know that the LORD will give victory to his
      anointed king.
   He will answer him from his holy heaven
      with mighty deeds of his powerful hand.
⁷ Some ⌊rely⌋ on chariots and others on horses,
   but we will boast in the name of the LORD our God.
⁸    They will sink to their knees and fall,
      but we will rise and stand firm.

⁹ Give victory to the king, O LORD.
   Answer us when we call.

## Psalm 21
*For the choir director; a psalm by David.*

¹ The king finds joy in your strength, O LORD.
   What great joy he has in your victory!

² You gave him his heart's desire.
   You did not refuse the prayer from his lips. *Selah*
³ You welcomed him with the blessings of good things
   and set a crown of fine gold on his head.
⁴ He asked you for life.
   You gave him a long life, forever and ever.
⁵ Because of your victory his glory is great.
   You place splendor and majesty on him.
⁶ Yes, you made him a blessing forever.
   You made him glad with the joy of your presence.
⁷ Indeed, the king trusts the Lord,
   and through the mercy of the Most High, he will not be moved.

⁸ Your hand will discover all your enemies.
   Your powerful hand will find all who hate you.
⁹ When you appear, you will make them ⌊burn⌋ like a blazing furnace.
   The Lord will swallow them up in his anger.
   Fire will devour them.
¹⁰ You will destroy their children from the earth
   and their offspring from among Adam's descendants.
¹¹ Although they scheme and plan evil against you,
   they will not succeed.
¹² They turn their backs ⌊and flee⌋
   because you aim your bow at their faces.

¹³ Arise, O Lord, in your strength.
   We will sing and make music to praise your power.

## Psalm 22

*For the choir director; according to* ayyeleth hashachar;*ᵃ*
*a psalm by David.*

¹ My God, my God,
   why have you abandoned me?
   Why are you so far away from helping me,
   so far away from the words of my groaning?
² My God,
   I cry out by day, but you do not answer—
   also at night, but I find no rest.

---

ᵃ 22:1 Unknown musical term.

³ Yet, you are holy, enthroned on the praises of Israel.
⁴ Our ancestors trusted you.
   They trusted, and you rescued them.
⁵ They cried to you and were saved.
   They trusted you and were never disappointed.

⁶ Yet, I am a worm and not a man.
I am scorned by humanity and despised by people.
⁷ All who see me make fun of me.
   Insults pour from their mouths.
     They shake their heads and say,
⁸      "Put yourself in the Lord's hands.
         Let the Lord save him!
         Let God rescue him since he is pleased with him!"
⁹ Indeed, you are the one who brought me out of the womb,
   the one who made me feel safe at my mother's breasts.
¹⁰ I was placed in your care from birth.
   From my mother's womb you have been my God.

¹¹ Do not be so far away from me.
   Trouble is near, and there is no one to help.
¹²    Many bulls have surrounded me.
       Strong bulls from Bashan have encircled me.
¹³    They have opened their mouths to attack me
       like ferocious, roaring lions.
¹⁴ I am poured out like water,
   and all my bones are out of joint.
     My heart is like wax.
       It has melted within me.
¹⁵ My strength is dried up like pieces of broken pottery.
My tongue sticks to the roof of my mouth.
   You lay me down in the dust of death.
¹⁶ Dogs have surrounded me.
A mob has encircled me.
   They have pierced my hands and feet.
¹⁷    I can count all my bones.
People stare.
   They gloat over me.
¹⁸    They divide my clothes among themselves.
   They throw dice for my clothing.

¹⁹ Do not be so far away, O Lord.
   Come quickly to help me, O my strength.
²⁰ Rescue my soul from the sword,
   my life from vicious dogs.

²¹ Save me from the mouth of the lion
    and from the horns of wild oxen.

You have answered me.

²² I will tell my people about your name.
   I will praise you within the congregation.
²³ All who fear the Lord, praise him!
   All you descendants of Jacob, glorify him!
      Stand in awe of him, all you descendants of Israel.
²⁴ The Lord has not despised or been disgusted
    with the plight of the oppressed one.
      He has not hidden his face from that person.
         The Lord heard when that oppressed person
           cried out to him for help.
²⁵ My praise comes from you while I am among those
    assembled for worship.
   I will fulfill my vows in the presence of those who fear
    the Lord.
²⁶    Oppressed people will eat until they are full.
   Those who look to the Lord will praise him.
      May you live forever.
²⁷ All the ends of the earth will remember and return
    to the Lord.
   All the families from all the nations will worship you
²⁸    because the kingdom belongs to the Lord
    and he rules the nations.
²⁹ All prosperous people on earth will eat and worship.
   All those who go down to the dust will kneel in front
      of him,
    even those who are barely alive.
³⁰ There will be descendants who serve him,
    a generation that will be told about the Lord.
³¹ They will tell people yet to be born about his
      righteousness—
   that he has finished it.

## Psalm 23
*A psalm by David.*

¹ The Lord is my shepherd.
   I am never in need.
²    He makes me lie down in green pastures.
     He leads me beside peaceful waters.
³    He renews my soul.

He guides me along the paths of righteousness
> for the sake of his name.
4 Even though I walk through the dark valley of death,
because you are with me, I fear no harm.
> Your rod and your staff give me courage.

5 You prepare a banquet for me while my enemies watch.
You anoint my head with oil.
> My cup overflows.

6 Certainly, goodness and mercy will stay close to me
> all the days of my life,
> and I will remain in the Lord's house for days
>> without end.

## Psalm 24
*A psalm by David.*

1 The earth and everything it contains are the Lord's.
The world and all who live in it are his.
2 He laid its foundation on the seas
> and set it firmly on the rivers.

3 Who may go up the Lord's mountain?
Who may stand in his holy place?
4 ⌊The one who⌋ has clean hands and a pure heart
> and does not long for what is false
> or lie when he is under oath.
5 ⌊This person⌋ will receive a blessing from the Lord
> and righteousness from God, his savior.
6 This is the person who seeks him,
> who searches for the face of the God of Jacob.[a]     *Selah*

7 Lift your heads, you gates.
Be lifted, you ancient doors,
> so that the king of glory may come in.

8 Who is this king of glory?
> The Lord, strong and mighty!
> The Lord, heroic in battle!

9 Lift your heads, you gates.

---

[a] 24:6 A few Hebrew manuscripts, Greek, Syriac; Masoretic Text "your face, Jacob."

> Be lifted, you ancient doors,
>> so that the king of glory may come in.

<sup>10</sup> Who, then, is this king of glory?
>> The LORD of Armies is the king of glory!     *Selah*

## Psalm 25<sup>*a*</sup>
*By David.*

<sup>1</sup> To you, O LORD, I lift my soul.
<sup>2</sup> I trust you, O my God.
>> Do not let me be put to shame.
>> Do not let my enemies triumph over me.

<sup>3</sup> No one who waits for you will ever be put to shame,
>> but all who are unfaithful will be put to shame.

<sup>4</sup> Make your ways known to me, O LORD,
>> and teach me your paths.

<sup>5</sup> Lead me in your truth and teach me
>> because you are God, my savior.
>> I wait all day long for you.

<sup>6</sup> Remember, O LORD, your compassionate and merciful deeds.
>> They have existed from eternity.

<sup>7</sup> Do not remember the sins of my youth or my rebellious ways.
>> Remember me, O LORD, in keeping with your mercy and your goodness.

<sup>8</sup> The LORD is good and decent.
>> That is why he teaches sinners the way they should live.

<sup>9</sup> He leads humble people to do what is right,
>> and he teaches them his way.

<sup>10</sup> Every path of the LORD is ⌊one of⌋ mercy and truth
>> for those who cling to his promise<sup>*b*</sup> and written instructions.

<sup>11</sup> For the sake of your name, O LORD,
>> remove my guilt, because it is great.

<sup>12</sup> Who, then, is this person that fears the LORD?
>> He is the one whom the LORD will teach which path to choose.

<sup>13</sup>    He will enjoy good things in life,

---

<sup>*a*</sup>25:1 Psalm 25 is a poem in Hebrew alphabetical order.
<sup>*b*</sup>25:10 Or "covenant."

and his descendants will inherit the land.
¹⁴ The Lord advises those who fear him.
   He reveals to them the intent of his promise.

¹⁵ My eyes are always on the Lord.
   He removes my feet from traps.
¹⁶ Turn to me, and have pity on me.
   I am lonely and oppressed.
¹⁷ Relieve my troubled heart,
   and bring me out of my distress.
¹⁸ Look at my misery and suffering,
   and forgive all my sins.
¹⁹ See how my enemies have increased in number,
   how they have hated me with vicious hatred!
²⁰ Protect my life, and rescue me!
  Do not let me be put to shame.
   I have taken refuge in you.
²¹ Integrity and honesty will protect me because
      I wait for you.
²² Rescue Israel, O God, from all its troubles!

## Psalm 26
*By David.*

¹ Judge me favorably, O Lord,
   because I have walked with integrity
      and I have trusted you without wavering.
² Examine me, O Lord, and test me.
  Look closely into my heart and mind.
³   I see your mercy in front of me.
   I walk in the light of your truth.
⁴   I did not sit with liars,
      and I will not be found among hypocrites.
⁵   I have hated the mob of evildoers
      and will not sit with wicked people.
⁶   I will wash my hands in innocence.
   I will walk around your altar, O Lord,
⁷      so that I may loudly sing a hymn of thanksgiving
         and tell about all your miracles.

⁸ O Lord, I love the house where you live,
   the place where your glory dwells.

⁹ Do not sweep away my soul along with hardened sinners
   or my life along with bloodthirsty people.

¹⁰     Evil schemes are in their hands.
         Their right hands are full of bribes.
¹¹ But I walk with integrity.
     Rescue me, and have pity on me.
¹² My feet stand on level ground.
     I will praise the Lord with the choirs in worship.

## Psalm 27
*By David.*

¹ The Lord is my light and my salvation.
     Who is there to fear?
  The Lord is my life's fortress.
     Who is there to be afraid of?

² Evildoers closed in on me to tear me to pieces.
     My opponents and enemies stumbled and fell.
³       Even though an army sets up camp against me,
           my heart will not be afraid.
         Even though a war breaks out against me,
           I will still have confidence ⌊in the Lord⌋.

⁴ I have asked one thing from the Lord.
  This I will seek:
       to remain in the Lord's house all the days of my life
         in order to gaze at the Lord's beauty
           and to search for an answer in his temple.
⁵ He hides me in his shelter when there is trouble.
  He keeps me hidden in his tent.
  He sets me high on a rock.
⁶ Now my head will be raised above my enemies
       who surround me.
  I will offer sacrifices with shouts of joy in his tent.
  I will sing and make music to praise the Lord.
⁷ Hear, O Lord, when I cry aloud.
  Have pity on me, and answer me.
⁸ ⌊When you said,⌋
     "Seek my face,"
       my heart said to you,
         "O Lord, I will seek your face."ᵃ
⁹       Do not hide your face from me.
         Do not angrily turn me away.

---

ᵃ 27:8 Greek "My heart said to you, 'I have sought your face. O Lord, I will seek your face.'"

You have been my help.
　　Do not leave me!
　　　Do not abandon me, O God, my savior!
¹⁰ 　　　　Even if my father and mother abandon me,
　　the Lord will take care of me.
¹¹ Teach me your way, O Lord.
　Lead me on a level path
　　because I have enemies who spy on me.
¹² Do not surrender me to the will of my opponents.
　　False witnesses have risen against me.
　　　They breathe out violence.
¹³ I believe that I will see the goodness of the Lord
　in this world of the living.

¹⁴ Wait with hope for the Lord.
　Be strong, and let your heart be courageous.
　Yes, wait with hope for the Lord.

## Psalm 28
*By David.*

¹ O Lord, I call to you.
　O my rock, do not turn a deaf ear to me.
　　If you remain silent,
　　　I will be like those who go into the pit.
² Hear my prayer for mercy when I call to you for help,
　　when I lift my hands toward your most holy place.
³ Do not drag me away with wicked people,
　　with troublemakers who speak of peace with
　　　　their neighbors
　　but have evil in their hearts.
⁴ Pay them back for what they have done,
　　for their evil deeds.
　Pay them back for what their hands have done,
　　and give them what they deserve.
⁵ The Lord will tear them down and never build them
　　　　up again,
　　because they never consider what he has done
　　　or what his hands have made.

⁶ Thank the Lord!
　　He has heard my prayer for mercy!
⁷ The Lord is my strength and my shield.
　My heart trusted him, so I received help.

> My heart is triumphant; I give thanks to him with
> my song.
> ⁸ The Lord is the strength of his people
> and a fortress for the victory of his Messiah.ᵃ
> ⁹ Save your people, and bless those who belong to you.
> Be their shepherd, and carry them forever.

## Psalm 29

*A psalm by David.*

> ¹ Give to the Lord, you heavenly beings.
> Give to the Lord glory and power.
> ² Give to the Lord the glory his name deserves.
> Worship the Lord in ⌊his⌋ holy splendor.
>
> ³ The voice of the Lord rolls over the water.
> The God of glory thunders.
> The Lord shouts over raging water.
> ⁴ The voice of the Lord is powerful.
> The voice of the Lord is majestic.
> ⁵ The voice of the Lord breaks the cedars.
> The Lord splinters the cedars of Lebanon.
> ⁶ He makes Lebanon skip along like a calf
> and Mount Sirion like a wild ox.
> ⁷ The voice of the Lord strikes with flashes of lightning.
> ⁸ The voice of the Lord makes the wilderness tremble.
> The Lord makes the wilderness of Kadesh tremble.
> ⁹ The voice of the Lord splits the oaks
> and strips ⌊the trees of⌋ the forests bare.
> Everyone in his temple is saying, "Glory!"
>
> ¹⁰ The Lord sat enthroned over the flood.
> The Lord sits enthroned as king forever.
> ¹¹ The Lord will give power to his people.
> The Lord will bless his people with peace.

## Psalm 30

*A psalm by David sung at the dedication of the temple.*

> ¹ I will honor you highly, O Lord,
> because you have pulled me out ⌊of the pit⌋
> and have not let my enemies rejoice over me.

---

ᵃ 28:8 Or "anointed one."

² O Lord my God,
    I cried out to you for help,
        and you healed me.
³ O Lord, you brought me up from the grave.
    You called me back to life
        from among those who had gone into the pit.
⁴ Make music to praise the Lord, you faithful people
        who belong to him.
    Remember his holiness by giving thanks.
⁵ His anger lasts only a moment.
    His favor lasts a lifetime.
        Weeping may last for the night,
            but there is a song of joy in the morning.

⁶ When all was well with me, I said,
    "I will never be shaken."
⁷ O Lord, by your favor you have made my mountain
        stand firm.
    When you hid your face, I was terrified.
⁸ I will cry out to you, O Lord.
    I will plead to the Lord for mercy:
⁹    "How will you profit if my blood is shed,
        if I go into the pit?
    Will the dust ⌊of my body⌋ give thanks to you?
    Will it tell about your truth?"
¹⁰ Hear, O Lord, and have pity on me!
    O Lord, be my helper!
¹¹ You have changed my sobbing into dancing.
    You have removed my sackcloth and clothed me with joy
¹²    so that my soul*ᵃ* may praise you with music and
            not be silent.
    O Lord my God, I will give thanks to you forever.

## Psalm 31
*For the choir director; a psalm by David.*

¹ I have taken refuge in you, O Lord.
    Never let me be put to shame.
        Save me because of your righteousness.
²    Turn your ear toward me.
    Rescue me quickly.
    Be a rock of refuge for me,
        a strong fortress to save me.

---
*ᵃ*30:12 Or "glory."

³ Indeed, you are my rock and my fortress.
　　For the sake of your name, lead me and guide me.
⁴ 　You are my refuge,
　　　so pull me out of the net that they have secretly
　　　　laid for me.
⁵ 　　　Into your hands I entrust my spirit.
　　　　You have rescued me, O Lord, God of truth.

⁶ I hate those who cling to false gods, but I trust the Lord.
⁷ I will rejoice and be glad because of your mercy.
　　You have seen my misery.
　　You have known the troubles in my soul.
⁸ 　You have not handed me over to the enemy.
　　You have set my feet in a place where I can move freely.

⁹ Have pity on me, O Lord, because I am in distress.
　　My eyes, my soul, and my body waste away from grief.
¹⁰ 　My life is exhausted from sorrow,
　　　my years from groaning.
　　My strength staggers under ⌊the weight of⌋ my guilt,
　　　and my bones waste away.
¹¹ I have become a disgrace because of all my opponents.
　　I have become someone dreaded by my friends,
　　　even by my neighbors.
　　　　Those who see me on the street run away from me.
¹² I have faded from memory as if I were dead
　　　and have become like a piece of broken pottery.
¹³ I have heard the whispering of many people—
　　　terror on every side—
　　　　while they made plans together against me.
　　　　They were plotting to take my life.

¹⁴ I trust you, O Lord.
　I said, "You are my God."

¹⁵ My future is in your hands.
　　Rescue me from my enemies, from those who
　　　persecute me.
¹⁶ 　Smile on me.
　　Save me with your mercy.
¹⁷ O Lord, I have called on you, so do not let me
　　　be put to shame.
　Let wicked people be put to shame.
　Let them be silent in the grave.
¹⁸ Let ⌊their⌋ lying lips be speechless,

since they speak against righteous people with
      arrogance and contempt.

¹⁹ Your kindness is so great!
   You reserve it for those who fear you.
      Adam's descendants watch
         as you show it to those who take refuge in you.
²⁰    You hide them in the secret place of your presence
         from those who scheme against them.
      You keep them in a shelter,
         safe from quarrelsome tongues.
²¹ Thank the Lord!
   He has shown me the miracle of his mercy
      in a city under attack.
²² When I was panic-stricken, I said,
      "I have been cut off from your sight."
   But you heard my pleas for mercy when I cried out
      to you for help.
²³ Love the Lord, all you godly ones!
   The Lord protects faithful people,
      but he pays back in full those who act arrogantly.
²⁴ Be strong, all who wait with hope for the Lord,
   and let your heart be courageous.

## Psalm 32

*A psalm by David; a maskil.*ᵃ

¹ Blessed is the person whose disobedience is forgiven
   and whose sin is pardoned.
² Blessed is the person whom the Lord no longer
      accuses of sin
   and who has no deceitful thoughts.

³ When I kept silent ⌊about my sins⌋,
   my bones began to weaken because of my groaning
      all day long.
⁴ Day and night your hand laid heavily on me.
   My strength shriveled in the summer heat.          *Selah*

⁵ I made my sins known to you, and I did not cover up
      my guilt.
   I decided to confess them to you, O Lord.
      Then you forgave all my sins.                   *Selah*

---
ᵃ 32:1 Unknown musical term.

⁶ For this reason let all godly people pray to you
    when you may be found.
        Then raging floodwater will not reach them.

⁷ You are my hiding place.
  You protect me from trouble.
  You surround me with joyous songs of salvation.    *Selah*

⁸ ⌊The Lord says,⌋
  "I will instruct you.
  I will teach you the way that you should go.
  I will advise you as my eyes watch over you.
⁹ Don't be stubborn like a horse or mule.
    ⌊They need⌋ a bit and bridle in their mouth
        to restrain them,
    or they will not come near you."

¹⁰ Many heartaches await wicked people,
    but mercy surrounds those who trust the Lord.

¹¹ Be glad and find joy in the Lord, you righteous people.
  Sing with joy, all whose motives are decent.

## Psalm 33

¹ Joyfully sing to the Lord, you righteous people.
    Praising ⌊the Lord⌋ is proper for decent people.
² Give thanks with a lyre to the Lord.
  Make music for him on a ten-stringed harp.
³ Sing a new song to him.
  Play beautifully and joyfully on stringed instruments.

⁴ The Lord's word is correct,
    and everything he does is trustworthy.
⁵ The Lord loves righteousness and justice.
    His mercy fills the earth.
⁶ The heavens were made by the Lord's word
    and all the stars by the breath of his mouth.
⁷ He gathers the water in the sea like a dam
    and puts the oceans in his storehouses.
⁸ Let all the earth fear the Lord.
  Let all who live in the world stand in awe of him.
⁹ He spoke, and it came into being.
  He gave the order, and there it stood.

¹⁰ The Lord blocks the plans of the nations.

He frustrates the schemes of the people of the world.
11  The Lord's plan stands firm forever.
His thoughts stand firm in every generation.
12 Blessed is the nation whose God is the Lord.
Blessed are the people he has chosen as his own.

13 The Lord looks down from heaven.
He sees all of Adam's descendants.
14 From the place where he sits enthroned,
he looks down upon all who live on earth.
15 The one who formed their hearts
understands everything they do.

16 No king achieves a victory with a large army.
No warrior rescues himself by his own great strength.
17 Horses are not a guarantee for victory.
Their great strength cannot help someone escape.
18 The Lord's eyes are on those who fear him,
on those who wait with hope for his mercy
19    to rescue their souls from death
and keep them alive during a famine.

20 We wait for the Lord.
He is our help and our shield.
21   In him our hearts find joy.
In his holy name we trust.
22 Let your mercy rest on us, O Lord,
since we wait with hope for you.

## Psalm 34[a]

*By David when he pretended to be insane in the presence of Abimelech; Abimelech threw him out, so David left.*

1 I will thank the Lord at all times.
My mouth will always praise him.
2 My soul will boast about the Lord.
Those who are oppressed will hear it and rejoice.
3 Praise the Lord's greatness with me.
Let us highly honor his name together.
4 I went to the Lord for help.
He answered me and rescued me from all my fears.
5 All who look to him will be radiant.
Their faces will never be covered with shame.

---

[a] 34:1 Psalm 34 is a poem in Hebrew alphabetical order.

⁶ Here is a poor man who called out.
  The Lord heard him and saved him from all his troubles.
⁷ The Messenger of the Lord camps around those
      who fear him,
  and he rescues them.
⁸ Taste and see that the Lord is good.
  Blessed is the person who takes refuge in him.
⁹ Fear the Lord, you holy people who belong to him.
  Those who fear him are never in need.
¹⁰ Young lions go hungry and may starve,
   but those who seek the Lord's help have all the good
       things they need.
¹¹ Come, children, listen to me.
   I will teach you the fear of the Lord.
¹² Which of you wants a full life?
  Who would like to live long enough to enjoy good things?
¹³   Keep your tongue from saying evil things
       and your lips from speaking deceitful things.
¹⁴   Turn away from evil, and do good.
   Seek peace, and pursue it!
¹⁵ The Lord's eyes are on righteous people.
  His ears hear their cry for help.
¹⁶ The Lord confronts those who do evil
    in order to wipe out all memory of them from the earth.
¹⁷ ⌊Righteous people⌋ cry out.
    The Lord hears and rescues them from all their troubles.
¹⁸ The Lord is near to those whose hearts are humble.
  He saves those whose spirits are crushed.
¹⁹ The righteous person has many troubles,
   but the Lord rescues him from all of them.
²⁰    The Lord guards all of his bones.
    Not one of them is broken.
²¹ Evil will kill wicked people,
   and those who hate righteous people will be condemned.
²² The Lord protects the souls of his servants.
  All who take refuge in him will never be condemned.

## Psalm 35
*By David.*

¹ O Lord, attack those who attack me.
    Fight against those who fight against me.
²    Use your shields, ⌊both⌋ small and large.
    Arise to help me.
³    Hold your spear to block the way of those who pursue me.

Say to my soul, "I am your savior."

4 Let those who seek my life be put to shame and disgraced.
  Let those who plan my downfall be turned back in
      confusion.
5 Let them be like husks blown by the wind
  as the Messenger of the LORD chases them.
6 Let their path be dark and slippery
  as the Messenger of the LORD pursues them.
7 For no reason they hid their net in a pit.
  For no reason they dug the pit ⌊to trap me⌋.
8 Let destruction surprise them.
  Let the net that they hid catch them.
  Let them fall into their own pit and be destroyed.
9 My soul will find joy in the LORD
  and be joyful about his salvation.
10 All my bones will say, "O LORD, who can compare
      with you?
    You rescue the weak person from the one who is too
        strong for him
      and weak and needy people from the one
        who robs them."

11 Malicious people bring charges against me.
  They ask me things I know nothing about.
12 I am devastated
  because they pay me back with evil instead of good.
13 But when they were sick, I wore sackcloth.
  I humbled myself with fasting.
    When my prayer returned unanswered,
14     I walked around as if I were mourning for my friend
        or my brother.
      I was bent over as if I were mourning for my mother.

15 Yet, when I stumbled,
    they rejoiced and gathered together.
    They gathered together against me.
      Unknown attackers tore me apart without stopping.
16     With crude and abusive mockers,
        they grit their teeth at me.
17 O Lord, how long will you look on?
    Rescue me from their attacks.
    Rescue my precious life from the lions.
18     I will give you thanks in a large gathering.
      I will praise you in a crowd ⌊of worshipers⌋.

¹⁹ Do not let my treacherous enemies gloat over me.
   Do not let those who hate me for no reason wink ⌊at me⌋.
²⁰    They do not talk about peace.
         Instead, they scheme against the peaceful people
            in the land.
²¹    They open their big mouths and say about me,
         "Aha! Aha! Our own eyes have seen it."
²² You have seen it, O Lord.
   Do not remain silent.
O Lord, do not be so far away from me.
²³    Wake up, and rise to my defense.
   Plead my case, O my God and my Lord.
²⁴    Judge me by your righteousness, O Lord my God.
Do not let them gloat over me
²⁵    or think, "Aha, just what we wanted!"
Do not let them say, "We have swallowed him up."
²⁶ Let those who gloat over my downfall
      be thoroughly put to shame and confused.
   Let those who promote themselves at my expense
      be clothed with shame and disgrace.
²⁷ Let those who are happy when I am declared innocent
      joyfully sing and rejoice.
   Let them continually say, "The Lord is great.
      He is happy when his servant has peace."
²⁸ Then my tongue will tell about your righteousness,
      about your praise all day long.

## Psalm 36

*For the choir director; by David, the Lord's servant.*

¹ There is an inspired truth about the wicked person
      who has rebellion in the depths of his heart:
         He is not terrified of God.
²    He flatters himself and does not hate or ⌊even⌋
         recognize his guilt.
³ The words from his mouth are ⌊nothing but⌋ trouble
      and deception.
   He has stopped doing what is wise and good.
⁴    He invents trouble while lying on his bed
         and chooses to go the wrong direction.
   He does not reject evil.

⁵ O Lord, your mercy reaches to the heavens,
      your faithfulness to the skies.

⁶ Your righteousness is like the mountains of God,
    your judgments like the deep ocean.
        You save people and animals, O Lord.
⁷ Your mercy is so precious, O God,
    that Adam's descendants take refuge
        in the shadow of your wings.
⁸    They are refreshed with the rich foods in your house,
        and you make them drink from the river
            of your pleasure.
⁹ Indeed, the fountain of life is with you.
    In your light we see light.
¹⁰ Continue to show your mercy to those who know you
    and your righteousness to those whose motives are
        decent.
¹¹ Do not let the feet of arrogant people step on me
    or the hands of wicked people push me away.
¹²    Look at the troublemakers who have fallen.
        They have been pushed down and are unable
            to stand up again.

## Psalm 37 ᵃ
*By David.*

¹ Do not be preoccupied with evildoers.
Do not envy those who do wicked things.
²    They will quickly dry up like grass
        and wither away like green plants.
³ Trust the Lord, and do good things.
Live in the land, and practice being faithful.
⁴ Be happy with the Lord,
    and he will give you the desires of your heart.
⁵ Entrust your ways to the Lord.
Trust him, and he will act ⌊on your behalf⌋.
⁶    He will make your righteousness shine like a light,
        your just cause like the noonday sun.
⁷ Surrender yourself to the Lord, and wait patiently for
        him.
    Do not be preoccupied with ⌊an evildoer⌋ who succeeds
        in his way
        when he carries out his schemes.
⁸ Let go of anger, and leave rage behind.
    Do not be preoccupied.
        It only leads to evil.

---

ᵃ 37:1 Psalm 37 is a poem in Hebrew alphabetical order.

⁹ Evildoers will be cut off ⌊from their inheritance⌋,
  but those who wait with hope for the LORD will inherit
    the land.

¹⁰ In a little while a wicked person will vanish.
    Then you can carefully examine where he was,
      but there will be no trace of him.
¹¹ Oppressed people will inherit the land
    and will enjoy unlimited peace.
¹² The wicked person plots against a righteous one
    and grits his teeth at him.
¹³ The Lord laughs at him
    because he has seen that his time is coming.
¹⁴ Wicked people pull out their swords and bend their bows
    to kill oppressed and needy people,
    to slaughter those who are decent.
¹⁵ ⌊But⌋ their own swords will pierce their hearts,
    and their bows will be broken.
¹⁶ The little that the righteous person has is better
    than the wealth of many wicked people.
¹⁷ The arms of wicked people will be broken,
    but the LORD continues to support righteous people.
¹⁸ The LORD knows the daily ⌊struggles⌋ of innocent people.
    Their inheritance will last forever.
¹⁹ They will not be put to shame in trying times.
   Even in times of famine they will be satisfied.
²⁰ But wicked people will disappear.
    The LORD's enemies will vanish like the best part
      of a meadow.
    They will vanish like smoke.
²¹ A wicked person borrows, but he does not repay.
   A righteous person is generous and giving.
²²   Those who are blessed by him will inherit the land.
    Those who are cursed by him will be cut off.

²³ A person's steps are directed by the LORD,
    and the LORD delights in his way.
²⁴ When he falls, he will not be thrown down headfirst
    because the LORD holds on to his hand.
²⁵ I have been young, and now I am old,
    but I have never seen a righteous person abandoned
      or his descendants begging for food.
²⁶     He is always generous and lends freely.
       His descendants are a blessing.
²⁷ Avoid evil, do good, and live forever.

²⁸ The LORD loves justice,
   and he will not abandon his godly ones.
 They will be kept safe forever,
   but the descendants of wicked people will be cut off.
²⁹ Righteous people will inherit the land
   and live there permanently.
³⁰ The mouth of the righteous person reflects on wisdom.
   His tongue speaks what is fair.
³¹ The teachings of his God are in his heart.
   His feet do not slip.
³² The wicked person watches the righteous person
   and seeks to kill him.
³³ But the LORD will not abandon him to the wicked
       person's power
   or condemn him when he is brought to trial.
³⁴ Wait with hope for the LORD, and follow his path,
   and he will honor you by giving you the land.
       When wicked people are cut off, you will see it.

³⁵ I have seen a wicked person ⌊acting like⌋ a tyrant,
   spreading himself out like a large cedar tree.
³⁶ But he moved on, and now there is no trace of him.
   I searched for him, but he could not be found.
³⁷ Notice the innocent person,
   and look at the decent person,
       because the peacemaker has a future.
³⁸      But rebels will be completely destroyed.
           The future of wicked people will be cut off.
³⁹ The victory for righteous people comes from the LORD.
   He is their fortress in times of trouble.
⁴⁰ The LORD helps them and rescues them.
 He rescues them from wicked people.
 He saves them because they have taken refuge in him.

## Psalm 38

*A psalm by David; to be kept in mind.*

¹ O LORD, do not angrily punish me
   or discipline me in your wrath.
²     Your arrows have struck me.
       Your hand has struck me hard.
³ No healthy spot is left on my body
   because of your rage.
 There is no peace in my bones
   because of my sin.

⁴ My guilt has overwhelmed me.
　　Like a heavy load, it is more than I can bear.
⁵ My wounds smell rotten.
　　They fester because of my stupidity.
⁶ I am bent over and bowed down very low.
　　All day I walk around in mourning.
⁷ My insides are filled with burning pain,
　　and no healthy spot is left on my body.
⁸ I am numb and completely devastated.
　I roar because my heart's in turmoil.
⁹ You know all my desires, O Lord,
　　and my groaning has not been hidden from you.
¹⁰ My heart is pounding.
　　I have lost my strength.
　　　　Even the light of my eyes has left me.

¹¹ My loved ones and my friends keep their distance
　　and my relatives stand far away because of my sickness.
¹² Those who seek my life lay traps for me.
　Those who are out to harm me talk about ruining me.
　　All day long they think of ways to deceive me.
¹³ But I am like a person who cannot hear
　　and like a person who cannot speak.
¹⁴ I am like one who cannot hear
　　and who can offer no arguments.

¹⁵ But I wait with hope for you, O Lord.
　You will answer, O Lord, my God.
¹⁶ I said, "Do not let them gloat over me.
　　When my foot slips,
　　　　do not let them promote themselves at my expense."
¹⁷ I am ready to fall.
　I am continually aware of my pain.
¹⁸ I confess my guilt.
　My sin troubles me.

¹⁹ My mortal enemies are growing stronger.
　　Many hate me for no reason.
²⁰ They pay me back with evil instead of good,
　　and they accuse me because I try to do what is good.

²¹ Do not abandon me, O Lord.
　O my God, do not be so distant from me.
²² Come quickly to help me, O Lord, my savior.

## Psalm 39

*For the choir director; for Jeduthun; a psalm by David.*

¹ I said,
"I will watch my ways so that I do not sin with my tongue.
I will bridle my mouth while wicked people are in
my presence."
² I remained totally speechless.
I kept silent, although it did me no good.
While I was deep in thought, my pain grew worse.
³ My heart burned like a fire flaring up within me.
Then I spoke with my tongue:
⁴ "Teach me, O Lord, about the end of my life.
Teach me about the number of days I have left
so that I may know how temporary my life is.
⁵ Indeed, you have made the length of my days ⌊only⌋
a few inches.
My life span is nothing compared to yours.
Certainly, everyone alive is like a whisper in the wind.
*Selah*
⁶ Each person who walks around is like a shadow.
They are busy for no reason.
They accumulate riches without knowing who will
get them."

⁷ And now, Lord, what am I waiting for?
My hope is in you!
⁸ Rescue me from all my rebellious acts.
Do not disgrace me in front of godless fools.
⁹ I remained speechless.
I did not open my mouth
because you are the one who has done this.
¹⁰ Remove the sickness you laid upon me.
My life is over because you struck me with your hand.
¹¹ With stern warnings you discipline people for their crimes.
Like a moth you eat away at what is dear to them.
Certainly, everyone is like a whisper in the wind.   *Selah*

¹² Listen to my prayer, O Lord.
Open your ear to my cry for help.
Do not be deaf to my tears,
for I am a foreign resident with you,
a stranger like all my ancestors.
¹³ Look away from me so that I may smile again
before I go away and am no more.

## Psalm 40

*For the choir director; a psalm by David.*

1 I waited patiently for the LORD.
    He turned to me and heard my cry for help.
2   He pulled me out of a horrible pit,
    out of the mud and clay.
  He set my feet on a rock
    and made my steps secure.
3   He placed a new song in my mouth,
    a song of praise to our God.
      Many will see this and worship.
    They will trust the LORD.
4 Blessed is the person
    who places his confidence in the LORD
      and does not rely on arrogant people
      or those who follow lies.
5 You have done many miraculous things, O LORD my God.
You have made many wonderful plans for us.
    No one compares to you!
I will tell others about your miracles,
    which are more than I can count.

6 You were not pleased with sacrifices and offerings.
You have dug out two ears for me.
You did not ask for burnt offerings or sacrifices for sin.
7   Then I said, "I have come!
    (It is written about me in the scroll of the book.)
8   I am happy to do your will, O my God."
Your teachings are deep within me.
9 I will announce the good news of righteousness
    among those assembled for worship.
      I will not close my lips.
        You know that, O LORD.
10 I have not buried your righteousness deep in my heart.
I have been outspoken about your faithfulness and
    your salvation.
I have not hidden your mercy and your truth
    from those assembled for worship.

11 Do not withhold your compassion from me, O LORD.
May your mercy and your truth always protect me.
12   Countless evils have surrounded me.
    My sins have caught up with me so that I can
      no longer see.

They outnumber the hairs on my head.
    I have lost heart.

¹³ O Lord, please rescue me!
  Come quickly to help me, O Lord!ᵃ
¹⁴ Let all those who seek to end my life
    be confused and put to shame.
  Let those who want my downfall
    be turned back and disgraced.
¹⁵ Let those who say to me, "Aha! Aha!"
    be stunned by their own shame.
¹⁶ Let all who seek you rejoice and be glad because of you.
  Let those who love your salvation continually say,
    "The Lord is great!"

¹⁷ But I am oppressed and needy.
  May the Lord think of me.
    You are my help and my savior.
      O my God, do not delay!

## Psalm 41
*For the choir director; a psalm by David.*

¹ Blessed is the one who has concern for helpless people.
    The Lord will rescue him in times of trouble.
²   The Lord will protect him and keep him alive.
    He will be blessed in the land.
      Do not place him at the mercy of his enemies.
³   The Lord will support him on his sickbed.
    You will restore this person to health when he is ill.

⁴ I said, "O Lord, have pity on me!
    Heal my soul because I have sinned against you."
⁵ My enemies say terrible things about me:
    "When will he die, and when will his family name
      disappear?"
⁶ When one of them comes to visit me, he speaks foolishly.
    His heart collects gossip.
      ⌊Then⌋ he leaves to tell others.
⁷ Everyone who hates me whispers about me.
  They think evil things about me and say,
⁸   "A devilish disease has attached itself to him.
    He will never leave his sickbed."

---

ᵃ40:13 Verses 13–17 are virtually identical in wording to Psalm 70.

9 Even my closest friend whom I trusted,
>   the one who ate my bread,
>>     has lifted his heel against me.
10 Have pity on me, O Lord!
>   Raise me up so that I can pay them back
11     and my enemy cannot shout in triumph over me.
>>     When you do this, I know that you are pleased with me.
12 You defend my integrity,
>   and you set me in your presence forever.

13         Thank the Lord God of Israel through all eternity!
>           Amen and amen!

## BOOK TWO
(Psalms 42–72)

### Psalm 42
*For the choir director; a maskil<sup>a</sup> by Korah's descendants.*

1 As a deer longs for flowing streams,
>   so my soul longs for you, O God.
2 My soul thirsts for God, for the living God.
>   When may I come to see God's face?
3 My tears are my food day and night.
>   People ask me all day long, "Where is your God?"
4 I will remember these things as I pour out my soul:
>   how I used to walk with the crowd
>>     and lead it in a procession to God's house.
>>       ⌊I sang⌋ songs of joy and thanksgiving
>>>         while crowds of people celebrated a festival.

5         Why are you discouraged, my soul?
>           Why are you so restless?
>>             Put your hope in God,
>>>               because I will still praise him.
>>>                 He is my savior and my God.

6 My soul is discouraged.
>   That is why I will remember you
>>     in the land of Jordan, on the peaks of Hermon,
>>>       on Mount Mizar.

---
<sup>a</sup> 42:1 Unknown musical term.

⁷ One deep sea calls to another at the roar of your
    waterspouts.
All the whitecaps on your waves have swept over me.
⁸ The LORD commands his mercy during the day,
    and at night his song is with me—
        a prayer to the God of my life.
⁹ I will ask God, my rock,
    "Why have you forgotten me?
    Why must I walk around in mourning
        while the enemy oppresses me?"
¹⁰ With a shattering blow to my bones,
    my enemies taunt me.
        They ask me all day long, "Where is your God?"

¹¹ Why are you discouraged, my soul?
Why are you so restless?
    Put your hope in God,
        because I will still praise him.
            He is my savior and my God.

## Psalm 43

¹ Judge me, O God,
    and plead my case against an ungodly nation.
Rescue me from deceitful and unjust people.
² You are my fortress, O God!
    Why have you rejected me?
    Why must I walk around in mourning
        while the enemy oppresses me?
³ Send your light and your truth.
    Let them guide me.
    Let them bring me to your holy mountain
        and to your dwelling place.
⁴ Then let me go to the altar of God, to God my ⌞highest⌟
    joy,
        and I will give thanks to you on the lyre, O God,
            my God.

⁵ Why are you discouraged, my soul?
Why are you so restless?
    Put your hope in God,
        because I will still praise him.
            He is my savior and my God.

## Psalm 44

*For the choir director; a* maskil *by Korah's descendants.*

1 O God,
  we have heard it with our own ears.
  Our ancestors have told us
    about the miracle you performed in their day,
    in days long ago.
2 By your power you forced nations ⌐out of the land¬,
  but you planted our ancestors ⌐there¬.
  You shattered many groups of people,
    but you set our ancestors free.[a]
3 It was not with their swords that they took possession
    of the land.
  They did not gain victory with their own strength.
  It was your right hand, your arm,
    and the light of your presence ⌐that did it¬,
    because you were pleased with them.

4 You alone are my king, O God.
  You won those victories for Jacob.
5   With you we can walk over our enemies.
    With your name we can trample those who attack us.
6     I do not rely on my bow,
      and my sword will never save me.
7 But you saved us from our enemies.
  You put to shame those who hate us.
8 All day long we praise our God.
    We give thanks to you forever.               *Selah*

9 But now you have rejected and disgraced us.
    You do not even go along with our armies.
10   You make us retreat from the enemy.
      Those who hate us rob us at will.
11   You hand us over to be butchered like sheep
      and scatter us among the nations.
12   You sell your people for almost nothing,
      and at that price you have gained nothing.
13   You made us a disgrace to our neighbors
      and an object of ridicule and contempt to those
        around us.
14   You made our ⌐defeat¬ a proverb among the nations
      so that people shake their heads at us.

---

[a] 44:2 Or "and you sent them away."

¹⁵ All day long my disgrace is in front of me.
    Shame covers my face
¹⁶    because of the words of those who insult
            and slander us,
        because of the presence of the enemy and the avenger.

¹⁷ Although all of this happened to us,
    we never forgot you.
    We never ignored your promise.*a*
¹⁸    Our hearts never turned away.
    Our feet never left your path.
¹⁹ Yet, you crushed us in a place for jackals
    and covered us with the shadow of death.

²⁰ If we forgot the name of our God
    or stretched out our hands to pray to another god,
²¹    wouldn't God find out,
            since he knows the secrets in our hearts?
²² Indeed, we are being killed all day long because of you.
    We are thought of as sheep to be slaughtered.

²³ Wake up! Why are you sleeping, O Lord?
    Awake! Do not reject us forever!
²⁴    Why do you hide your face?
    Why do you forget our suffering and misery?
²⁵    Our souls are bowing in the dust.
    Our bodies cling to the ground.
²⁶        Arise! Help us!
        Rescue us because of your mercy!

## Psalm 45

*For the choir director; according to* shoshannim;*b a maskil
by Korah's descendants; a love song.*

¹ My heart is overflowing with good news.
    I will direct my song to the king.
    My tongue is a pen for a skillful writer.

² You are the most handsome of Adam's descendants.
    Grace is poured on your lips.
        That is why God has blessed you forever.

---
*a* 44:17 Or "covenant."
*b* 45:1 Unknown musical term.

³ O warrior, strap your sword to your side
    with your splendor and majesty.
⁴ Ride on victoriously in your majesty
    for the cause of truth, humility, and righteousness.
Let your right hand teach you awe-inspiring things.
⁵ Your arrows are sharp in the heart of the king's enemies.
    Nations fall beneath you.
⁶ Your throne, O God, is forever and ever.
The scepter in your kingdom is a scepter for justice.
⁷ You have loved what is right and hated what is wrong.
    That is why God, your God, has anointed you,
        rather than your companions, with the oil of joy.
⁸ All your robes are ⌞fragrant⌟ with myrrh, aloes, and cassia.
From ivory palaces the music of stringed instruments delights you.
⁹ The daughters of kings are among your noble ladies.
The queen takes her place at your right hand
    and wears gold from Ophir.

¹⁰ Listen, daughter! Look closely!
Turn your ear ⌞toward me⌟.
Forget your people, and forget your father's house.
¹¹     The king longs for your beauty.
    He is your Lord.
        Worship him.

¹² The people of Tyre, the richest people,
    want to win your favor with a gift.
¹³ The daughter of the king is glorious inside ⌞the palace⌟.
Her dress is embroidered with gold.
¹⁴ Wearing a colorful gown, she is brought to the king.
Her bridesmaids follow her.
    They will be brought to you.
¹⁵     With joy and delight they are brought in.
    They enter the palace of the king.

¹⁶ Your sons will take the place of your father.
You will make them princes over the whole earth.

¹⁷ I will cause your name to be remembered throughout every generation.
That is why the nations will give thanks to you
    forever and ever.

## Psalm 46

*For the choir director; a song by the descendants of Korah; according to alamoth.*<sup>a</sup>

1 God is our refuge and strength,
    an ever-present help in times of trouble.
2 That is why we are not afraid
    even when the earth quakes
        or the mountains topple into the depths of the sea.
3        Water roars and foams,
            and mountains shake at the surging waves.  *Selah*

4 There is a river
    whose streams bring joy to the city of God,
        the holy place where the Most High lives.
5 God is in that city.
    It cannot fall.
        God will help it at the break of dawn.
6 Nations are in turmoil, and kingdoms topple.
    The earth melts at the sound of ⌊God's⌋ voice.

7 The Lord of Armies is with us.
    The God of Jacob is our stronghold.              *Selah*

8 Come, see the works of the Lord,
    the devastation he has brought to the earth.
9     He puts an end to wars all over the earth.
        He breaks an archer's bow.
        He cuts spears in two.
        He burns chariots.
10 Let go ⌊of your concerns⌋!
    Then you will know that I am God.
        I rule the nations.
        I rule the earth.

11 The Lord of Armies is with us.
    The God of Jacob is our stronghold.              *Selah*

## Psalm 47

*For the choir director; a psalm by Korah's descendants.*

1 Clap your hands, all you people.
    Shout to God with a loud, joyful song.

---

<sup>a</sup>46:1 Unknown musical term.

² We must fear the LORD, the Most High.
    He is the great king of the whole earth.
³   He brings people under our authority
    and ⌞puts⌟ nations under our feet.
⁴   He chooses our inheritance for us,
    the pride of Jacob, whom he loved.    *Selah*

⁵ God has gone up with a joyful shout.
    The LORD has gone up with the sound of a ram's horn.
⁶   Make music to praise God.
    Play music for him!
  Make music to praise our king.
    Play music for him!
⁷ God is the king of the whole earth.
    Make your best music for him!
⁸ God rules the nations.
He sits upon his holy throne.

⁹ The influential people from the nations gather together
    as the people of the God of Abraham.
The rulers of the earth belong to God.
    He rules everything.

## Psalm 48

*A song; a psalm by Korah's descendants.*

¹ The LORD is great.
He should be highly praised.
    His holy mountain is in the city of our God.
²     Its beautiful peak is the joy of the whole earth.
  Mount Zion is on the northern ridge.
    It is the city of the great king.
³ God is in its palaces.
He has proved that he is a stronghold.

⁴ The kings have gathered.
    They marched together.
⁵     ⌞When⌟ they saw ⌞Mount Zion⌟,
    they were astonished.
        They were terrified and ran away in fear.
⁶     Trembling seized them
        like the trembling that a woman experiences
            during labor.
⁷   With the east wind you smash the ships of Tarshish.

⁸ The things we had only heard about, we have now seen
　　in the city of the L ORD of Armies,
　　in the city of our God.
　　　　God makes Zion stand firm forever.　　　　Selah
⁹ Inside your temple we carefully reflect on your mercy,
　　O God.
¹⁰ Like your name, O God,
　　your praise ⌊reaches⌋ to the ends of the earth.
　Your right hand is filled with righteousness.
¹¹ Let Mount Zion be glad
　　and the cities of Judah rejoice
　　　because of your judgments.

¹² Walk around Zion.
　　Go around it.
　　　　Count its towers.
¹³ 　　　　Examine its embankments.
　　　　　　Walk through its palaces.
　Then you can tell the next generation,
¹⁴ 　"This God is our God forever and ever.
　　　He will lead us beyond death."

## Psalm 49

*For the choir director; a psalm by Korah's descendants.*

¹ Listen to this, all you people.
　Open your ears, all who live in the world—
² 　　common people and important ones,
　　　rich people and poor ones.
³ My mouth will speak wise sayings,
　　the insights I have carefully considered.
⁴ I will turn my attention to a proverb.
　I will explain my riddle with the ⌊music of⌋ a lyre.
⁵ 　Why should I be afraid in times of trouble,
　　　when slanderers surround me with evil?
⁶ 　　　They trust their riches
　　　　　and brag about their abundant wealth.

⁷ No one can ever buy back another person
　　or pay God a ransom for his life.
⁸ 　　The price to be paid for his soul is too costly.
　　　　He must always give up
⁹ 　　　　　in order to live forever and never see the pit.

¹⁰ Indeed, one can see that wise people die,

that foolish and stupid people meet the same end.
    They leave their riches to others.
<sup>11</sup> Although they named their lands after themselves,
    their graves[a] have become their homes for ages to come,
    their dwelling places throughout every generation.

<sup>12</sup> But mortals will not continue here with what
    they treasure.
    They are like animals that die.

<sup>13</sup> This is the final outcome for fools and their followers
    who are delighted by what they say:         *Selah*
<sup>14</sup>     Like sheep, they are driven to hell
      with death as their shepherd.
        (Decent people will rule them in the morning.)
      Their forms will decay in the grave,
        far away from their comfortable homes.
<sup>15</sup> But God will buy me back from the power of hell
    because he will take me.         *Selah*
<sup>16</sup> Do not be afraid when someone becomes rich,
    when the greatness of his house increases.
<sup>17</sup>     He will not take anything with him when he dies.
      His greatness cannot follow him.
<sup>18</sup> Even though he blesses himself while he is alive
    (and they praise you when you do well for yourself),
<sup>19</sup>     he must join the generation of his ancestors,
      who will never see light ⌊again⌋.

<sup>20</sup> Mortals, with what they treasure, still don't have
    understanding.
    They are like animals that die.

## Psalm 50

*A psalm by Asaph.*

<sup>1</sup> The L<small>ORD</small>, the only true God, has spoken.
    He has summoned the earth
      from where the sun rises to where it sets.
<sup>2</sup> God shines from Zion,
    the perfection of beauty.
<sup>3</sup> Our God will come and will not remain silent.
    A devouring fire is in front of him
      and a raging storm around him.

---

[a] 49:11 Greek, Syriac, Targum; Masoretic Text "their insides."

⁴ He summons heaven and earth to judge his people:
⁵ "Gather around me, my godly people
      who have made a pledge to me through sacrifices."

⁶ The heavens announce his righteousness
      because God is the judge.                                    *Selah*

⁷ "Listen, my people, and I will speak.
   Listen, Israel, and I will testify against you:
      I am God, your God!
⁸ I am not criticizing you for your sacrifices
         or burnt offerings,
      which are always in front of me.
⁹ ⌊But⌋ I will not accept ⌊another⌋ young bull from
         your household
      or a single male goat from your pens.
¹⁰ Every creature in the forest,
      ⌊even⌋ the cattle on a thousand hills, is mine.
¹¹ I know every bird in the mountains.
   Everything that moves in the fields is mine.
¹² If I were hungry, I would not tell you,
      because the world and all that it contains are mine.
¹³ Do I eat the meat of bulls or drink the blood of goats?
¹⁴ Bring ⌊your⌋ thanks to God as a sacrifice,
      and keep your vows to the Most High.
¹⁵     Call on me in times of trouble.
         I will rescue you, and you will honor me."

¹⁶ But God says to wicked people,
      "How dare you quote my decrees
         and mouth my promises!*ᵃ*
¹⁷    You hate discipline.
      You toss my words behind you.
¹⁸       When you see a thief, you want to make friends
               with him.
         You keep company with people who commit adultery.
¹⁹       You let your mouth say anything evil.
         Your tongue plans deceit.
²⁰       You sit and talk against your own brother.
         You slander your own mother's son.
²¹    When you did these things, I remained silent.
         ⌊That⌋ made you think I was like you.

---
*ᵃ*50:16 Or "covenant."

>     I will argue my point with you
>         and lay it all out for you to see.
> 22 Consider this, you people who forget God.
>     Otherwise, I will tear you to pieces,
>         and there will be no one left to rescue you.
> 23 Whoever offers thanks as a sacrifice honors me.
>     I will let everyone who continues in my way
>         see the salvation that comes from God."

## Psalm 51

*For the choir director; a psalm by David when the prophet Nathan came to him after David's adultery with Bathsheba.*

> 1 Have pity on me, O God, in keeping with your mercy.
>     In keeping with your unlimited compassion, wipe out
>         my rebellious acts.
> 2 Wash me thoroughly from my guilt,
>     and cleanse me from my sin.
> 3     I admit that I am rebellious.
>     My sin is always in front of me.
> 4 I have sinned against you, especially you.
>     I have done what you consider evil.
>         So you hand down justice when you speak,
>             and you are blameless when you judge.
>
> 5 Indeed, I was born guilty.
>     I was a sinner when my mother conceived me.
> 6 Yet, you desire truth and sincerity.
>     Deep down inside me you teach me wisdom.
> 7 Purify me from sin with hyssop,[a] and I will be clean.[b]
>   Wash me, and I will be whiter than snow.
> 8     Let me hear ⌞sounds of⌟ joy and gladness.
>     Let the bones that you have broken dance.
> 9 Hide your face from my sins,
>     and wipe out all that I have done wrong.
>
> 10 Create a clean heart in me, O God,
>     and renew a faithful spirit within me.
> 11 Do not force me away from your presence,
>     and do not take your Holy Spirit from me.
> 12 Restore the joy of your salvation to me,
>     and provide me with a spirit of willing obedience.

---

[a] 51:7 Branches from the hyssop plant were used in purification rites.
[b] 51:7 "Clean" refers to anything that Moses' Teachings say is presentable to God.

¹³ ⌊Then⌋ I will teach your ways to those who are rebellious,
  and sinners will return to you.
¹⁴ Rescue me from the guilt of murder,
  O God, my savior.
 Let my tongue sing joyfully about your righteousness!
¹⁵ O Lord, open my lips,
  and my mouth will tell about your praise.
¹⁶ You are not happy with any sacrifice.
  Otherwise, I would offer one ⌊to you⌋.
 You are not pleased with burnt offerings.
¹⁷  The sacrifice pleasing to God is a broken spirit.
  O God, you do not despise a broken and sorrowful heart.
¹⁸ Favor Zion with your goodness.
 Rebuild the walls of Jerusalem.
¹⁹  Then you will be pleased with sacrifices offered in the
     right spirit—
  with burnt offerings and whole burnt offerings.
   Young bulls will be offered on your altar.

## Psalm 52

*For the choir director; a maskil; a psalm by David when Doeg (who was from Edom) told Saul that David had come to Ahimelech's home.*

¹ Why do you brag about the evil you've done, you hero?
  The mercy of God lasts all day long!
² Your tongue makes up threats.
  It's like a sharp razor, you master of deceit.
³ You prefer evil to good.
 You prefer lying to speaking the truth.          *Selah*
⁴ You love every destructive accusation, you
    deceitful tongue!

⁵ But God will ruin you forever.
  He will grab you and drag you out of your tent.
  He will pull your roots out of this world of the living.
                                                  *Selah*
⁶   Righteous people will see ⌊this⌋ and be struck with
     fear.
   They will laugh at you and say,
⁷    "Look at this person who refused to make God
      his fortress!
     Instead, he trusted his great wealth
       and became strong through his greed."

⁸ But I am like a large olive tree in God's house.
  I trust the mercy of God forever and ever.
⁹ I will give thanks to you forever
    for what you have done.
  In the presence of your godly people,
    I will wait with hope in your good name.

## Psalm 53[a]

*For the choir director; according to* mahalath,[b]
*a maskil by David.*

¹ Godless fools say in their hearts,
    "There is no God."
  They are corrupt.
  They do disgusting things.
    There is no one who does good things.
² God looks down from heaven on Adam's descendants
    to see if there is anyone who acts wisely,
      if there is anyone who seeks help from God.
³   Everyone has fallen away.
      Together they have become rotten to the core.
        No one, not even one person, does good things.
⁴ Are all those troublemakers,
    those who devour my people as if they were
      devouring food,
      so ignorant that they do not call on God?
⁵ There they are—panic-stricken—
    ⌊but⌋ there was no reason to panic,
      because God has scattered the bones
        of those who set up camp against you.
  You put them to shame.
    After all, God has rejected them.

⁶ If only salvation for Israel would come from Zion!
  When God restores the fortunes of his people,
    Jacob will rejoice.
    Israel will be glad.

---

[a] 53:1 Psalm 53 is virtually identical in wording to Psalm 14.
[b] 53:1 Unknown musical term.

## Psalm 54

*For the choir director; on stringed instruments; a maskil by David when people from the city of Ziph told Saul that David was hiding among them.*

1 O God, save me by your name,
    and defend me with your might.
2 O God, hear my prayer,
    and open your ears to the words from my mouth.

3 Strangers have attacked me.
Ruthless people seek my life.
    They do not think about God.                    *Selah*

4 God is my helper!
The Lord is the provider for my life.
5   My enemies spy on me.
        Pay them back with evil.
        Destroy them with your truth!

6 I will make a sacrifice to you along with a freewill offering.
I will give thanks to your good name, O LORD.
7   Your name rescues me from every trouble.
        My eyes will gloat over my enemies.

## Psalm 55

*For the choir director; on stringed instruments;
a maskil by David.*

1 Open your ears to my prayer, O God.
Do not hide from my plea for mercy.
2 Pay attention to me, and answer me.
    My thoughts are restless, and I am confused
3       because my enemy shouts at me
            and a wicked person persecutes me.
                They bring misery crashing down on me,
                and they attack me out of anger.
4 My heart is in turmoil.
    The terrors of death have seized me.
5   Fear and trembling have overcome me.
    Horror has overwhelmed me.
6 I said, "If only I had wings like a dove—
    I would fly away and find rest.
7   Indeed, I would run far away.
    I would stay in the desert.                    *Selah*

⁸ I would hurry to find shelter
   from the raging wind and storm."

⁹ Completely confuse their language, O Lord,
   because I see violence and conflict in the city.
¹⁰ Day and night they go around on ⌞top of⌟ the city walls.
   Trouble and misery are everywhere.
¹¹ Destruction is everywhere.
   Oppression and fraud never leave the streets.*

¹² If an enemy had insulted me,
   then I could bear it.
 If someone who hated me had attacked me,
   then I could hide from him.
¹³ But it is you, my equal,
   my best friend,
      one I knew so well!
¹⁴    We used to talk to each other in complete confidence
         and walk into God's house with the festival crowds.

¹⁵ Let death suddenly take ⌞wicked people⌟!
   Let them go into the grave while they are still alive,
      because evil lives in their homes as well as in their hearts.
¹⁶ But I call on God,
   and the LORD saves me.
¹⁷ Morning, noon, and night I complain and groan,
   and he listens to my voice.
¹⁸ With ⌞his⌟ peace, he will rescue my soul
   from the war waged against me,
      because there are many ⌞soldiers fighting⌟ against me.
¹⁹ God will listen.
   The one who has sat enthroned from the beginning
      will deal with them.                                    *Selah*
         They never change. They never fear God.
²⁰ ⌞My best friend⌟ has betrayed his friends.
   He has broken his solemn promise.
²¹ His speech is smoother than butter,
   but there is war in his heart.
 His words are more soothing than oil,
   but they are like swords ready to attack.
²² Turn your burdens over to the LORD,
   and he will take care of you.
      He will never let the righteous person stumble.

---

*55:11 Or "its marketplace."

²³ But you, O God, will throw ⌞wicked people⌟ into the
     deepest pit.
        Bloodthirsty and deceitful people will not live out
            half their days.
        But I will trust you.

## Psalm 56
*For the choir director; according to* yonath elem rechokim;[a]
*a miktam by David when the Philistines captured
him in Gath.*

¹ Have pity on me, O God, because people are harassing me.
    All day long warriors oppress me.
² All day long my enemies spy on me.
    They harass me.
        There are so many fighting against me.
³ Even when I am afraid, I still trust you.

⁴ I praise God's word.
  I trust God.
  I am not afraid.
      What can mere flesh ⌞and blood⌟ do to me?

⁵ All day long my enemies twist my words.
  Their every thought is an evil plan against me.
⁶ They attack, and then they hide.
  They watch my every step as they wait to take my life.
⁷ With the wrong they do, can they escape?
  O God, angrily make the nations fall.
⁸ (You have kept a record of my wanderings.
      Put my tears in your bottle.
          They are already in your book.)
⁹ Then my enemies will retreat when I call ⌞to you⌟.
  This I know: God is on my side.

¹⁰ I praise God's word.
   I praise the LORD's word.
¹¹ I trust God.
   I am not afraid.
       What can mortals do to me?

¹² I am bound by my vows to you, O God.

---
[a]56:1 Unknown musical term.

I will keep my vows by offering songs of thanksgiving
to you.
¹³ You have rescued me from death.
You have kept my feet from stumbling
so that I could walk in your presence, in the
light of life.

## Psalm 57

*For the choir director; al tashcheth;*<sup>a</sup> *a miktam by David when he fled from Saul into the cave.*

¹ Have pity on me, O God. Have pity on me,
because my soul takes refuge in you.
I will take refuge in the shadow of your wings
until destructive storms pass by.
² I call to God Most High,
to the God who does everything for me.
³ He sends his help from heaven and saves me.
He disgraces the one who is harassing me.      *Selah*
God sends his mercy and his truth!
⁴ My soul is surrounded by lions.
I must lie down with man-eating lions.
Their teeth are spears and arrows.
Their tongues are sharp swords.
⁵ May you be honored above the heavens, O God.
Let your glory extend over the whole earth.

⁶ ⌊My enemies⌋ spread out a net to catch me.
(My soul is bowed down.)
They dug a pit to trap me,
but then they fell into it.      *Selah*
⁷ My heart is confident, O God.
My heart is confident.
I want to sing and make music.<sup>b</sup>
⁸ Wake up, my soul!<sup>c</sup>
Wake up, harp and lyre!
I want to wake up at dawn.
⁹ I want to give thanks to you among the people, O Lord.
I want to make music to praise you among the nations
¹⁰ because your mercy is as high as the heavens.
Your truth reaches the skies.

---

<sup>a</sup>57:1 Unknown musical term.
<sup>b</sup>57:7 Verses 7–11 are virtually identical in wording to Psalm 108:1–5.
<sup>c</sup>57:8 Or "my glory."

¹¹ May you be honored above the heavens, O God.
  Let your glory extend over the whole earth.

## Psalm 58
*For the choir director; al tashcheth; a miktam by David.*

¹ Do you rulers really give fair verdicts?
  Do you judge Adam's descendants fairly?
² No, you invent new crimes on earth,
    and your hands spread violence.

³ ⌞Even⌟ inside the womb wicked people are strangers
    ⌞to God⌟.
  From their birth liars go astray.
⁴ They have poisonous venom like snakes.
    They are like a deaf cobra that shuts its ears
⁵   so that it cannot hear the voice of a snake charmer
      or of anyone trained to cast spells.

⁶ O God, knock the teeth out of their mouths.
    Break the young lions' teeth, O LORD.
⁷ Let them disappear like water that drains away.
    When they aim their bows, let their arrows miss
      the target.
⁸ Let them become like a snail that leaves behind
      a slimy trail
    or like a stillborn child who never sees the sun.
⁹ Let ⌞God⌟ sweep them away
    faster than a cooking pot is heated by burning twigs.

¹⁰ Righteous people will rejoice when they see ⌞God⌟
      take revenge.
  They will wash their feet in the blood of wicked people.
¹¹ Then people will say,
    "Righteous people certainly have a reward.
    There is a God who judges on earth."

## Psalm 59
*For the choir director; al tashcheth; a miktam by David
when Saul sent men to watch David's home and kill him.*

¹ Rescue me from my enemies, O my God.
    Protect me from those who attack me.
² Rescue me from troublemakers.
    Save me from bloodthirsty people.

³ They lie in ambush for me right here!
Fierce men attack me, O Lord,
    but not because of any disobedience,
⁴        or any sin, or any guilt on my part.
They hurry to take positions against me.
Wake up, and help me; see ⌊for yourself⌋.
⁵ O Lord God of Armies, God of Israel,
    arise to punish all the nations.
    Have no pity on any traitors.                    *Selah*

⁶    They return in the evening.
    They howl like dogs.
    They prowl the city.

⁷ See what pours out of their mouths—
    swords from their lips!
        ⌊They think,⌋ "Who will hear us?"
⁸ O Lord, you laugh at them.
    You make fun of all the nations.

⁹    O my strength, I watch for you!
        God is my stronghold, my merciful God!

¹⁰ God will come to meet me.
    He will let me gloat over those who spy on me.
¹¹ Do not kill them.
    Otherwise, my people may forget.
    Make them wander aimlessly by your power.
    Bring them down, O Lord, our shield,
¹²    ⌊because of⌋ the sins from their mouths
        and the words on their lips.
    Let them be trapped by their own arrogance
        because they speak curses and lies.
¹³ Destroy them in your rage.
    Destroy them until not one of them is left.
        Then they will know that God rules Jacob
            to the ends of the earth.              *Selah*

¹⁴    They return in the evening.
    They howl like dogs.
    They prowl the city.

¹⁵ They wander around to find something to eat.
    If they are not full enough,
        they will stay all night.

¹⁶ But I will sing about your strength.
　　In the morning I will joyfully sing about your mercy.
　　　　You have been my stronghold
　　　　　　and a place of safety in times of trouble.

¹⁷ 　　O my strength, I will make music to praise you!
　　　God is my stronghold, my merciful God!

## Psalm 60

*For the choir director; according to* shushan eduth;[a]
*a miktam by David; for teaching. When David fought Aram Naharaim and Aram Zobah, and ⌊when⌋ Joab came back and killed 12,000 men from Edom in the Dead Sea region.*

¹ O God, you have rejected us.
　　You have broken down our defenses.
　　You have been angry.
　　　　Restore us!
² You made the land quake.
　You split it wide open.
　　Heal the cracks in it
　　　　because it is falling apart.
³ You have made your people experience hardships.
　You have given us wine that makes us stagger.
⁴ Yet, you have raised a flag for those who fear you
　　so that they can rally to it
　　　　when attacked by bows ⌊and arrows⌋.　　　Selah
⁵ 　Save ⌊us⌋ with your powerful hand, and answer us
　　so that those who are dear to you may be rescued.[b]

⁶ God has promised the following through his holiness:
　　"I will triumph!
　　　I will divide Shechem.
　　　I will measure the valley of Succoth.
⁷ 　　Gilead is mine.
　　　Manasseh is mine.
　　　Ephraim is the helmet on my head.
　　　Judah is my scepter.
⁸ 　　Moab is my washtub.
　　　I will throw my shoe over Edom.
　　　I will shout in triumph over Philistia."

---

[a] 60:1 Unknown musical term.
[b] 60:5 Verses 5–12 are virtually identical in wording to Psalm 108:6–13.

⁹ Who will bring me into the fortified city?
Who will lead me to Edom?
¹⁰ Isn't it you, O God, who rejected us?
Isn't it you, O God, who refused to accompany
our armies?

¹¹ Give us help against the enemy
because human assistance is worthless.
¹² With God we will display great strength.
He will trample our enemies.

## Psalm 61

*For the choir director; on a stringed instrument; by David.*

¹ Listen to my cry for help, O God.
Pay attention to my prayer.
² From the ends of the earth, I call to you
when I begin to lose heart.
Lead me to the rock that is high above me.
³ You have been my refuge,
a tower of strength against the enemy.
⁴ I would like to be a guest in your tent forever
and to take refuge under the protection
of your wings.                                    *Selah*
⁵ O God, you have heard my vows.
You have given me the inheritance
that belongs to those who fear your name.
⁶ Add days upon days to the life of the king.
May his years endure throughout every generation.
⁷ May he sit enthroned in the presence of God forever.
May mercy and truth protect him.
⁸ Then I will make music to praise your name forever,
as I keep my vows day after day.

## Psalm 62

*For the choir director; according to Jeduthun; a psalm by David.*

¹ My soul waits calmly for God alone.
My salvation comes from him.
² He alone is my rock and my savior—my stronghold.
I cannot be severely shaken.

³ How long will all of you attack a person?
How long will you try to murder him,
as though he were a leaning wall or a sagging fence?

4   They plan to force him out of his high position.
    They are happy to lie.
    They bless with their mouths,
        but in their hearts they curse.                    Selah

5 Wait calmly for God alone, my soul,
    because my hope comes from him.
6 He alone is my rock and my savior—my stronghold.
    I cannot be shaken.

7 My salvation and my glory depend on God.
    God is the rock of my strength, my refuge.
8 Trust him at all times, you people.
    Pour out your hearts in his presence.
        God is our refuge.                                  Selah

9 Common people are only a whisper in the wind.
    Important people are only a delusion.
        When all of them are weighed on a scale, they amount
            to nothing.
        They are less than a whisper in the wind.
10 Do not count on extortion ⌊to make you rich⌋.
    Do not hope to gain anything through robbery.
        When riches increase, do not depend on them.

11 God has spoken once.
    I have heard it ⌊said⌋ twice:
        "Power belongs to God.
12       Mercy belongs to you, O Lord.
            You reward a person based on what he has done."

## Psalm 63
*A psalm by David when he was in the wilderness of Judah.*

1 O God, you are my God.
    At dawn I search for you.
        My soul thirsts for you.
        My body longs for you
            in a dry, parched land where there is no water.
2 So I look for you in the holy place
    to see your power and your glory.
3 My lips will praise you
    because your mercy is better than life ⌊itself⌋.
4 So I will thank you as long as I live.
    I will lift up my hands ⌊to pray⌋ in your name.

⁵ You satisfy my soul with the richest foods.
  My mouth will sing ⌜your⌝ praise with joyful lips.
⁶ As I lie on my bed, I remember you.
  Through the long hours of the night, I think about you.
⁷ You have been my help.
  In the shadow of your wings, I sing joyfully.
⁸ My soul clings to you.
  Your right hand supports me.

⁹ But those who try to destroy my life
   will go into the depths of the earth.
¹⁰    They will be cut down by swords.
        Their dead bodies will be left as food for jackals.
¹¹ But the king will find joy in God.
   Everyone who takes an oath by God will brag,
     but the mouths of liars will be shut.

## Psalm 64

*For the choir director; a psalm by David.*

¹ Hear my voice, O God, when I complain.
  Protect my life from a terrifying enemy.
² Hide me from the secret plots of criminals,
    from the mob of troublemakers.
³     They sharpen their tongues like swords.
        They aim bitter words like arrows
⁴        to shoot at innocent people from their hiding
           places.
        They shoot at them suddenly, without any fear.
⁵     They encourage one another in their evil plans.
      They talk about setting traps and say,
        "Who can see them?"
⁶     They search for the perfect crime and say,
        "We have perfected a foolproof scheme!"
          Human nature and the human heart are
            a mystery!

⁷ But God will shoot them with an arrow.
    Suddenly, they will be struck dead.
⁸ They will trip over their own tongues.
    Everyone who sees them will shake his head.
⁹ Everyone will be afraid and conclude,
    "This is an act of God!"
      They will learn from what he has done.

¹⁰ Righteous people will find joy in the LORD and take
        refuge in him.
    Everyone whose motives are decent will be able to brag.

## Psalm 65
*For the choir director; a psalm by David; a song.*

¹ You are praised with silence in Zion, O God,
        and vows ⌞made⌟ to you must be kept.
² You are the one who hears prayers.
        Everyone will come to you.
³ Various sins overwhelm me.
        You are the one who forgives our rebellious acts.
⁴ Blessed is the person you choose
        and invite to live with you in your courtyards.
            We will be filled with good food from your house,
                from your holy temple.

⁵ You answer us with awe-inspiring acts ⌞done⌟
        in righteousness,
    O God, our savior,
        the hope of all the ends of the earth and of the most
            distant sea,
⁶       the one who set the mountains in place with
            his strength,
        the one who is clothed with power,
⁷       the one who calms the roar of the seas,
            their crashing waves,
                and the uproar of the nations.
⁸ Those who live at the ends of the earth are in awe of your
        miraculous signs.
    The lands of the morning sunrise and evening sunset
        sing joyfully.

⁹ You take care of the earth, and you water it.
    You make it much richer than it was.
        (The river of God is filled with water.)
    You provide grain for them.
        Indeed, you even prepare the ground.
¹⁰ You drench plowed fields ⌞with rain⌟
        and level their clumps of soil.
    You soften them with showers
        and bless what grows in them.
¹¹ You crown the year with your goodness,
        and richness overflows wherever you are.

¹² The pastures in the desert overflow ⌞with richness⌟.
　　The hills are surrounded with joy.
¹³ 　　The pastures are covered with flocks.
　　The valleys are carpeted with grain.
　　　　All of them shout triumphantly. Indeed, they sing.

## Psalm 66
*For the choir director; a song; a psalm.*

¹ Shout happily to God, all the earth!
² Make music to praise the glory of his name.
　Make his praise glorious.
³ Say to God,
　　"How awe-inspiring are your deeds!
　　　Your power is so great that your enemies will cringe
　　　　in front of you.
⁴ 　The whole earth will worship you.
　　　It will make music to praise you.
　　　It will make music to praise your name."　　*Selah*
⁵ Come and see what God has done—
　　his awe-inspiring deeds for Adam's descendants.
⁶ 　He turned the sea into dry land.
　　　They crossed the river on foot.
　　　　We rejoiced because of what he did there.
⁷ 　He rules forever with his might.
　　His eyes watch the nations.
　　　Rebels will not be able to oppose him.　　*Selah*

⁸ Thank our God, you nations.
　Make the sound of his praise heard.
⁹ 　He has kept us alive
　　　and has not allowed us to fall.
¹⁰ You have tested us, O God.
　You have refined us in the same way silver is refined.
¹¹ You have trapped us in a net.
　You have laid burdens on our backs.
¹² You let people ride over our heads.
　　We went through fire and water,
　　　but then you brought us out and refreshed us.

¹³ I will come into your temple with burnt offerings.
　I will keep my vows to you,
¹⁴ 　the vows made by my lips and spoken by my
　　　⌞own⌟ mouth
　　when I was in trouble.

ⁱ⁵ I will offer you a sacrifice of fattened livestock
     for burnt offerings
        with the smoke from rams.
   I will offer cattle and goats.                    *Selah*

¹⁶ Come and listen, all who fear God,
     and I will tell you what he has done for me.
¹⁷    With my mouth I cried out to him.
        High praise was on my tongue.
¹⁸ If I had thought about doing anything sinful,
     the Lord would not have listened ⌊to me⌋.
¹⁹ But God has heard me.
   He has paid attention to my prayer.

²⁰ Thanks be to God,
     who has not rejected my prayer
        or taken away his mercy from me.

## Psalm 67
*For the choir director; on stringed instruments; a psalm; a song.*

¹ May God have pity on us and bless us!
   May he smile on us.                               *Selah*
²    Then your ways will be known on earth,
        your salvation throughout all nations.

³ Let everyone give thanks to you, O God.
   Let everyone give thanks to you.
⁴ Let the nations be glad and sing joyfully
     because you judge everyone with justice
        and guide the nations on the earth.          *Selah*
⁵ Let the people give thanks to you, O God.
   Let all the people give thanks to you.
⁶    The earth has yielded its harvest.
   May God, our God, bless us.
⁷ May God bless us,
     and may all the ends of the earth worship him.

## Psalm 68
*For the choir director; a psalm by David; a song.*

¹ God will arise.
   His enemies will be scattered.
   Those who hate him will flee from him.
²    Blow them away like smoke.

Let wicked people melt in God's presence like wax
next to a fire.

³ But let righteous people rejoice.
Let them celebrate in God's presence.
Let them overflow with joy.
⁴ Sing to God; make music to praise his name.
Make a highway for him to ride through the deserts.*ᵃ*
The Lᴏʀᴅ is his name.
Celebrate in his presence.

⁵ The God who is in his holy dwelling place
is the father of the fatherless and the defender of widows.
⁶ God places lonely people in families.
He leads prisoners out of prison into productive lives,
but rebellious people must live in an
unproductive land.

⁷ O God, when you went in front of your people,
when you marched through the desert,     *Selah*
⁸     the earth quaked and the sky poured
in the presence of the God of Sinai,
in the presence of the God of Israel.

⁹ You watered the land with plenty of rain, O God.
You refreshed it when your land was exhausted.
¹⁰     Your flock settled there.
Out of your goodness, O God,
you provided for oppressed people.

¹¹ The Lord gives instructions.
The women who announce the good news are
a large army.
¹²     ⌊They say,⌋ "The kings of the armies flee; they run away.
The women who remained at home will divide
the goods.
¹³     Though you stayed among the sheep pens,
⌊you will be like⌋ the wings of a dove covered
with silver,
its feathers with yellow gold.
¹⁴     Meanwhile, the Almighty was still scattering
kings there
like snow falling on Mount Zalmon."

---

*ᵃ*68:4 Or "Lift a song to him who rides upon the clouds."

¹⁵ The mountain of Bashan is the mountain of God.
  The mountain of Bashan is the mountain with many peaks.
¹⁶   Why do you look with envy, you mountains with
        many peaks,
      at the mountain where God has chosen to live?
      Certainly, the LORD will live there forever.

¹⁷ The chariots of God are twenty thousand in number,
    thousands upon thousands.
      The Lord is among them.
        ⌊The God of⌋ Sinai is in his holy place.
¹⁸ You went to the highest place.
  You took prisoners captive.
  You received gifts from people,
      even from rebellious people, so that the LORD God
        may live there.

¹⁹ Thanks be to the Lord,
    who daily carries our burdens for us.
      God is our salvation.                              *Selah*
²⁰ Our God is the God of victories.
  The Almighty LORD is our escape from death.

²¹ Certainly, God will crush the heads of his enemies
    ⌊and destroy even⌋ the hair on the heads
      of those who continue to be guilty.
²² The Lord said, "I will bring them back from Bashan.
  I will bring them back from the depths of the sea
²³    so that you, ⌊my people,⌋ may bathe$^a$ your feet in blood
      and the tongues of your dogs
        may lick the blood of your enemies."

²⁴ Your festival processions, O God, can be seen by everyone.
    They are the processions for my God, my king, into the
        holy place.
²⁵    The singers are in front.
    The musicians are behind them.
    The young women beating tambourines are
        between them.
²⁶    Thank God, the Lord, the source of Israel,
        with the choirs.
²⁷    Benjamin, the youngest, is leading them,
      ⌊next⌋ the leaders of Judah with their noisy crowds,

---

$^a$68:23 Greek, Targum, Syriac; Masoretic Text "shatter."

⌞then⌟ the leaders of Zebulun,
⌞then⌟ the leaders of Naphtali.

²⁸ Your God has decided you will be strong.
  Display your strength, O God,
    as you have for us before.
²⁹ Kings will bring you gifts
    because of your temple high above Jerusalem.
³⁰ Threaten the beast who is among the cattails,
    the herd of bulls with the calves of the nations,
      until it humbles itself with pieces of silver.
  Scatter the people who find joy in war.
³¹ Ambassadors will come from Egypt.
  Sudan will stretch out its hands to God ⌞in prayer⌟.

³² You kingdoms of the world, sing to God.
  Make music to praise the Lord.                                    *Selah*
³³    God rides through the ancient heaven,
        the highest heaven.
  Listen! He makes his voice heard, his powerful voice.
³⁴    Acknowledge the power of God.
        His majesty is over Israel, and his power is in the skies.

³⁵ God, the God of Israel, is awe-inspiring in his holy place.
  He gives strength and power to his people.
    Thanks be to God!

## Psalm 69

*For the choir director; according to* shoshannim; *by David.*

¹ Save me, O God!
  The water is already up to my neck!
² I am sinking in deep mud.
  There is nothing to stand on.
  I am in deep water.
  A flood is sweeping me away.
³ I am exhausted from crying for help.
  My throat is hoarse.
  My eyes are strained ⌞from⌟ looking for my God.
⁴    Those who hate me for no reason
      outnumber the hairs on my head.
  Those who want to destroy me are mighty.
    They have no reason to be my enemies.
  I am forced to pay back what I did not steal.

⁵ O God, you know my stupidity,
    and the things of which I am guilty are not hidden
            from you.
⁶ Do not let those who wait with hope for you
    be put to shame because of me, O Almighty LORD
            of Armies.
  Do not let those who come to you for help
    be humiliated because of me, O God of Israel.

⁷ Indeed, for your sake I have endured insults.
    Humiliation has covered my face.
⁸ I have become a stranger to my ⌊own⌋ brothers,
    a foreigner to my mother's sons.
⁹ Indeed, devotion for your house has consumed me,
    and the insults of those who insult you have fallen on me.
¹⁰ I cried and fasted, but I was insulted for it.
¹¹ I dressed myself in sackcloth, but I became the object
            of ridicule.
¹²    Those who sit at the gate gossip about me,
    and drunkards make up songs about me.

¹³ May my prayer come to you at an acceptable time, O LORD.
    O God, out of the greatness of your mercy,
        answer me with the truth of your salvation.
¹⁴ Rescue me from the mud.
    Do not let me sink ⌊into it⌋.
  I want to be rescued from those who hate me
    and from the deep water.
¹⁵ Do not let floodwaters sweep me away.
    Do not let the ocean swallow me up,
        or the pit close its mouth over me.
¹⁶ Answer me, O LORD, because your mercy is good.
  Out of your unlimited compassion, turn to me.
¹⁷ I am in trouble, so do not hide your face from me.
    Answer me quickly!
¹⁸ Come close, and defend my soul.
    Set me free because of my enemies.

¹⁹ You know that I have been insulted, put to shame,
        and humiliated.
    All my opponents are in front of you.
²⁰  Insults have broken my heart, and I am sick.
      I looked for sympathy, but there was none.
      I looked for people to comfort me, but I found no one.
²¹      They poisoned my food,

and when I was thirsty, they gave me vinegar
to drink.

²² Let the table set for them become a trap
and a snare for their friends.
²³ Let their vision become clouded so that they cannot see.
Let their thighs continually shake.

²⁴ Pour your rage on them.
Let your burning anger catch up with them.
²⁵ Let their camp be deserted
and their tents empty.

²⁶ They persecute the one you have struck,
and they talk about the pain of those you have wounded.
²⁷ Charge them with one crime after another.
Do not let them be found innocent.
²⁸ Let their ⌐names⌐ be erased from the Book of Life.
Do not let them be listed with righteous people.

²⁹ I am suffering and in pain.
Let your saving power protect me, O God.
³⁰ I want to praise God's name with a song.
I want to praise his great name with a song of thanksgiving.
³¹    This will please the LORD more than ⌐sacrificing⌐ an ox
or a bull with horns and hoofs.
³² Oppressed people will see ⌐this⌐ and rejoice.
May the hearts of those who look to God for help
be refreshed.

³³ The LORD listens to needy people.
He does not despise his own who are in prison.
³⁴ Let heaven and earth, the seas, and everything that
moves in them, praise him.
³⁵ When God saves Zion, he will rebuild the cities of Judah.
His servants will live there and take possession of it.
³⁶    The descendants of his servants will inherit it.
Those who love him will live there.

## Psalm 70[a]

*For the choir director; by David; to be kept in mind.*

¹ Come quickly to rescue me, O God!

---

[a] 70:1 Psalm 70 is virtually identical in wording to Psalm 40:13–17.

Come quickly to help me, O Lord!
² Let those who seek my life
 be confused and put to shame.
Let those who want my downfall
 be turned back and disgraced.
³ Let those who say, "Aha! Aha!"
 be turned back because of their own shame.
⁴ Let all who seek you rejoice and be glad because of you.
Let those who love your salvation continually say,
 "God is great!"

⁵ But I am oppressed and needy.
O God, come to me quickly.
 You are my help and my savior.
  O Lord, do not delay!

## Psalm 71

¹ I have taken refuge in you, O Lord.
 Never let me be put to shame.
² Rescue me and free me because of your righteousness.
Turn your ear toward me, and save me.
³   Be a rock on which I may live,
  a place where I may always go.
   You gave the order to save me!
Indeed, you are my rock and my fortress.
⁴ My God, free me from the hands of a wicked person,
 from the grasp of one who is cruel and unjust.
⁵ You are my hope, O Almighty Lord.
You have been my confidence ever since I was young.
⁶ I depended on you before I was born.
 You took me from my mother's womb.
  My songs of praise constantly speak about you.
⁷ I have become an example to many people,
 but you are my strong refuge.
⁸ My mouth is filled with your praise,
 with your glory all day long.

⁹ Do not reject me when I am old
 or abandon me when I lose my strength.
¹⁰ My enemies talk about me.
 They watch me as they plot to take my life.
¹¹ They say, "God has abandoned him.
 Pursue him and grab him because there is no one
  to rescue him."
¹² O God, do not be so distant from me.

O my God, come quickly to help me.
¹³ Let those who accuse me come to a shameful end.
Let those who want my downfall be covered
with disgrace and humiliation.
¹⁴ But I will always have hope.
I will praise you more and more.
¹⁵ My mouth will tell about your righteousness,
about your salvation all day long.
Even then, it is more than I can understand.
¹⁶ I will come with the mighty deeds of the Almighty LORD.
I will praise your righteousness, yours alone.

¹⁷ O God, you have taught me ever since I was young,
and I still talk about the miracles you have done.
¹⁸ Even when I am old and gray, do not abandon me, O God.
Let me live to tell the people of this age
what your strength has accomplished,
to tell about your power to all who will come.

¹⁹ Your righteousness reaches to the heavens, O God.
You have done great things.
O God, who is like you?
²⁰ You have made me endure many terrible troubles.
You restore me to life again.
You bring me back from the depths of the earth.
²¹ You comfort me and make me greater than ever.

²² Because of your faithfulness, O my God,
even I will give thanks to you as I play on a lyre.
I will make music with a harp to praise you, O Holy One
of Israel.
²³ My lips will sing with joy when I make music to praise you.
My soul, which you have rescued, also will sing joyfully.
²⁴ My tongue will tell about your righteousness all day long,
because those who wanted my downfall
have been disgraced and put to shame.

## Psalm 72

*By Solomon.*

¹ O God, give the king your justice
and the king's son*ᵃ* your righteousness

---

*ᵃ*72:1 According to ancient Jewish and Christian tradition, "king" and "king's son" refer to the Messiah.

² so that he may judge your people with righteousness
and your oppressed ˻people˼ with justice.

³ May the mountains bring peace to the people
and the hills bring righteousness.
⁴ May he grant justice to the people who are oppressed.
May he save the children of needy people
and crush their oppressor.
⁵ May they fear you as long as the sun and moon ˻shine˼—
throughout every generation.
⁶ May he be like rain that falls on ˻freshly˼ cut grass,
like showers that water the land.
⁷ May righteous people blossom in his day.
May there be unlimited peace until the moon
no longer ˻shines˼.

⁸ May he rule from sea to sea,
from the Euphrates River to the ends of the earth.
⁹ May the people of the desert kneel in front of him.
May his enemies lick the dust.
¹⁰ May the kings from Tarshish and the islands bring presents.
May the kings from Sheba and Seba bring gifts.
¹¹ May all kings worship him.
May all nations serve him.

¹² He will rescue the needy person who cries for help
and the oppressed person who has no one's help.
¹³ He will have pity on the poor and needy
and will save the lives of the needy.
¹⁴ He will rescue them from oppression and violence.
Their blood will be precious in his sight.

¹⁵ May he live long.
May the gold from Sheba be given to him.
May ˻the people˼ pray for him continually.
May ˻they˼ praise him all day long.
¹⁶ May there be plenty of grain in the land.
May it wave ˻in the breeze˼ on the mountaintops,
its fruit like ˻the treetops of˼ Lebanon.
May those from the city flourish like the grass
on the ground.
¹⁷ May his name endure forever.
May his name continue as long as the sun ˻shines˼.
May all nations be blessed through him and call
him blessed.

¹⁸ Thank the LORD God, the God of Israel,
   who alone does miracles.
¹⁹ Thanks be to his glorious name forever.
   May the whole earth be filled with his glory.
      Amen and amen!

²⁰ The prayers by David, son of Jesse, end here.

## BOOK THREE
(Psalms 73–89)

### Psalm 73
*A psalm by Asaph.*

¹ God is truly good to Israel,
   to those whose lives are pure.

² But my feet had almost stumbled.
      They had almost slipped
³     because I was envious of arrogant people
         when I saw the prosperity that wicked people enjoy.

⁴ They suffer no pain.
Their bodies are healthy.
⁵ They have no drudgery in their lives like ordinary people.
They are not plagued ⌊with problems⌋ like others.
⁶ That is why they wear arrogance like a necklace
   and acts of violence like clothing.
⁷ Their eyes peer out from their fat faces,
   and their imaginations run wild.
⁸ They ridicule.
They speak maliciously.
They speak arrogantly about oppression.
⁹ They verbally attack heaven,
   and they order people around on earth.
¹⁰ That is why God's people turn to wickedness
   and swallow their words.
¹¹ Then wicked people ask, "What does God know?"
   "Does the Most High know anything?"
¹² Look how wicked they are!
   They never have a worry.
      They grow more and more wealthy.

¹³ I've received no reward for keeping my life pure
   and washing my hands of any blame.

¹⁴ I'm plagued ⌊with problems⌋ all day long,
   and every morning my punishment ⌊begins again⌋.
¹⁵ If I had said, "I will continue to talk like that,"
   I would have betrayed God's people.

¹⁶ But when I tried to understand this,
   it was too difficult for me.
¹⁷ Only when I came into God's holy place
   did I ⌊finally⌋ understand what would happen to them.

¹⁸ You put them in slippery places
   and make them fall into ruin.
¹⁹ They are suddenly destroyed.
  They are completely swept away by terror!
²⁰ As ⌊someone⌋ gets rid of a dream when he wakes up,
   so you, O Lord, get rid of the thought of them
      when you wake up.

²¹ When my heart was filled with bitterness
   and my mind was seized ⌊with envy⌋,
²²     I was stupid, and I did not understand.
   I was like a dumb animal in your presence.
²³ Yet, I am always with you.
   You hold on to my right hand.
²⁴     With your advice you guide me,
      and in the end you will take me to glory.
²⁵ As long as I have you,
   I don't need anyone else in heaven or on earth.
²⁶ My body and mind may waste away,
   but God remains the foundation of my life
      and my inheritance forever.
²⁷ Without a doubt, those who are far from you will die.
  You destroy all who are unfaithful to you.

²⁸ Being united with God is my highest good.
   I have made the Almighty LORD my refuge
      so that I may report everything that he has done.

## Psalm 74
*A maskil[a] by Asaph.*

¹ Why, O God, have you rejected us forever?

---
[a] 74:1 Unknown musical term.

Why does your anger
   smolder against the sheep in your care?

2 Remember your congregation.
   Long ago you made it your own.
   You bought this tribe to be your possession.
      This tribe is Mount Zion, where you have made
         your home.
3 Turn your steps toward these pathetic ruins.
   The enemy has destroyed everything in the holy temple.

4 Your opponents have roared inside your meeting place.
   They have set up their own emblems as symbols.
5     Starting from its entrance, they hacked away
         like a woodcutter in a forest.
6     They smashed all its carved paneling with axes
         and hatchets.
7     They burned your holy place to the ground.
      They dishonored the place where you live among us.
8     They said to themselves, "We will crush them."
      They burned every meeting place of God in the land.

9 We no longer see miraculous signs.
   There are no prophets anymore.
      No one knows how long this will last.
10 How long, O God, will the enemy insult us?
   Will the enemy despise you forever?
11 Why do you hold back your hand, especially your
      right hand?
   Take your hands out of your pockets.
      Destroy your enemies!

12 And yet, from long ago God has been my king,
      the one who has been victorious throughout the earth.
13    You stirred up the sea with your own strength.
      You smashed the heads of sea monsters in the water.
14    You crushed the heads of Leviathan
         and gave them to the creatures of the desert for food.
15    You opened the springs and brooks.
      You dried up the ever-flowing rivers.
16       The day and the night are yours.
      You set the moon and the sun in their places.
17    You determined all the boundaries of the earth.
      You created summer and winter.

¹⁸ Remember how the enemy insulted you, O Lord.
Remember how an entire nation of godless fools
despised your name.
¹⁹ Do not hand over the soul of your dove to wild animals.
Do not forget the life of your oppressed people forever.
²⁰ Consider your promise*ᵃ*
because every dark corner of the land is filled
with violence.
²¹ Do not let oppressed people come back in disgrace.
Let weak and needy people praise your name.
²² Arise, O God!
Fight for your own cause!
Remember how godless fools insult you all day long.
²³ Do not forget the shouting of your opponents.
Do not forget the uproar made by those who attack you.

## Psalm 75
*For the choir director; al tashcheth; a psalm by Asaph; a song.*

¹ We give thanks to you, O God; we give thanks.
You are present, and your miracles confirm that.

² When I choose the right time,
I will judge fairly.
³ When the earth and everyone who lives on it begin to melt,
I will make its foundations as solid as rock.        *Selah*
⁴ I said to those who brag, "Don't brag,"
and to wicked people,
"Don't raise your weapons.
⁵     Don't raise your weapons so proudly
or speak so defiantly."

⁶ The ⌊authority⌋ to reward someone does not ⌊come⌋
from the east,
from the west,
or ⌊even⌋ from the wilderness.
⁷ God alone is the judge.
He punishes one person and rewards another.
⁸ A cup is in the Lord's hand.
(Its foaming wine is thoroughly mixed with spices.)
He will empty it,
⌊and⌋ all the wicked people on earth
will have to drink every last drop.

---
*ᵃ*74:20 Or "covenant."

⁹ But I will speak ⌊about your miracles⌋ forever.
   I will make music to praise the God of Jacob.
¹⁰ I will destroy all the weapons of wicked people,
     but the weapons of righteous people will be
       raised proudly.

## Psalm 76
*For the choir director; on stringed instruments; a psalm by Asaph; a song.*

¹ God is known in Judah.
  His name is great in Israel.
² His tent is in Salem.
  His home is in Zion.
³   There he destroyed flaming arrows,
       shields, swords, and weapons of war.                    *Selah*

⁴ You are the radiant one.
  You are more majestic than the ancient mountains.[a]
⁵   Brave people were robbed.
      They died.
         None of the warriors were able to lift a hand.
⁶         At your stern warning, O God of Jacob,
            chariot riders and horses were put to sleep.

⁷ You alone must be feared!
  Who can stand in your presence when you become angry?
⁸   From heaven you announced a verdict.
      The earth was fearful and silent
⁹      when you rose to judge, O God,
         when you rose to save every oppressed person
           on earth.                                           *Selah*

¹⁰ Even angry mortals will praise you.
   You will wear the remainder of ⌊their⌋ anger.
¹¹   Make vows to the LORD your God, and keep them.
       Let everyone around him bring gifts to the one who
         must be feared.
¹²      He cuts short the lives of influential people.
        He terrifies the kings of the earth.

---

*a* 76:4 Greek, Syriac; Masoretic Text "mountains of prey."

## Psalm 77

*For the choir director; according to Jeduthun; a psalm by Asaph.*

¹ Loudly, I cried to God.
  Loudly, I cried to God
    so that he would open his ears to ⌊hear⌋ me.
² On the day I was in trouble, I went to the Lord for help.
  At night I stretched out my hands in prayer without
      growing tired.
    Yet, my soul refused to be comforted.

³ I sigh as I remember God.
  I begin to lose hope as I think about him.           *Selah*
⁴ (You keep my eyelids open.)
  I am so upset that I cannot speak.
⁵ I have considered the days of old,
    the years long ago.
⁶ I remember my song in the night
    and reflect ⌊on it⌋.
  My spirit searches ⌊for an answer⌋:
⁷ Will the Lord reject ⌊me⌋ for all time?
  Will he ever accept me?
⁸ Has his mercy come to an end forever?
  Has his promise been canceled throughout every
      generation?
⁹ Has God forgotten to be merciful?
  Has he locked up his compassion because of
      his anger?                                       *Selah*
¹⁰ Then I said, "It makes me feel sick
      that the power of the Most High is no longer
        the same."

¹¹ I will remember the deeds of the Lord.
   I will remember your ancient miracles.
¹² I will reflect on all your actions
     and think about what you have done.

¹³ O God, your ways are holy!
     What god is as great as our God?
¹⁴ You are the God who performs miracles.
   You have made your strength known among the nations.
¹⁵ With your might you have defended your people,
     the descendants of Jacob and Joseph.            *Selah*

¹⁶ The water saw you, O God.
   The water saw you and shook.
      Even the depths of the sea trembled.
¹⁷ The clouds poured out water.
   The sky thundered.
      Even your arrows flashed in every direction.
¹⁸ The sound of your thunder rumbled in the sky.
      Streaks of lightning lit up the world.
         The earth trembled and shook.

¹⁹ Your road went through the sea.
      Your path went through raging water,
         but your footprints could not be seen.
²⁰ Like a shepherd, you led your people.
   You had Moses and Aaron take them by the hand.

## Psalm 78
A maskil *by Asaph.*

¹ Open your ears to my teachings, my people.
  Turn your ears to the words from my mouth.
²    I will open my mouth to illustrate points.
     I will explain what has been hidden long ago,
³        things that we have heard and known about,
         things that our parents have told us.
⁴            We will not hide them from our children.
             We will tell the next generation
                about the LORD's power and great deeds
                   and the miraculous things he has done.

⁵ He established written instructions for Jacob's people.
  He gave his teachings to Israel.
  He commanded our ancestors to make them known
         to their children
⁶    so that the next generation would know them.
        Children yet to be born ⌞would learn them⌟.
        They will grow up and tell their children
⁷           to trust God, to remember what he has done,
            and to obey his commands.
⁸        Then they will not be like their ancestors,
         a stubborn and rebellious generation.
            Their hearts were not loyal.
            Their spirits were not faithful to God.

⁹ The men of Ephraim, well-equipped with bows
⌊and arrows⌋,
turned ⌊and ran⌋ on the day of battle.
¹⁰     They had not been faithful to God's promise.ᵃ
They refused to follow his teachings.
¹¹     They forgot what he had done—
the miracles that he had shown them.

¹² In front of their ancestors he performed miracles
in the land of Egypt, in the fields of Zoan.
¹³     He divided the sea and led them through it.
He made the waters stand up like a wall.
¹⁴     He guided them by a cloud during the day
and by a fiery light throughout the night.
¹⁵     He split rocks in the desert.
He gave them plenty to drink, an ocean of water.
¹⁶     He made streams come out of a rock.
He made the water flow like rivers.

¹⁷ They continued to sin against him,
to rebel in the desert against the Most High.
¹⁸ They deliberately tested God by demanding the food
they craved.
¹⁹ They spoke against God by saying,
"Can God prepare a banquet in the desert?
²⁰     True, he did strike a rock,
and water did gush out,
and the streams did overflow.
But can he also give us bread or provide us, his people,
with meat?"

²¹ When the LORD heard this, he became furious.
His fire burned against Jacob
and his anger flared up at Israel
²²     because they did not believe God
or trust him to save them.

²³ In spite of that, he commanded the clouds above
and opened the doors of heaven.
²⁴     He rained manna down on them to eat
and gave them grain from heaven.
²⁵     Humans ate the bread of the mighty ones,
and God sent them plenty of food.

---

ᵃ78:10 Or "covenant."

²⁶ He made the east wind blow in the heavens
and guided the south wind with his might.
²⁷ He rained meat down on them like dust,
birds like the sand on the seashore.
²⁸ He made the birds fall in the middle of his camp,
all around his dwelling place.

²⁹ They ate more than enough.
He gave them what they wanted,
³⁰ but they still wanted more.
While the food was still in their mouths,
³¹ the anger of God flared up against them.
He killed their strongest men
and slaughtered the best young men in Israel.

³² In spite of all this, they continued to sin,
and they no longer believed in his miracles.
³³ He brought their days to an end like a whisper
in the wind.
He brought their years to an end in terror.
³⁴ When he killed ⌞some of⌟ them, ⌞the rest⌟ searched
for him.
They turned from their sins and eagerly looked
for God.
³⁵ They remembered that God was their rock,
that the Most High was their defender.
³⁶ They flattered him with their mouths
and lied to him with their tongues.
³⁷ Their hearts were not loyal to him.
They were not faithful to his promise.

³⁸ But he is compassionate.
He forgave their sin.
He did not destroy them.
He restrained his anger many times.
He did not display all of his fury.
³⁹ He remembered that they were only flesh and blood,
a breeze that blows and does not return.

⁴⁰ How often they rebelled against him in the wilderness!
How often they caused him grief in the desert!
⁴¹ Again and again they tested God,
and they pushed the Holy One of Israel to the limit.
⁴² They did not remember his power—
the day he freed them from their oppressor,

⁴³ when he performed his miraculous signs in Egypt,
  his wonders in the fields of Zoan.

⁴⁴ He turned their rivers into blood
  so that they could not drink from their streams.
⁴⁵ He sent a swarm of flies that bit them
  and frogs that ruined them.
⁴⁶ He gave their crops to grasshoppers
  and their produce to locusts.
⁴⁷ He killed their vines with hail
  and their fig trees with frost.
⁴⁸ He let the hail strike their cattle
  and bolts of lightning strike their livestock.
⁴⁹ He sent his burning anger, rage, fury, and hostility
    against them.
  He sent an army of destroying angels.
⁵⁰ He cleared a path for his anger.
  He did not spare them.
  He let the plague take their lives.
⁵¹ He slaughtered every firstborn in Egypt,
    the ones born in the tents of Ham when their fathers
      were young.

⁵² But he led his own people out like sheep
    and guided them like a flock through the wilderness.
⁵³   He led them safely.
      They had no fear while the sea covered
        their enemies.
⁵⁴ He brought them into his holy land,
    to this mountain that his power had won.
⁵⁵   He forced nations out of their way
      and gave them the land of the nations as their
        inheritance.
        He settled the tribes of Israel in their own tents.

⁵⁶ They tested God Most High and rebelled against him.
  They did not obey his written instructions.
⁵⁷ They were disloyal and treacherous like their ancestors.
  They were like arrows shot from a defective bow.
⁵⁸ They made him angry because of their illegal
    worship sites.
  They made him furious because they worshiped idols.

⁵⁹ When God heard, he became furious.
  He completely rejected Israel.

⁶⁰ He abandoned his dwelling place in Shiloh,
   the tent where he had lived among humans.
⁶¹ He allowed his power to be taken captive
   and handed his glory over to an oppressor.
⁶² He let swords kill his people.
   He was furious with those who belonged to him.
⁶³ Fire consumed his best young men,
   so his virgins heard no wedding songs.
⁶⁴ His priests were cut down with swords.
   The widows ⌊of his priests⌋ could not even weep ⌊for them⌋.
⁶⁵ Then the Lord woke up like one who had been sleeping,
   like a warrior sobering up from ⌊too much⌋ wine.
⁶⁶ He struck his enemies from behind
   and disgraced them forever.

⁶⁷ He rejected the tent of Joseph.
  He did not choose the tribe of Ephraim,
⁶⁸ but he chose the tribe of Judah,
   Mount Zion which he loved.
⁶⁹ He built his holy place to be like the high heavens,
   like the earth which he made to last for a long time.

⁷⁰ He chose his servant David.
  He took him from the sheep pens.
⁷¹ He brought him from tending the ewes that had lambs
   so that David could be the shepherd of the people of Jacob,
    of Israel, the people who belonged to the Lord.
⁷² With unselfish devotion David became their shepherd.
  With skill he guided them.

## Psalm 79

*A psalm by Asaph.*

¹ O God, the nations have invaded the land that belongs to you.
   They have dishonored your holy temple.
   They have left Jerusalem in ruins.
² They have given the dead bodies of your servants
    to the birds for food.
   They have given the flesh of your godly ones
    to the animals.
³ They have shed the blood of your people around Jerusalem

as though it were water.
   There is no one to bury your people.

4 We have become a disgrace to our neighbors,
   an object of ridicule and contempt to those around us.
5 How long, O Lord?
   Will you remain angry forever?
   Will your fury continue to burn like fire?
6 Pour your fury on the nations that do not know you,
   on the kingdoms that have not called you.
7    They have devoured Jacob.
   They have destroyed his home.
8 Do not hold the crimes of our ancestors against us.
Reach out to us soon with your compassion,
   because we are helpless.
9 Help us, O God, our savior, for the glory of your name.
Rescue us, and forgive our sins for the honor
         of your name.

10 Why should the nations ⌊be allowed to⌋ say,
   "Where is their God?"
Let us watch as the nations learn
   that there is punishment for shedding the blood of
         your servants.
11 Let the groans of prisoners come into your presence.
   With your powerful arm rescue those who are
         condemned to death.
12 Pay each one of our neighbors back
   with seven times the number of insults they used to
         insult you, O Lord.
13 Then we, your people, the flock in your pasture,
   will give thanks to you forever.
      We will praise you throughout every generation.

## Psalm 80

*For the choir director; according to shoshannim eduth;*
*by Asaph; a psalm.*

1 Open your ears, O Shepherd of Israel,
   the one who leads ⌊the descendants of⌋ Joseph like sheep,
   the one who is enthroned over the angels.[a]
2 Appear in front of Ephraim, Benjamin, and Manasseh.
Wake up your power, and come to save us.

---
[a] 80:1 Or "cherubim."

³ O God, restore us and smile on us
    so that we may be saved.

⁴ O LORD God, commander of armies, how long will you
        smolder in anger
    against the prayer of your people?
⁵ You made them eat tears as food.
    You often made them drink ⌊their own⌋ tears.
⁶ You made us a source of conflict to our neighbors,
    and our enemies made fun of us.

⁷ O God, commander of armies, restore us and smile on us
    so that we may be saved.

⁸ You brought a vine from Egypt.
    You forced out the nations and planted it.
⁹ You cleared the ground for it
    so that it took root and filled the land.
¹⁰    Its shade covered the mountains.
        Its branches covered the mighty cedars.
¹¹    It reached out with its branches to the
            Mediterranean Sea.
        Its shoots reached the Euphrates River.

¹² Why did you break down the stone fences around this vine?
    All who pass by are picking its fruit.
¹³    Wild boars from the forest graze on it.
        Wild animals devour it.
¹⁴ O God, commander of armies, come back!
    Look from heaven and see!
    Come to help this vine.
¹⁵ Take care of what your right hand planted,
    the son you strengthened for yourself.
¹⁶    The vine has been cut down and burned.
        Let them be destroyed by the threatening look
            on your face.

¹⁷ Let your power rest on the man you have chosen,
    the son of man you strengthened for yourself.
¹⁸    Then we will never turn away from you.
        Give us life again, and we will call on you.

¹⁹ O LORD God, commander of armies, restore us,
    and smile on us
    so that we may be saved.

## Psalm 81

*For the choir director; on the* gittith;[a] *by Asaph.*

1. Sing joyfully to God, our strength.
   Shout happily to the God of Jacob.
2. Begin a psalm, and strike a tambourine.
   Play lyres and harps with their pleasant music.
3. Blow the ram's horn on the day of the new moon,
   on the day of the full moon,
   on our festival days.
4. This is a law for Israel,
   a legal decision from the God of Jacob.
5. These are the instructions God set in place for Joseph
   when Joseph rose to power over Egypt.

   I heard a message I did not understand:
6. "I removed the burden from his shoulder.
   His hands were freed from the basket.
7. When you were in trouble, you called out ⌊to me⌋,
   and I rescued you.
   I was hidden in thunder, but I answered you.
   I tested your ⌊loyalty⌋ at the oasis of Meribah.    *Selah*
8. Listen, my people, and I will warn you.
   Israel, if you would only listen to me!
9. Never keep any strange god among you.
   Never worship a foreign god.
10. I am the LORD your God, the one who brought you
    out of Egypt.
    Open your mouth wide, and I will fill it.

11. "But my people did not listen to me.
    Israel wanted nothing to do with me.
12. So I let them go their own stubborn ways
    and follow their own advice.
13. If only my people would listen to me!
    If only Israel would follow me!
14. I would quickly defeat their enemies.
    I would turn my power against their foes.
15. Those who hate the LORD would cringe in front of him,
    and their time ⌊for punishment⌋ would last forever.
16. But I would feed Israel with the finest wheat
    and satisfy them with honey from a rock."

---

[a] 81:1 Unknown musical term.

## Psalm 82

*A psalm by Asaph.*

1 God takes his place in his own assembly.
  He pronounces judgment among the gods:
2   "How long are you going to judge unfairly?
    How long are you going to side with
        wicked people?"                          *Selah*

3 Defend weak people and orphans.
  Protect the rights of the oppressed and the poor.
4 Rescue weak and needy people.
    Help them escape the power of wicked people.

5 Wicked people do not know or understand anything.
    As they walk around in the dark,
        all the foundations of the earth shake.
6 I said, "You are gods.
    You are all sons of the Most High.
7       You will certainly die like humans
        and fall like any prince."

8 Arise, O God!
    Judge the earth, because all the nations belong to you.

## Psalm 83

*A song; a psalm by Asaph.*

1 O God, do not remain silent.
    Do not turn a deaf ear to me.
    Do not keep quiet, O God.

2 Look, your enemies are in an uproar.
    Those who hate you hold their heads high.
3       They make plans in secret against your people
        and plot together against those you treasure.
4       They say, "Let's wipe out their nation
        so that the name of Israel will no longer
            be remembered."
5       They agree completely on their plan.
        They form an alliance against you:
6           the tents from Edom and Ishmael,
            Moab and Hagar,
7           Gebal, Ammon, and Amalek,
            Philistia, along with those who live in Tyre.

⁸ Even Assyria has joined them.
They helped the descendants of Lot. *Selah*
⁹ Do to them what you did to Midian,
to Sisera and Jabin at the Kishon River.
¹⁰ They were destroyed at Endor.
They became manure to fertilize the ground.
¹¹ Treat their influential people as you treated Oreb
and Zeeb.
Treat all their leaders like Zebah and Zalmunna.
¹² They said, "Let's take God's pasturelands for ourselves."
¹³ O my God, blow them away like tumbleweeds,ᵃ
like husks in the wind.
¹⁴ Pursue them with your storms,
and terrify them with your windstorms
¹⁵ the way fire burns a forest
and flames set mountains on fire.ᵇ
¹⁶ Let their faces blush with shame, O LORD,
so that they must look to you for help.
¹⁷ Let them be put to shame and terrified forever.
Let them die in disgrace
¹⁸ so that they must acknowledge you.
Your name is the LORD.
You alone are the Most High God of the whole earth.

## Psalm 84

*For the choir director; on the* gittith; *a psalm by Korah's descendants.*

¹ Your dwelling place is lovely, O LORD of Armies!
² My soul longs and yearns
for the LORD's courtyards.
My whole body shouts for joy to the living God.
³ Even sparrows find a home,
and swallows find a nest for themselves.
There they hatch their young
near your altars, O LORD of Armies,
my king and my God.
⁴ Blessed are those who live in your house.
They are always praising you. *Selah*

⁵ Blessed are those who find strength in you.
Their hearts are on the road ⌊that leads to you⌋.

---
ᵃ 83:13 Or "whirling dust."
ᵇ 83:15 Verse 15 (in Hebrew) has been placed in front of verse 14 to express the complex Hebrew sentence structure more clearly in English.

⁶ As they pass through a valley where balsam
        trees grow,ᵃ
    they make it a place of springs.
        The early rains cover it with blessings.ᵇ
⁷ Their strength grows as they go along
    until each one of them appears
        in front of God in Zion.

⁸ O Lord God, commander of armies, hear my prayer.
    Open your ears, O God of Jacob.                    Selah
⁹ Look at our shield, O God.
    Look with favor on the face of your anointed one.
¹⁰ One day in your courtyards is better than a thousand
        ⌊anywhere else⌋.
    I would rather stand in the entrance to my God's house
        than live inside wicked people's homes.
¹¹ The Lord God is a sun and shield.
    The Lord grants favor and honor.
    He does not hold back any blessing
        from those who live innocently.

¹² O Lord of Armies, blessed is the person who trusts you.

## Psalm 85

*For the choir director; a psalm by Korah's descendants.*

¹ You favored your land, O Lord.
    You restored the fortunes of Jacob.
² You removed your people's guilt.
    You pardoned all their sins.                       Selah
³ You laid aside all your fury.
    You turned away from your burning anger.

⁴ Restore us, O God, our savior.
    Put an end to your anger against us.
⁵ Will you be angry with us forever?
    Will you ever let go of your anger in the generations
        to come?
⁶ Won't you restore our lives again
    so that your people may find joy in you?
⁷ Show us your mercy, O Lord,
    by giving us your salvation.

---
ᵃ 84:6 Or "As they pass through the valley of Weeping."
ᵇ 84:6 Or "pools."

⁸ I want to hear what God the Lord says,
    because he promises peace to his people, to his
        godly ones.
    But they must not go back to their stupidity.
⁹ Indeed, his salvation is near those who fear him,
    and ⌊his⌋ glory will remain in our land.

¹⁰ Mercy and truth have met.
    Righteousness and peace have kissed.
¹¹ Truth sprouts from the ground,
    and righteousness looks down from heaven.
¹² The Lord will certainly give us what is good,
    and our land will produce crops.
¹³ Righteousness will go ahead of him
    and make a path for his steps.

## Psalm 86

*A prayer by David.*

¹ Turn your ear ⌊toward me⌋, O Lord.
    Answer me, because I am oppressed and needy.
² Protect me, because I am faithful ⌊to you⌋.
    Save your servant who trusts you. You are my God.
³ Have pity on me, O Lord,
    because I call out to you all day long.
⁴ Give me joy, O Lord,
    because I lift my soul to you.
⁵ You, O Lord, are good and forgiving,
    full of mercy toward everyone who calls out to you.
⁶ Open your ears to my prayer, O Lord.
    Pay attention when I plead for mercy.
⁷    When I am in trouble, I call out to you
        because you answer me.

⁸ No god is like you, O Lord.
    No one can do what you do.
⁹ All the nations that you have made
    will bow in your presence, O Lord.
        They will honor you.
¹⁰ Indeed, you are great, a worker of miracles.
    You alone are God.
¹¹ Teach me your way, O Lord,
    so that I may live in your truth.
    Focus my heart on fearing you.

¹² I will give thanks to you with all my heart, O Lord my God.
I will honor you forever
¹³ because your mercy toward me is great.
You have rescued me from the depths of hell.

¹⁴ O God, arrogant people attack me,
and a mob of ruthless people seeks my life.
They think nothing of you.
¹⁵ But you, O Lord, are a compassionate and merciful God.
You are patient, always faithful and ready to forgive.
¹⁶ Turn toward me, and have pity on me.
Give me your strength because I am your servant.
Save me because I am the son of your female servant.
¹⁷ Grant me some proof of your goodness
so that those who hate me may see it and be put to shame.
You, O Lord, have helped me and comforted me.

## Psalm 87

*By Korah's descendants; a psalm; a song.*

¹ ⌊The city⌋ the Lord has founded ⌊stands⌋ on holy mountains.
² The Lord loves the city of Zion
more than any other place in Jacob.
³ Glorious things are said about you, O city of God!　*Selah*

⁴ ⌊The Lord says,⌋ "I will add Egypt and Babylon
as well as Philistia, Tyre, and Sudan
to the list of those who acknowledge me.
Each nation ⌊will claim that it⌋ was born there."

⁵ But it will be said of Zion,
"Every race is born in it.
The Most High will make it secure."
⁶ The Lord will record this in the Book of Nations:
"Every race ⌊claims that it⌋ was born there."　*Selah*
⁷ Singers and dancers will sing,
"Zion is the source of all our blessings."

## Psalm 88

*A song; a psalm by Korah's descendants; for the choir director; according to* mahalath leannoth;*ᵃ a* maskil *by Heman the Ezrahite.*

¹ O Lord God, my savior,
   I cry out to you during the day and at night.
²    Let my prayer come into your presence.
        Turn your ear to hear my cries.
³ My soul is filled with troubles,
    and my life comes closer to the grave.
⁴    I am numbered with those who go into the pit.
     I am like a man without any strength—
⁵       abandoned with the dead,
           like those who have been killed and lie in graves,
           like those whom you no longer remember,
              who are cut off from your power.
⁶ You have put me in the bottom of the pit—in deep,
    dark places.
⁷ Your rage lies heavily on me.
    You make all your waves pound on me.            *Selah*
⁸ You have taken my friends far away from me.
    You made me disgusting to them.
       I'm shut in, and I can't get out.
⁹      My eyes grow weak because of my suffering.
          All day long I call out to you, O Lord.
             I stretch out my hands to you ⌞in prayer⌟.

¹⁰ Will you perform miracles for those who are dead?
     Will the spirits of the dead rise and give thanks to you?
                                                                   *Selah*
¹¹ Will anyone tell about your mercy in Sheol
     or about your faithfulness in Abaddon?
¹² Will anyone know about your miracles in that dark place
     or about your righteousness in the place where
        forgotten people live?

¹³ I cry out to you for help, O Lord,
     and in the morning my prayer will come into
        your presence.

¹⁴ Why do you reject my soul, O Lord?
     Why do you hide your face from me?

---
ᵃ 88:1 Unknown musical term.

¹⁵ Ever since I was young, I have been suffering and
near death.
I have endured your terrors, and now I am in despair.
¹⁶ Your burning anger has swept over me.
Your terrors have destroyed me.
¹⁷ They swirl around me all day long like water.
They surround me on all sides.
¹⁸ You have taken my loved ones and friends
far away from me.
Darkness is my only friend!

## Psalm 89
*A maskil by Ethan the Ezrahite.*

¹ I will sing forever about the evidence of your mercy,
O Lord.
I will tell about your faithfulness to every generation.
² I said, "Your mercy will last forever.
Your faithfulness stands firm in the heavens."

³ ⌊You said,⌋ "I have made a promise*ᵃ* to my chosen one.
I swore this oath to my servant David:
⁴ 'I will make your dynasty continue forever.
I built your throne to last throughout every
generation.'" *Selah*

⁵ O Lord, the heavens praise your miracles
and your faithfulness in the assembly of the holy ones.
⁶ Who in the skies can compare with the Lord?
Who among the heavenly beings is like the Lord?
⁷ God is terrifying in the council of the holy ones.
He is greater and more awe-inspiring than those who
surround him.
⁸ O Lord God of Armies, who is like you?
Mighty Lord, even your faithfulness surrounds you.
⁹ You rule the raging sea.
When its waves rise, you quiet them.
¹⁰ You crushed Rahab;*ᵇ* it was like a corpse.
With your strong arm you scattered your enemies.
¹¹ The heavens are yours.
The earth is also yours.
You made the world and everything in it.

---
*ᵃ*89:3 Or "covenant."
*ᵇ*89:10 Rahab is the name of a demonic creature who opposes God.

¹² You created north and south.
    Mount Tabor and Mount Hermon sing your
        name joyfully.
¹³ Your arm is mighty.
    Your hand is strong.
    Your right hand is lifted high.
¹⁴ Righteousness and justice are the foundations
        of your throne.
    Mercy and truth stand in front of you.
¹⁵ Blessed are the people who know how to praise you.
    They walk in the light of your presence, O Lord.
¹⁶ They find joy in your name all day long.
    They are joyful in your righteousness
¹⁷     because you are the glory of their strength.
    By your favor you give us victory.
¹⁸ Our shield belongs to the Lord.
    Our king belongs to the Holy One of Israel.

¹⁹ Once in a vision you said to your faithful ones:
    "I set a boy above warriors.
    I have raised up one chosen from the people.
²⁰ I found my servant David.
    I anointed him with my holy oil.
²¹ My hand is ready to help him.
    My arm will also give him strength.
²² No enemy will take him by surprise.
    No wicked person will mistreat him.
²³ I will crush his enemies in front of him
    and defeat those who hate him.
²⁴ My faithfulness and mercy will be with him,
    and in my name he will be victorious.
²⁵ I will put his ⌞left⌟ hand on the sea
    and his right hand on the rivers.
²⁶ He will call out to me,
    'You are my Father, my God, and the rock of my
        salvation.'
²⁷ Yes, I will make him the firstborn.
    He will be the Most High to the kings of the earth.
²⁸ My mercy will stay with him forever.
    My promise to him is unbreakable.
²⁹ I will make his dynasty endure forever
    and his throne like the days of heaven.

³⁰ "If his descendants abandon my teachings
    and do not live by my rules,

³¹ if they violate my laws
   and do not obey my commandments,
³² then with a rod I will punish their rebellion
   and their crimes with beatings.
³³ But I will not take my mercy away from him
   or allow my truth to become a lie.
³⁴ I will not dishonor my promise
   or alter my own agreement.
³⁵ On my holiness I have taken an oath once and for all:
   I will not lie to David.
³⁶ His dynasty will last forever.
   His throne will be in my presence like the sun.
³⁷    Like the moon his throne will stand firm forever.
      It will be like a faithful witness in heaven."

³⁸ But you have despised, rejected,
   and become angry with your anointed one.
³⁹ You have refused to recognize the promise to your
      servant
   and have thrown his crown into the dirt.
⁴⁰ You have broken through all his walls
   and have laid his fortified cities in ruins.
⁴¹    (Everyone who passed by robbed him.
      He has become the object of his neighbors' scorn.)
⁴² You held the right hand of his enemies high
   and made all of his adversaries rejoice.
⁴³ You even took his sword out of his hand
   and failed to support him in battle.
⁴⁴ You put an end to his splendor
   and hurled his throne to the ground.
⁴⁵ You cut short the days of his youth
   and covered him with shame.                    *Selah*

⁴⁶ How long, O Lord? Will you hide yourself forever?
   How long will your anger continue to burn like fire?
⁴⁷ Remember how short my life is!
   Have you created Adam's descendants for no reason?
⁴⁸    Can a mortal go on living and never see death?
      Who can set himself free from the power
         of the grave?                            *Selah*
⁴⁹    Where is the evidence of your mercy, Lord?
      You swore an oath to David
         on ⌊the basis of⌋ your faithfulness.

⁵⁰ Remember, O LORD,ᵃ how your servantᵇ has been insulted.
   Remember how I have carried in my heart ⌊the insults⌋
      from so many people.
⁵¹ Your enemies insulted ⌊me⌋.
   They insulted your Messiahᶜ every step he took.

⁵²       Thank the LORD forever.
        Amen and amen!

## BOOK FOUR
(Psalms 90–106)

### Psalm 90
*A prayer by Moses, the man of God.*

¹ O Lord, you have been our refuge throughout every
      generation.
² Before the mountains were born,
   before you gave birth to the earth and the world,
      you were God.
   You are God from everlasting to everlasting.

³ You turn mortals back into dust
   and say, "Return, descendants of Adam."
⁴ Indeed, in your sight a thousand years are like a single day,
   like yesterday—already past—
   like an hour in the night.
⁵ You sweep mortals away.
   They are a dream.
   They sprout again in the morning like cut grass.
⁶   In the morning they blossom and sprout.
     In the evening they wither and dry up.

⁷ Indeed, your anger consumes us.
   Your rage terrifies us.
⁸   You have set our sins in front of you.
     You have put our secret sins in the light
         of your presence.
⁹ Indeed, all our days slip away because of your fury.
   We live out our years like one ⌊long⌋ sigh.

---

ᵃ 89:50 Many Hebrew manuscripts; other Hebrew manuscripts "Lord."
ᵇ 89:50 Many Hebrew manuscripts, Greek, Syriac; other Hebrew manuscripts "your servants."
ᶜ 89:51 Or "anointed one."

¹⁰ Each of us lives for 70 years—
    or even 80 if we are in good health.
        But the best of them ⌊bring⌋ trouble and misery.
        Indeed, they are soon gone, and we fly away.
¹¹ Who fully understands the power of your anger?
    A person fears you more when he better understands
        your fury.
¹² Teach us to number each of our days
    so that we may grow in wisdom.

¹³ Return, LORD! How long … ?
    Change your plans about ⌊us,⌋ your servants.
¹⁴ Satisfy us every morning with your mercy
    so that we may sing joyfully and rejoice all our days.
¹⁵ Make us rejoice for as many days as you have made
        us suffer,
    for as many years as we have experienced evil.
¹⁶ Let ⌊us,⌋ your servants, see what you can do.
    Let our children see your glorious power.
¹⁷ Let the kindness of the Lord our God be with us.
    Make us successful in everything we do.
        Yes, make us successful in everything we do.

## Psalm 91

¹ Whoever lives under the shelter of the Most High
    will remain in the shadow of the Almighty.
² I will say to the LORD,
    "⌊You are⌋ my refuge and my fortress, my God in whom
        I trust."

³ He is the one who will rescue you from hunters' traps
    and from deadly plagues.
⁴ He will cover you with his feathers,
    and under his wings you will find refuge.
        His truth is your shield and armor.

⁵ You do not need to fear
    terrors of the night,
    arrows that fly during the day,
⁶     plagues that roam the dark,
    epidemics that strike at noon.
⁷     They will not come near you,
        even though a thousand may fall dead beside you
        or ten thousand at your right side.

⁸ You only have to look with your eyes
    to see the punishment of wicked people.

⁹ You, O Lord, are my refuge!

You have made the Most High your home.
¹⁰    No harm will come to you.
    No sickness will come near your house.
¹¹ He will put his angels in charge of you
    to protect you in all your ways.
¹²        They will carry you in their hands
            so that you never hit your foot against a rock.
¹³        You will step on lions and cobras.
          You will trample young lions and snakes.

¹⁴ Because you love me, I will rescue you.
    I will protect you because you know my name.
¹⁵ When you call to me, I will answer you.
    I will be with you when you are in trouble.
    I will save you and honor you.
¹⁶    I will satisfy you with a long life.
    I will show you how I will save you.

## Psalm 92

*A psalm; a song; for the day of rest—a holy day.*

¹ It is good to give thanks to the Lord,
    to make music to praise your name, O Most High.
² It is good to announce your mercy in the morning
    and your faithfulness in the evening
³        on a ten-stringed instrument and a harp
            and with a melody on a lyre.

⁴ You made me find joy in what you have done, O Lord.
  I will sing joyfully about the works of your hands.
⁵    How spectacular are your works, O Lord!
    How very deep are your thoughts!

⁶ A stupid person cannot know
    and a fool cannot understand
⁷        that wicked people sprout like grass
            and all troublemakers blossom ⌊like flowers⌋,
            only to be destroyed forever.

⁸ But you, O Lord, are highly honored forever.
⁹ Now look at your enemies, O Lord.
  Now look at your enemies.
    They disappear, and all troublemakers are scattered.

¹⁰ But you make me as strong as a wild bull,
    and soothing lotion is poured on me.
¹¹ My eyes gloat over those who spy on me.
  My ears hear ⌊the cries⌋ of evildoers attacking me.

¹² Righteous people flourish like palm trees
    and grow tall like the cedars in Lebanon.
¹³   They are planted in the Lord's house.
    They blossom in our God's courtyards.
¹⁴     Even when they are old, they still bear fruit.
    They are always healthy and fresh.
¹⁵       They make it known that the Lord is decent.
      He is my rock.
      He is never unfair.

## Psalm 93

¹ The Lord rules as king! He is clothed with majesty.
  The Lord has clothed himself; he has armed himself
    with power.
    The world was set in place; it cannot be moved.

² Your throne was set in place a long time ago.
  You are eternal.

³ The ocean rises, O Lord.
  The ocean rises with a roar.
  The ocean rises with its pounding waves.
⁴   The Lord above is mighty—
    mightier than the sound of raging water,
    mightier than the foaming waves of the sea.

⁵ Your written testimonies are completely reliable.
  O Lord, holiness is what makes your house beautiful
    for days without end.

## Psalm 94

¹ O Lord, God of vengeance,
    O God of vengeance, appear!
² Arise, O Judge of the earth.
  Give arrogant people what they deserve.

3 How long, O Lord, will wicked people triumph?
   How long?

4 They ramble.
   They speak arrogantly.
     All troublemakers brag about themselves.
5 They crush your people, O Lord.
   They make those who belong to you suffer.
6     They kill widows and foreigners, and they
         murder orphans.
7     They say, "The Lord doesn't see it.
         The God of Jacob doesn't even pay attention to it."

8 Pay attention, you stupid people!
   When will you become wise, you fools?
9    God created ears.
       Do you think he can't hear?
     He formed eyes.
       Do you think he can't see?
10   He disciplines nations.
       Do you think he can't punish?
     He teaches people.
       Do you think he doesn't know anything?
11     The Lord knows that people's thoughts are pointless.

12 O Lord, blessed is the person
     whom you discipline and instruct from your teachings.
13   You give him peace and quiet from times of trouble
       while a pit is dug to trap wicked people.

14 The Lord will never desert his people
     or abandon those who belong to him.
15   The decisions of judges will again become fair,
       and everyone whose motives are decent will
         pursue justice.

16 Who will stand up for me against evildoers?
   Who will stand by my side against troublemakers?
17   If the Lord had not come to help me,
       my soul would have quickly fallen silent ⌊in death⌋.

18 When I said, "My feet are slipping,"
     your mercy, O Lord, continued to hold me up.
19 When I worried about many things,
     your assuring words soothed my soul.

²⁰ Are wicked rulers who use the law to do unlawful things
    able to be your partners?
²¹   They join forces to take the lives of righteous people.
     They condemn innocent people to death.
²² The Lord has become my stronghold.
   My God has become my rock of refuge.
²³   He has turned their own wickedness against them.
     He will destroy them because of their sins.
        The Lord our God will destroy them.

## Psalm 95

¹ Come, let's sing joyfully to the Lord.
   Let's shout happily to the rock of our salvation.
²   Let's come into his presence with a song of
        thanksgiving.
    Let's shout happily to him with psalms.
³ The Lord is a great God and a great king above all gods.
⁴   In his hand are the deep places of the earth,
       and the mountain peaks are his.
⁵   The sea is his.
       He made it, and his hands formed the dry land.

⁶ Come, let's worship and bow down.
   Let's kneel in front of the Lord, our maker,
⁷      because he is our God
          and we are the people in his care,
          the flock that he leads.

  If only you would listen to him today!
⁸    "Do not be stubborn like ⌊my people were⌋ at Meribah,
     like the time at Massah in the desert.
⁹       Your ancestors challenged me and tested me there,
        although they had seen what I had done.
¹⁰   For 40 years I was disgusted with those people.
     So I said, 'They are a people whose hearts continue
        to stray.
     They have not learned my ways.'
¹¹   That is why I angrily took this solemn oath:
     'They will never enter my place of rest!' "

## Psalm 96

¹ Sing to the Lord a new song!
   Sing to the Lord, all the earth!
² Sing to the Lord! Praise his name!
   Day after day announce that the Lord saves his people.

3 Tell people about his glory.
  Tell all the nations about his miracles.

4 The Lord is great!
  He should be highly praised.
  He should be feared more than all ⌊other⌋ gods
5   because all the gods of the nations are idols.
  The Lord made the heavens.
6   Splendor and majesty are in his presence.
  Strength and beauty are in his holy place.

7 Give to the Lord, you families of the nations.
  Give to the Lord glory and power.
8 Give to the Lord the glory he deserves.
  Bring an offering, and come into his courtyards.
9 Worship the Lord in ⌊his⌋ holy splendor.
  Tremble in his presence, all the earth!

10 Say to the nations, "The Lord rules as king!"
  The earth stands firm; it cannot be moved.
  He will judge people fairly.
11   Let the heavens rejoice and the earth be glad.
  Let the sea and everything in it roar like thunder.
12   Let the fields and everything in them rejoice.
    Then all the trees in the forest will sing joyfully
13     in the Lord's presence because he is coming.
      He is coming to judge the earth.
        He will judge the world with righteousness
        and its people with his truth.

## Psalm 97

1 The Lord rules as king.
  Let the earth rejoice.
  Let all the islands be joyful.
2 Clouds and darkness surround him.
  Righteousness and justice are the foundations
    of his throne.
3 Fire spreads ahead of him.
  It burns his enemies who surround him.
4 His flashes of lightning light up the world.
  The earth sees them and trembles.
5 The mountains melt like wax in the presence of the Lord,
  in the presence of the Lord of the whole earth.
6 The heavens tell about his righteousness,
  and all the people of the world see his glory.

⁷ Everyone who worships idols
    and brags about false gods will be put to shame.
  All the gods will bow to him.

⁸ Zion hears about this and rejoices.
    The people of Judah are delighted with your judgments,
      O Lord.
⁹ You, O Lord, the Most High, are above the whole earth.
    You are highest. You are above all the gods.
¹⁰ Let those who love the Lord hate evil.
    The one who guards the lives of his godly ones
      will rescue them from the power of wicked people.
¹¹ Light dawns for righteous people*ᵃ*
    and joy for those whose motives are decent.
¹² Find joy in the Lord, you righteous people.
  Give thanks to him as you remember how holy he is.

## Psalm 98

*A psalm.*

¹ Sing a new song to the Lord
    because he has done miraculous things.
      His right hand and his holy arm have gained victory
        for him.
² The Lord has made his salvation known.
    He has uncovered his righteousness for the nations
      to see.
³   He has not forgotten to be merciful and faithful
  to Israel's descendants.
    All the ends of the earth have seen how our God
      saves ⌊them⌋.

⁴ Shout happily to the Lord, all the earth.
  Break out into joyful singing, and make music.
⁵ Make music to the Lord with a lyre,
    with a lyre and the melody of a psalm,
⁶   with trumpets and the playing of a ram's horn.
  Shout happily in the presence of the king, the Lord.

⁷ Let the sea, everything in it,
    the world, and those who live in it roar like thunder.
⁸ Let the rivers clap their hands

---

*ᵃ*97:11 One Hebrew manuscript, Greek, Syriac, Latin; other Hebrew manuscripts "Light is planted for righteous people."

and the mountains sing joyfully
9     in the Lord's presence
         because he is coming to judge the earth.
         He will judge the world with justice
            and its people with fairness.

## Psalm 99

1 The Lord rules as king.
    Let the people tremble.
  He is enthroned over the angels.*
    Let the earth quake.
2 The Lord is mighty in Zion.
    He is high above all people.
3     Let them give thanks to your great and fearful name.

   He is holy!

4 The king's strength is that he loves justice.
    You have established fairness.
    You have done what is fair and right for Jacob.

5 Highly honor the Lord our God.
  Bow down at his footstool.

   He is holy!

6 Moses and Aaron were among his priests.
  Samuel was among those who prayed to him.
     They called to the Lord, and he answered them.
7      He spoke to them from a column of smoke.
     They obeyed his written instructions and the laws that
        he gave them.
8 O Lord, our God, you answered them.
     You showed them that you are a forgiving God
        and that you are a God who punishes their
           ⌊sinful⌋ deeds.

9 Highly honor the Lord our God.
  Bow at his holy mountain.

   The Lord our God is holy!

---

*99:1 Or "cherubim."

## Psalm 100

*A psalm of thanksgiving.*

1 Shout happily to the Lord, all the earth.
2 Serve the Lord cheerfully.
  Come into his presence with a joyful song.
3 Realize that the Lord alone is God.
    He made us, and we are his.[a]
    We are his people and the sheep in his care.
4 Enter his gates with a song of thanksgiving.
  Come into his courtyards with a song of praise.
  Give thanks to him; praise his name.

5 The Lord is good.
    His mercy endures forever.
    His faithfulness endures throughout every generation.

## Psalm 101

*A psalm by David.*

1 I will sing about mercy and justice.
  O Lord, I will make music to praise you.
2 I want to understand the path to integrity.
    When will you come to me?

  I will live in my own home with integrity.
3    I will not put anything wicked in front of my eyes.
  I hate what unfaithful people do.
    I want no part of it.
4 I will keep far away from devious minds.
    I will have nothing to do with evil.
5 I will destroy anyone who secretly slanders his neighbor.
    I will not tolerate anyone with a conceited look or
        arrogant heart.
6 My eyes will be watching the faithful people in the land
    so that they may live with me.
      The person who lives with integrity will serve me.

7 The one who does deceitful things will not stay
    in my home.
  The one who tells lies will not remain in my presence.

---

[a]100:3 Many Hebrew manuscripts, Greek, Targum, Latin; other Hebrew manuscripts "and not we ourselves."

⁸ Every morning I will destroy all the wicked people
    in the land
  to rid the Lord's city of all troublemakers.

## Psalm 102

*A prayer by someone who is suffering, when he is weary
and pours out his troubles in the Lord's presence.*

¹ O Lord, hear my prayer,
    and let my cry for help come to you.
²     Do not hide your face from me when I am in trouble.
    Turn your ear toward me.
    Answer me quickly when I call.
³ My days disappear like smoke.
  My bones burn like hot coals.
⁴ My heart is beaten down and withered like grass
    because I have forgotten about eating.
⁵ I am nothing but skin and bones
    because of my loud groans.
⁶ I am like a desert owl,
    like an owl living in the ruins.
⁷ I lie awake.
  I am like a lonely bird on a rooftop.
⁸ All day long my enemies insult me.
    Those who ridicule me use my name as a curse.
⁹ I eat ashes like bread
    and my tears are mixed with my drink
¹⁰     because of your hostility and anger,
    because you have picked me up and thrown me away.
¹¹ My days are like a shadow that is getting longer,
    and I wither away like grass.

¹² But you, O Lord, remain forever.
    You are remembered throughout every generation.
¹³     You will rise and have compassion on Zion,
        because it is time to grant a favor to it.
            Indeed, the appointed time has come.
¹⁴            Your servants value Zion's stones,
                and they pity its rubble.
¹⁵ The nations will fear the Lord's name.
  All the kings of the earth will fear your glory.
¹⁶ When the Lord builds Zion,
    he will appear in his glory.
¹⁷     He will turn his attention to the prayers
        of those who have been abandoned.

He will not despise their prayers.
<sup>18</sup> This will be written down for a future generation
  so that a people yet to be created may praise the LORD:
<sup>19</sup>   "The LORD looked down from his holy place
      high above.
    From heaven he looked at the earth.
<sup>20</sup>     He heard the groans of the prisoners
      and set free those who were condemned to death.
<sup>21</sup>       The LORD's name is announced in Zion
        and his praise in Jerusalem
<sup>22</sup>         when nations and kingdoms gather
          to worship the LORD."

<sup>23</sup> He has weakened my strength along the way.
  He has reduced ⌊the number of⌋ my days.
<sup>24</sup> I said, "My God, don't take me now in the middle of my life.
  Your years ⌊continue on⌋ throughout every generation.
<sup>25</sup>   Long ago you laid the foundation of the earth.
  Even the heavens are the works of your hands.
<sup>26</sup>     They will come to an end, but you will still go on.
    They will all wear out like clothing.
      You will change them like clothes,
        and they will be thrown away.
<sup>27</sup>         But you remain the same, and your life
          will never end.
<sup>28</sup>     The children of your servants will go on living ⌊here⌋.
    Their descendants will be secure in your presence."

## Psalm 103
*By David.*

<sup>1</sup> Praise the LORD, my soul!
  Praise his holy name, all that is within me.
<sup>2</sup> Praise the LORD, my soul,
  and never forget all the good he has done:
<sup>3</sup>   He is the one who forgives all your sins,
    the one who heals all your diseases,
<sup>4</sup>     the one who rescues your life from the pit,
    the one who crowns you with mercy and
      compassion,
<sup>5</sup>       the one who fills your life with blessings
      so that you become young again like an eagle.

<sup>6</sup> The LORD does what is right and fair
  for all who are oppressed.

7 He let Moses know his ways.
   He let the Israelites know the things he had done.
8 The LORD is compassionate, merciful, patient,
   and always ready to forgive.

9 He will not always accuse us of wrong
   or be angry ⌞with us⌟ forever.
10 He has not treated us as we deserve for our sins
   or paid us back for our wrongs.

11 As high as the heavens are above the earth—
   that is how vast his mercy is toward those who fear him.
12 As far as the east is from the west—
   that is how far he has removed our rebellious acts
      from himself.
13 As a father has compassion for his children,
   so the LORD has compassion for those who fear him.

14 He certainly knows what we are made of.
   He bears in mind that we are dust.
15 Human life is as short-lived as grass.
   It blossoms like a flower in the field.
16    When the wind blows over the flower, it disappears,
      and there is no longer any sign of it.

17 But from everlasting to everlasting,
   the LORD's mercy is on those who fear him.
      His righteousness belongs
         to their children and grandchildren,
18       to those who are faithful to his promise,[a]
         to those who remember to follow his guiding
            principles.
19 The LORD has set his throne in heaven.
   His kingdom rules everything.

20 Praise the LORD, all his angels,
   you mighty beings who carry out his orders
   and are ready to obey his spoken orders.
21 Praise the LORD, all his armies,
   his servants who carry out his will.
22 Praise the LORD, all his creatures
   in all the places of his empire.
   Praise the LORD, my soul!

---

[a] 103:18 Or "covenant."

## Psalm 104

1 Praise the Lord, my soul!
 O Lord my God, you are very great.
  You are clothed with splendor and majesty.
2  You cover yourself with light as though it were a robe.
  You stretch out the heavens as though they were curtains.
3  You lay the beams of your home in the water.
  You use the clouds for your chariot.
  You move on the wings of the wind.
4  You make your angels winds
   and your servants flames of fire.

5 You set the earth on its foundations
  so that it can never be shaken.
6 You covered the earth with an ocean as though it
   were a robe.
  Water stood above the mountains
7   and fled because of your threat.
  Water ran away at the sound of your thunder.
8   The mountains rose and the valleys sank
    to the place you appointed for them.
9   Water cannot cross the boundary you set
    and cannot come back to cover the earth.

10 You make water gush from springs into valleys.
   It flows between the mountains.
11    Every wild animal drinks ⌊from them⌋.
    Wild donkeys quench their thirst.
12    The birds live by the streams.
    They sing among the branches.
13 You water the mountains from your home above.
  You fill the earth with the fruits of your labors.

14 You make grass grow for cattle
   and make vegetables for humans to use
    in order to get food from the ground.
15 You make wine to cheer human hearts,
   olive oil to make faces shine,
    and bread to strengthen human hearts.
16 The Lord's trees, the cedars in Lebanon which he planted,
   drink their fill.
17    Birds build their nests in them.
    Storks make their homes in fir trees.
18 The high mountains are for wild goats.
  The rocks are a refuge for badgers.

¹⁹ He created the moon, which marks the seasons,
  and the sun, which knows when to set.
²⁰   He brings darkness, and it is nighttime,
    when all the wild animals in the forest come out.
²¹     The young lions roar for their prey
      and seek their food from God.
²² When the sun rises,
  they gather and lie down in their dens.
²³   Then people go to do their work,
    to do their tasks until evening.

²⁴ What a large number of things you have made, O Lord!
  You made them all by wisdom.
    The earth is filled with your creatures.
²⁵   The sea is so big and wide with countless creatures,
    living things both large and small.
²⁶   Ships sail on it,
    and Leviathan, which you made, plays in it.
²⁷ All of them look to you to give them their food at the right time.
²⁸   You give it to them, and they gather it up.
  You open your hand, and they are filled with blessings.
²⁹   You hide your face, and they are terrified.
  You take away their breath, and they die and return to dust.
³⁰   You send out your Spirit, and they are created.
  You renew the face of the earth.

³¹ May the glory of the Lord endure forever.
  May the Lord find joy in what he has made.
³²   He looks at the earth, and it trembles.
  He touches the mountains, and they smoke.
³³     I will sing to the Lord throughout my life.
      I will make music to praise my God as long as I live.
³⁴ May my thoughts be pleasing to him.
    I will find joy in the Lord.
³⁵ May sinners vanish from the world.
  May there no longer be any wicked people.
  Praise the Lord, my soul!

Hallelujah!

## Psalm 105

¹ Give thanks to the Lord.
  Call on him.

Make known among the nations what he has done.
² Sing to him.
Make music to praise him.
Meditate on all the miracles he has performed.
³ Brag about his holy name.
Let the hearts of those who seek the LORD rejoice.
⁴ Search for the LORD and his strength.
Always seek his presence.
⁵ Remember the miracles he performed,
    the amazing things he did, and the judgments
        he pronounced,
⁶     you descendants of his servant Abraham,
    you descendants of Jacob, his chosen ones.

⁷ He is the LORD our God.
    His judgments are pronounced throughout the earth.
⁸ He always remembers his promise,[a]
    the word that he commanded for a thousand
        generations,
⁹     the promise that he made to Abraham,
    and his sworn oath to Isaac.
¹⁰ He confirmed it as a law for Jacob,
    as an everlasting promise to Israel,
¹¹     by saying, "I will give you the land of Canaan.
    It is your share of the inheritance."

¹² While the people of Israel were few in number,
    a small group of foreigners living in that land,
¹³     they wandered from nation to nation,
    from one kingdom to another.
¹⁴ He didn't permit anyone to oppress them.
    He warned kings about them:
¹⁵     "Do not touch my anointed ones
    or harm my prophets."

¹⁶ He brought famine to the land.
    He took away their food supply.
¹⁷ He sent a man ahead of them.
    He sent Joseph, who was sold as a slave.
¹⁸     They hurt his feet with shackles,
        and cut into his neck with an iron collar.
¹⁹         The LORD's promise tested him through fiery trials
        until his prediction came true.

---

[a] 105:8 Or "covenant."

20 The king sent someone to release him.
  The ruler of nations set him free.
21 He made Joseph the master of his palace
  and the ruler of all his possessions.
22   Joseph trained the king's officers the way he wanted
    and taught his respected leaders wisdom.

23 Then Israel came to Egypt.
  Jacob lived as a foreigner in the land of Ham.
24 The LORD made his people grow rapidly in number
  and stronger than their enemies.
25 He changed their minds so that they hated his people,
  and they dealt treacherously with his servants.
26 He sent his servant Moses, and he sent Aaron, whom he
    had chosen.
27   They displayed his miraculous signs among them
    and did amazing things in the land of Ham.
28 He sent darkness and made ⌊their land⌋ dark.
  They did not rebel against his orders.
29 He turned their water into blood
  and caused their fish to die.
30 He made their land swarm with frogs,
  even in the kings' bedrooms.
31 He spoke, and swarms of flies and gnats
  infested their whole territory.
32 He gave them hail and lightning
  instead of rain throughout their land.
33 He struck their grapevines and fig trees
  and smashed the trees in their territory.
34 He spoke, and countless locusts and grasshoppers came.
35   They devoured all the plants in the land.
  They devoured the crops in the fields.
36 He killed all the firstborn sons,
    the first ones born in the land when their fathers
      were young.
37 He brought Israel out with silver and gold,
  and no one among his tribes stumbled.
38 The Egyptians were terrified of Israel,
  so they were glad when Israel left.
39 He spread out a cloud as a protective covering
  and a fire to light up the night.
40 The Israelites asked, and he brought them quail
  and filled them with bread from heaven.
41 He opened a rock, and water gushed
  and flowed like a river through the dry places.

⁴² He remembered his holy promise to his servant Abraham.
⁴³ He brought his people out with joy,
>   his chosen ones with a song of joy.
⁴⁴ He gave them the lands of ⌊other⌋ nations,
>   and they inherited what others had worked for
⁴⁵   so that they would obey his laws
>       and follow his teachings.

Hallelujah!

## Psalm 106

¹ Hallelujah!

Give thanks to the LORD because he is good,
>   because his mercy endures forever.
² Who can speak about all the mighty things the LORD
>       has done?
Who can announce all the things for which he is worthy
>       of praise?
³ Blessed are those who defend justice
>   and do what is right at all times.

⁴ Remember me, O LORD, when you show favor
>       to your people.
Come to help me with your salvation
⁵   so that I may see the prosperity of your chosen ones,
>       find joy in our people's happiness,
>           and brag with the people who belong to you.

⁶ We have sinned, and so did our ancestors.
We have done wrong.
We are guilty.
⁷   When our ancestors were in Egypt,
>       they gave no thought to your miracles.
>           They did not remember your numerous acts
>               of mercy,
>           so they rebelled at the sea, the Red Sea.

⁸ He saved them because of his reputation
>   so that he could make his mighty power known.
⁹ He angrily commanded the Red Sea, and it dried up.
He led them through deep water as though it were a desert.
¹⁰ He rescued them from the power of the one who
>       hated them.
He rescued them from the enemy.

¹¹ Water covered their adversaries.
   Not one Egyptian survived.
¹²     Then our ancestors believed what he said.
         They sang his praise.

¹³ They quickly forgot what he did.
   They did not wait for his advice.
¹⁴ They had an unreasonable desire ⌊for food⌋
         in the wilderness.
   In the desert they tested God.
¹⁵     He gave them what they asked for.
         He ⌊also⌋ gave them a degenerative disease.

¹⁶ In the camp certain men became envious of Moses.
   They also became envious of Aaron, the LORD's holy one.
¹⁷     The ground split open and swallowed Dathan.
         It buried Abiram's followers.
¹⁸         A fire broke out among their followers.
             Flames burned up wicked people.

¹⁹ At Mount Horeb they made ⌊a statue of⌋ a calf.
   They worshiped an idol made of metal.
²⁰     They traded their glorious God*ᵃ*
         for the statue of a bull that eats grass.
²¹ They forgot God, their savior,
   the one who did spectacular things in Egypt,
²²     miracles in the land of Ham,
         and terrifying things at the Red Sea.
²³ God said he was going to destroy them,
   but Moses, his chosen one, stood in his way
         to prevent him from exterminating them.

²⁴ They refused ⌊to enter⌋ the pleasant land.
   They did not believe what he said.
²⁵ They complained in their tents.
   They did not obey the LORD.
²⁶     Raising his hand, he swore
         that he would kill them in the wilderness,
²⁷         kill their descendants among the nations,
             and scatter them throughout various lands.

²⁸ They joined in worshiping the god Baal while they
         were at Peor,

---

ᵃ 106:20 Or "their glory."

and they ate what was sacrificed to the dead.
<sup>29</sup> They infuriated God by what they did,
and a plague broke out among them.
<sup>30</sup> Then Phinehas stood between God and the people,
and the plague was stopped.
<sup>31</sup> Because of this, Phinehas was considered
righteous forever,
throughout every generation.
<sup>32</sup> They made God angry by the water at Meribah.
Things turned out badly for Moses because of what
they did,
<sup>33</sup> since they made him bitter so that he spoke recklessly.

<sup>34</sup> They did not destroy the people as the LORD had told them.
<sup>35</sup> Instead, they intermarried with other nations.
They learned to do what other nations did,
<sup>36</sup> and they worshiped their idols,
which became a trap for them.
<sup>37</sup> They sacrificed their sons and daughters to demons.
<sup>38</sup> They shed innocent blood,
the blood of their own sons and daughters
whom they sacrificed to the idols of Canaan.
The land became polluted with blood.
<sup>39</sup> They became filthy because of what they did.
They behaved like prostitutes.
<sup>40</sup> The LORD burned with anger against his own people.
He was disgusted with those who belonged to him.
<sup>41</sup> He handed them over to other nations,
and those who hated them ruled them.
<sup>42</sup> Their enemies oppressed them
and made them subject to their power.
<sup>43</sup> He rescued them many times,
but they continued to plot rebellion against him
and to sink deeper because of their sin.
<sup>44</sup> He saw that they were suffering
when he heard their cry for help.
<sup>45</sup> He remembered his promise*[a]* to them.
In keeping with his rich mercy, he changed his plans.
<sup>46</sup> He let them find compassion
from all those who held them captive.

<sup>47</sup> Rescue us, O LORD our God, and gather us from
the nations

---

*[a]* 106:45 Or "covenant."

so that we may give thanks to your holy name
and make your praise our glory.

⁴⁸ Thanks be to the Lord God of Israel
from everlasting to everlasting.
Let all the people say amen.

Hallelujah!

# BOOK FIVE
(Psalms 107–150)

## Psalm 107

¹ Give thanks to the Lord because he is good,
because his mercy endures forever.

² Let the people the Lord defended repeat these words.
They are the people he defended from the power of
their enemies
³ and gathered from other countries,
from the east and from the west,
from the north and from the south.
⁴ They wandered around the desert on a deserted road
without finding an inhabited city.
⁵ They were hungry and thirsty.
They began to lose hope.
⁶ In their distress they cried out to the Lord.
He rescued them from their troubles.
⁷ He led them on a road that went straight to an
inhabited city.

⁸ Let them give thanks to the Lord because of his mercy.
He performed his miracles for Adam's descendants.
⁹ He gave plenty to drink to those who were thirsty.
He filled those who were hungry with good food.
¹⁰ Those who lived in the dark, in death's shadow
were prisoners in misery.
They were held in iron chains
¹¹ because they had rebelled against God's words
and had despised the advice given by
the Most High.
¹² So he humbled them with hard work.
They fell down, but no one was there to help them.
¹³ In their distress they cried out to the Lord.
He saved them from their troubles.

¹⁴ He brought them out of the dark, out of death's shadow.
　　He broke apart their chains.

¹⁵ Let them give thanks to the Lord because of his mercy.
　　He performed his miracles for Adam's descendants.
¹⁶ 　He shattered bronze gates
　　　and cut iron bars in two.
¹⁷ 　Fools suffered because of their disobedience
　　　and because of their crimes.
¹⁸ 　All food was disgusting to them,
　　　and they came near death's gates.
¹⁹ In their distress they cried out to the Lord.
　　He saved them from their troubles.
²⁰ 　He sent his message and healed them.
　　He rescued them from the grave.

²¹ Let them give thanks to the Lord because of his mercy.
　　He performed his miracles for Adam's descendants.
²² Let them bring songs of thanksgiving as their sacrifice.
　Let them tell in joyful songs what he has done.
²³ 　Those who sail on the sea in ships,
　　　who do business on the high seas,
²⁴ 　　　have seen what the Lord can do,
　　　　the miracles he performed in the depths of the sea.
²⁵ 　He spoke, and a storm began to blow,
　　　and it made the waves rise high.
²⁶ 　The sailors aboard ship rose toward the sky.
　　　They plunged into the depths.
　　　　Their courage melted in ⌊the face of⌋ disaster.
²⁷ 　They reeled and staggered like drunks,
　　　and all their skills as sailors became useless.
²⁸ In their distress they cried out to the Lord.
　　He led them from their troubles.
²⁹ 　He made the storm calm down,
　　　and the waves became still.
³⁰ 　　The sailors were glad that the storm was quiet.
　　He guided them to the harbor they had longed for.

³¹ Let them give thanks to the Lord because of his mercy.
　　He performed his miracles for Adam's descendants.
³² Let them glorify him when the people are gathered
　　　for worship.
　Let them praise him in the company of respected leaders.
³³ 　He changes rivers into a desert,
　　　springs into thirsty ground,

³⁴     and fertile ground into a layer of salt
       because of the wickedness of the people
          living there.
³⁵ He changes deserts into lakes
   and dry ground into springs.
³⁶    There he settles those who are hungry,
     and they build cities to live in.
³⁷    They plant in fields and vineyards
     that produce crops.
³⁸ He blesses them, and their numbers multiply,
   and he does not allow a shortage of cattle.

³⁹ They became few in number and were humiliated
   because of oppression, disaster, and sorrow.
⁴⁰    He poured contempt on their influential people
     and made them stumble around in
         a pathless desert.
⁴¹    But now he lifts needy people high above suffering
     and makes their families like flocks.
⁴²       Decent people will see this and rejoice,
         but all the wicked people will shut
            their mouths.

⁴³ Let those who ⌊think⌋ they are wise
   pay attention to these things
     so that they may understand the LORD's blessings.

## Psalm 108ᵃ
*A song; a psalm by David.*

¹ My heart is confident, O God.
I want to sing and make music even with my soul.ᵇ
²   Wake up, harp and lyre!
I want to wake up at dawn.
³ I want to give thanks to you among the people, O LORD.
I want to make music to praise you among the nations
⁴   because your mercy is higher than the heavens.
    Your truth reaches the skies.

⁵ May you be honored above the heavens, O God.
Let your glory extend over the whole earth.

---

ᵃ108:1 Verses 1-5 are virtually identical in wording to Psalm 57:7-11; verses 6-13 are virtually identical in wording to Psalm 60:5-12.
ᵇ108:1 Or "my glory."

⁶ Save ⌊us⌋ with your powerful hand, and answer us
    so that those who are dear to you may be rescued.

⁷ God has promised the following through his holiness:
  "I will triumph!
    I will divide Shechem.
    I will measure the valley of Succoth.
⁸     Gilead is mine.
    Manasseh is mine.
    Ephraim is the helmet on my head.
    Judah is my scepter.
⁹     Moab is my washtub.
    I will throw my shoe over Edom.
    I will shout in triumph over Philistia."

¹⁰ Who will bring me into the fortified city?
  Who will lead me to Edom?
¹¹   Isn't it you, O God, who rejected us?
    Isn't it you, O God, who refused to accompany
      our armies?

¹² Give us help against the enemy
    because human assistance is worthless.
¹³     With God we will display great strength.
    He will trample our enemies.

## Psalm 109

*For the choir director; a psalm by David.*

¹ O God, whom I praise, do not turn a deaf ear to me.
² Wicked and deceitful people have opened their mouths
    against me.
  They speak against me with lying tongues.
³   They surround me with hateful words.
  They fight against me for no reason.
⁴ In return for my love, they accuse me,
    but I pray for them.[a]
⁵ They reward me with evil instead of good
    and with hatred instead of love.

⁶ ⌊I said,⌋ "Appoint the evil one to oppose him.
    Let Satan stand beside him.
⁷     When he stands trial,

---
[a] 109:4 Or "but I am a man of prayer."

      let him be found guilty.
      Let his prayer be considered sinful.
⁸   Let his days be few ⌊in number⌋.
      Let someone else take his position.

⁹   "Let his children become fatherless and his wife
          a widow.
¹⁰  Let his children wander around and beg.
        Let them seek help far from their ruined homes.
¹¹  Let a creditor take everything he owns.
      Let strangers steal what he has worked for.
¹²  Let no one be kind to him anymore.
      Let no one show any pity to his fatherless children.
¹³  Let his descendants be cut off
        and their family name be wiped out by the
          next generation.
¹⁴  Let the LORD remember the guilt of his ancestors
        and not wipe out his mother's sin.
¹⁵     Let their guilt and sin always remain on record
           in front of the LORD.
    Let the LORD remove every memory of him[a] from
        the earth,
¹⁶     because he did not remember to be kind.

    "He drove oppressed, needy,
        and brokenhearted people to their graves.
¹⁷  He loved to put curses ⌊on others⌋,
      so he, too, was cursed.
    He did not like to bless ⌊others⌋,
      so he never received a blessing.
¹⁸  He wore cursing as though it were clothing,
      so cursing entered his body like water
          and his bones like oil.
¹⁹  Let cursing be his clothing,
      a belt he always wears."

²⁰ This is how the LORD rewards those who accuse me,
    those who say evil things against me.

²¹ O Lord Almighty, deal with me out of the goodness
        of your name.
    Rescue me because of your mercy.
²² I am oppressed and needy.

---

[a] 109:15 Or "them."

I can feel the pain in my heart.
²³ I fade away like a lengthening shadow.
I have been shaken off like a grasshopper.
²⁴ My knees give way because I have been fasting.
My body has become lean, without any fat.
²⁵ I have become the victim of my enemies' insults.
They look at me and shake their heads.
²⁶ Help me, O LORD my God.
Save me because of your mercy.
²⁷ Then they will know that this is your doing,
that you, O LORD, are the one who saved me.
²⁸ They may curse, but you will bless.
Let those who attack me be ashamed,
but let me rejoice.
²⁹ Let those who accuse me wear disgrace as though
it were clothing.
Let them be wrapped in their shame as though
it were a robe.

³⁰ With my mouth I will give many thanks to the LORD.
I will praise him among many people,
³¹ because he stands beside needy people
to save them from those who would condemn them
to death.

## Psalm 110

*A psalm by David.*

¹ The LORD said to my Lord,
"Take the honored position—the one next to me
[God the Father] on the heavenly throne
until I put your enemies under your control."[a]

² The LORD will extend your powerful scepter from Zion.
Rule your enemies who surround you.

³ Your people will volunteer when you call up
your army.
Your young people will come to you in holy splendor
like dew in the early morning.[b]

---

[a]110:1 Or "Sit at my right hand, until I make your enemies your footstool."
[b]110:3 Or "You have the dew of your youth."

4 The Lord has taken an oath and will not change his mind:
    "You are a priest forever, in the way Melchizedek
        was a priest."

5 The Lord is at your right side.
    He will crush kings on the day of his anger.
6 He will pass judgment on the nations
    and fill them with dead bodies.
        Throughout the earth he will crush ⌊their⌋ heads.
7 He will drink from the brook along the road.
    He will hold his head high.

## Psalm 111[a]

1 Hallelujah!

I will give thanks to the Lord with all my heart
    in the company of decent people and in the
        congregation.
2 The Lord's deeds are spectacular.
    They should be studied by all who enjoy them.
3 His work is glorious and majestic.
    His righteousness continues forever.
4 He has made his miracles unforgettable.
    The Lord is merciful and compassionate.
5 He provides food for those who fear him.
    He always remembers his promise.[b]
6 He has revealed the power of his works to his people
    by giving them the lands of other nations as an
        inheritance.
7 His works are done with truth and justice.
    All his guiding principles are trustworthy.
8    They last forever and ever.
        They are carried out with truth and decency.
9 He has sent salvation to his people.
    He has ordered that his promise should continue forever.
        His name is holy and terrifying.
10 The fear of the Lord is the beginning of wisdom.
    Good sense is shown by everyone who follows
        ⌊God's guiding principles⌋.
    His praise continues forever.

---

[a] 111:1 Psalm 111 is a poem in Hebrew alphabetical order.
[b] 111:5 Or "covenant."

## Psalm 112[a]

¹ Hallelujah!

Blessed is the person who fears the LORD
  and is happy to obey his commands.
² His descendants will grow strong on the earth.
  The family of a decent person will be blessed.
³ Wealth and riches will be in his home.
  His righteousness continues forever.
⁴ Light will shine in the dark for a decent person.
  He is merciful, compassionate, and fair.

⁵ All goes well for the person who is generous and
    lends willingly.
  He earns an honest living.
⁶ He will never fail.
  A righteous person will always be remembered.
⁷ He is not afraid of bad news.
  His heart remains secure, full of confidence
    in the LORD.
⁸ His heart is steady, and he is not afraid.
  In the end he will look triumphantly at
    his enemies.
⁹ He gives freely to poor people.
  His righteousness continues forever.
  His head is raised in honor.
¹⁰ The wicked person sees this and becomes angry.
  He angrily grits his teeth and disappears.
    The hope that wicked people have will vanish.

## Psalm 113

¹ Hallelujah!

You servants of the LORD, praise him.
Praise the name of the LORD.
² Thank the name of the LORD now and forever.
³ From where the sun rises to where the sun sets,
  the name of the LORD should be praised.
⁴ The LORD is high above all the nations.
  His glory is above the heavens.
⁵ Who is like the LORD our God?
  He is seated on his high throne.
⁶ He bends down to look at heaven and earth.

---

[a] 112:1 Psalm 112 is a poem in Hebrew alphabetical order.

⁷   He lifts the poor from the dust.
      He lifts the needy from a garbage heap.
⁸   He seats them with influential people,
      with the influential leaders of his people.
⁹   He makes a woman who is in a childless home
      a joyful mother.

Hallelujah!

## Psalm 114

¹ When Israel left Egypt,
   when Jacob's family left people who spoke a foreign
         language,
² Judah became his holy place and Israel became
         his kingdom.
³   The Red Sea looked at this and ran away.
      The Jordan River turned back.
⁴      The mountains jumped like rams.
         The hills jumped like lambs.
⁵   Red Sea, why did you run away?
      Jordan River, what made you turn back?
⁶      Mountains, what made you jump like rams?
         Hills, what made you jump like lambs?
⁷ Earth, tremble in the presence of the Lord,
   in the presence of the God of Jacob.
⁸      He turns a rock into a pool filled with water
         and turns flint into a spring flowing with water.

## Psalm 115

¹ Don't give glory to us, O Lord.
   Don't give glory to us.
      Instead, give glory to your name
         because of your mercy and faithfulness.
² Why should other nations say, "Where is their God?"
³   Our God is in heaven.
      He does whatever he wants.
⁴ Their idols are made of silver and gold.
      They were made by human hands.ᵃ
⁵      They have mouths, but they cannot speak.
         They have eyes, but they cannot see.
⁶      They have ears, but they cannot hear.
         They have noses, but they cannot smell.
⁷      They have hands, but they cannot feel.

---

ᵃ115:4 Verses 4–8 are virtually identical in wording to Psalm 135:15–18.

They have feet, but they cannot walk.
They cannot ₗevenⱼ make a sound with their throats.
⁸ Those who make idols end up like them.
So does everyone who trusts them.

⁹ Israel, trust the LORD.
He is your helper and your shield.
¹⁰ Descendants of Aaron, trust the LORD.
He is your helper and your shield.
¹¹ If you fear the LORD, trust the LORD.
He is your helper and your shield.

¹² The LORD, who is ₗalwaysⱼ thinking about us, will bless us.
He will bless the descendants of Israel.
He will bless the descendants of Aaron.
¹³ He will bless those who fear the LORD,
from the least important to the most important.
¹⁴ May the LORD continue to bless you and your children.
¹⁵ You will be blessed by the LORD, the maker of heaven
and earth.
¹⁶ The highest heaven belongs to the LORD,
but he has given the earth to the descendants of Adam.
¹⁷ Those who are dead do not praise the LORD,
nor do those who go into the silence ₗof the graveⱼ.
¹⁸ But we will thank the LORD now and forever.

Hallelujah!

## Psalm 116

¹ I love the LORD because he hears my voice, my pleas
for mercy.
² I will call on him as long as I live
because he turns his ear toward me.
³ The ropes of death became tangled around me.
The horrors of the grave took hold of me.
I experienced pain and agony.
⁴ But I kept calling on the name of the LORD:
"Please, LORD, rescue me!"

⁵ The LORD is merciful and righteous.
Our God is compassionate.
⁶ The LORD protects defenseless people.
When I was weak, he saved me.
⁷ Be at peace again, my soul,
because the LORD has been good to you.

8. You saved me from death.
   You saved my eyes from tears ⌊and⌋ my feet from stumbling.
9. I will walk in the Lord's presence in this world
     of the living.
10. I kept my faith even when I said,
    "I am suffering terribly."
11. I also said when I was panic-stricken,
    "Everyone is undependable."
12. How can I repay the Lord
     for all the good that he has done for me?
13. I will take the cup of salvation
     and call on the name of the Lord.
14. I will keep my vows to the Lord
     in the presence of all his people.
15. Precious in the sight of the Lord
     is the death of his faithful ones.
16. O Lord, I am indeed your servant.
     I am your servant,
        the son of your female servant.
    You have freed me from my chains.
17. I will bring a song of thanksgiving to you as a sacrifice.
    I will call on the name of the Lord.
18. I will keep my vows to the Lord
     in the presence of all his people,
19.    in the courtyards of the Lord's house,
         in the middle of Jerusalem.

Hallelujah!

## Psalm 117

1. Praise the Lord, all you nations!
   Praise him, all you people of the world!
2.   His mercy toward us is powerful.
      The Lord's faithfulness endures forever.

Hallelujah!

## Psalm 118

1. Give thanks to the Lord because he is good,
     because his mercy endures forever.
2.   Israel should say,
       "His mercy endures forever."
3.   The descendants of Aaron should say,
       "His mercy endures forever."

⁴ Those who fear the Lord should say,
  "His mercy endures forever."

⁵ During times of trouble I called on the Lord.
  The Lord answered me ⌊and⌋ set me free ⌊from all of them⌋.
⁶ The Lord is on my side.
  I am not afraid.
    What can mortals do to me?
⁷ The Lord is on my side as my helper.
  I will see ⌊the defeat of⌋ those who hate me.
⁸ It is better to depend on the Lord
  than to trust mortals.
⁹ It is better to depend on the Lord
  than to trust influential people.

¹⁰ All the nations surrounded me,
   ⌊but armed⌋ with the name of the Lord, I defeated them.
¹¹ They surrounded me. Yes, they surrounded me,
   ⌊but armed⌋ with the name of the Lord, I defeated them.
¹² They swarmed around me like bees,
   but they were extinguished like burning thornbushes.
     ⌊So armed⌋ with the name of the Lord, I defeated them.
¹³ They pushed hard to make me fall,
   but the Lord helped me.
¹⁴ The Lord is my strength and my song.
   He is my savior.

¹⁵ The sound of joyful singing and victory is heard
   in the tents of righteous people.
     The right hand of the Lord displays strength.
¹⁶   The right hand of the Lord is held high.
     The right hand of the Lord displays strength.
¹⁷ I will not die,
   but I will live and tell what the Lord has done.
¹⁸ The Lord disciplined me severely,
   but he did not allow me to be killed.

¹⁹ Open the gates of righteousness for me.
   I will go through them ⌊and⌋ give thanks to the Lord.
²⁰ This is the gate of the Lord
   through which righteous people will enter.

²¹ I give thanks to you,
   because you have answered me.

You are my savior.
²² The stone that the builders rejected
  has become the cornerstone.
²³ The LORD is responsible for this,
  and it is amazing for us to see.
²⁴ This is the day the LORD has made.
  Let's rejoice and be glad today!
²⁵ We beg you, O LORD, save us!
  We beg you, O LORD, give us success!
²⁶   Blessed is the one who comes in the name of the LORD.
    We bless you from the LORD's house.
²⁷ The LORD is God, and he has given us light.
  March in a festival procession
    with branches to the horns of the altar.
²⁸ You are my God, and I give thanks to you.
  My God, I honor you highly.

²⁹ Give thanks to the LORD because he is good,
  because his mercy endures forever.

## Psalm 119 [a]

¹ Blessed are those whose lives have integrity,
  those who follow the teachings of the LORD.
² Blessed are those who obey his written instructions.
  They wholeheartedly search for him.
³   They do nothing wrong.
    They follow his directions.
⁴ You have commanded
  that your guiding principles be carefully followed.
⁵ I pray that my ways may become firmly established
  so that I can obey your laws.
⁶   Then I will never feel ashamed
    when I study all your commandments.
⁷ I will give thanks to you
  as I learn your regulations, which are based on your
    righteousness.
⁸ I will obey your laws.
  Never abandon me.

⁹ How can a young person keep his life pure?
  ⌊He can do it⌋ by holding on to your word.
¹⁰ I wholeheartedly searched for you.
  Do not let me wander away from your commandments.

---

[a] 119:1 Psalm 119 is a poem in Hebrew alphabetical order.

¹¹ I have treasured your promise in my heart
 so that I may not sin against you.
¹² Thanks be to you, O Lord.
 Teach me your laws.
¹³ With my lips I have repeated
 every regulation that ⌐comes¬ from your mouth.
¹⁴ I find joy in the way ⌐shown by¬ your written instructions
 more than I find joy in all kinds of riches.
¹⁵ I want to reflect on your guiding principles
 and study your ways.
¹⁶ Your laws make me happy.
 I never forget your word.

¹⁷ Be kind to me so that I may live
 and hold on to your word.
¹⁸ Uncover my eyes
 so that I may see the miraculous things
 in your teachings.
¹⁹ I am a foreigner in this world.
 Do not hide your commandments from me.
²⁰ My soul is overwhelmed with endless longing for your
 regulations.
²¹ You threaten arrogant people, who are condemned
 and wander away from your commandments.
²² Remove the insults and contempt that have fallen on me
 because I have obeyed your written instructions.
²³ Even though influential people plot against me,
 I reflect on your laws.
²⁴ Indeed, your written instructions make me happy.
 They are my best friends.

²⁵ I am close to death.
 Give me a new life as you promised.
²⁶ I told you what I have done, and you answered me.
 Teach me your laws.
²⁷  Help me understand your guiding principles
 so that I may reflect on your miracles.
²⁸ I am drowning in tears.
 Strengthen me as you promised.
²⁹  Turn me away from a life of lies.
 Graciously provide me with your teachings.
³⁰ I have chosen a life of faithfulness.
 I have set your regulations in front of me.
³¹ I have clung tightly to your written instructions.
 O Lord, do not let me be put to shame.

³² I will eagerly pursue your commandments
   because you continue to increase my understanding.

³³ Teach me, O LORD, how to live by your laws,
   and I will obey them to the end.
³⁴ Help me understand so that I can follow your teachings.
   I will guard them with all my heart.
³⁵ Lead me on the path of your commandments,
   because I am happy with them.
³⁶ Direct my heart toward your written instructions
   rather than getting rich in underhanded ways.
³⁷ Turn my eyes away from worthless things.
   Give me a new life in your ways.
³⁸ Keep your promise to me
   so that I can fear you.
³⁹ Take away insults, which I dread,
   because your regulations are good.
⁴⁰ I long for your guiding principles.
   Give me a new life in your righteousness.

⁴¹ Let your blessings reach me, O LORD.
   Save me as you promised.
⁴²    Then I will have an answer for the one who insults me
         since I trust your word.
⁴³ Do not take so much as a single word of truth from
      my mouth.
   My hope is based on your regulations.
⁴⁴    I will follow your teachings forever and ever.
⁴⁵    I will walk around freely
         because I sought out your guiding principles.
⁴⁶    I will speak about your written instructions in the
            presence of kings
         and not feel ashamed.
⁴⁷    Your commandments, which I love, make me happy.
⁴⁸    I lift my hands ⌊in prayer⌋ because of your
            commandments,
         which I love.
      I will reflect on your laws.

⁴⁹ Remember the word ⌊you gave⌋ me.
   Through it you gave me hope.
⁵⁰ This is my comfort in my misery:
   Your promise gave me a new life.
⁵¹ Arrogant people have mocked me with cruelty,
   yet I have not turned away from your teachings.

⁵² I remembered your regulations from long ago, O Lord,
　　and I found comfort ⌊in them⌋.
⁵³ I am burning with anger because of wicked people,
　　who abandon your teachings.
⁵⁴ Your laws have become like psalms to me
　　in this place where I am only a foreigner.
⁵⁵ At night I remember your name, O Lord,
　　and I follow your teachings.
⁵⁶ This has happened to me
　　because I have obeyed your guiding principles.

⁵⁷ You are my inheritance, O Lord.
　　I promised to hold on to your words.
⁵⁸ With all my heart I want to win your favor.
　　Be kind to me as you promised.
⁵⁹ I have thought about my life,
　　and I have directed my feet back to your written
　　　　instructions.
⁶⁰ Without any hesitation I hurry to obey your
　　　commandments.
⁶¹ ⌊Though⌋ the ropes of wicked people are tied around me,
　　I never forget your teachings.
⁶² At midnight I wake up to give thanks to you
　　for the regulations, which are based on your
　　　righteousness.
⁶³ I am a friend to everyone who fears you
　　and to everyone who follows your guiding principles.
⁶⁴ Your mercy, O Lord, fills the earth.
　　Teach me your laws.

⁶⁵ You have treated me well, O Lord,
　　as you promised.
⁶⁶ Teach me ⌊to use⌋ good judgment and knowledge,
　　because I believe in your commandments.
⁶⁷ Before you made me suffer, I used to wander off,
　　but now I hold on to your word.
⁶⁸ You are good, and you do good things.
　　Teach me your laws.
⁶⁹ Arrogant people have smeared me with lies,
　　⌊yet⌋ I obey your guiding principles with all my heart.
⁷⁰ Their hearts are cold and insensitive,
　　⌊yet⌋ I am happy with your teachings.
⁷¹ It was good that I had to suffer
　　in order to learn your laws.

⁷² The teachings ⌐that come⌐ from your mouth are worth more to me
    than thousands in gold or silver.

⁷³ Your hands created me and made me what I am.
    Help me understand so that I may learn your commandments.
⁷⁴ Those who fear you will see me and rejoice,
    because my hope is based on your word.
⁷⁵ I know that your regulations are fair, O Lord,
    and that you were right to make me suffer.
⁷⁶ Let your mercy comfort me
    as you promised.
⁷⁷ Let your compassion reach me so that I may live,
    because your teachings make me happy.
⁷⁸ Let arrogant people be put to shame
    because they lied about me,
        ⌐yet⌐ I reflect on your guiding principles.
⁷⁹ Let those who fear you turn to me
    so that they can come to know your written instructions.
⁸⁰ Let my heart be filled with integrity in regard to your laws
    so that I will not be put to shame.

⁸¹ My soul is weak from waiting for you to save me.
    My hope is based on your word.
⁸² My eyes have become strained from looking for your promise.
    I ask, "When will you comfort me?"
⁸³ Although I have become like a shriveled and dried out wineskin,
    I have not forgotten your laws.
⁸⁴ What is left of my life?
  When will you bring those who persecute me to justice?
⁸⁵   Arrogant people have dug pits to trap me
    in defiance of your teachings.
⁸⁶     (All your commandments are reliable.)
  Those people persecute me with lies. Help me!
⁸⁷   They almost wiped me off ⌐the face of⌐ the earth.
    But I did not abandon your guiding principles.
⁸⁸ Give me a new life through your mercy
    so that I may obey the written instructions,
        ⌐which came⌐ from your mouth.

⁸⁹ O Lord, your word is established in heaven forever.

⁹⁰ Your faithfulness endures throughout every generation.
   You set the earth in place, and it continues to stand.
⁹¹ All things continue to stand today because of
      your regulations,
   since they are all your servants.
⁹² If your teachings had not made me happy,
   then I would have died in my misery.
⁹³ I will never forget your guiding principles,
   because you gave me a new life through them.
⁹⁴ I am yours.
   Save me, because I have searched for your guiding
      principles.
⁹⁵ The wicked people have waited for me in order
      to destroy me,
   ⌞yet⌟ I want to understand your written instructions.
⁹⁶ I have seen a limit to everything else,
   ⌞but⌟ your commandments have no limit.

⁹⁷ Oh, how I love your teachings!
   They are in my thoughts all day long.
⁹⁸ Your commandments make me wiser than my enemies,
   because your commandments are always with me.
⁹⁹ I have more insight than all my teachers,
   because your written instructions are in my thoughts.
¹⁰⁰ I have more wisdom than those with many years
      of experience,
   because I have obeyed your guiding principles.
¹⁰¹ I have kept my feet ⌞from walking⌟ on any evil path
   in order to obey your word.
¹⁰² I have not neglected your regulations,
   because you have taught me.
¹⁰³ How sweet the taste of your promise is!
   It tastes sweeter than honey.
¹⁰⁴ From your guiding principles I gain understanding.
   That is why I hate every path that leads to lying.

¹⁰⁵ Your word is a lamp for my feet
   and a light for my path.
¹⁰⁶ I took an oath, and I will keep it.
   I took an oath to follow your regulations,
      which are based on your righteousness.
¹⁰⁷ I have suffered so much.
   Give me a new life, O LORD, as you promised.
¹⁰⁸ Please accept the praise I gladly give you, O LORD,
   and teach me your regulations.

¹⁰⁹ I always take my life into my own hands,
   but I never forget your teachings.
¹¹⁰ Wicked people have set a trap for me,
   but I have never wandered away from your
      guiding principles.
¹¹¹ Your written instructions are mine forever.
   They are the joy of my heart.
¹¹² I have decided to obey your laws.
   They offer a reward that never ends.

¹¹³ I hate two-faced people,
   but I love your teachings.
¹¹⁴ You are my hiding place and my shield.
   My hope is based on your word.
¹¹⁵ Get away from me, you evildoers,
   so that I can obey the commandments of my God.
¹¹⁶ Help me God, as you promised, so that I may live.
   Do not turn my hope into disappointment.
¹¹⁷ Hold me, and I will be safe,
   and I will always respect your laws.
¹¹⁸ You reject all who wander away from your laws,
   because their lies mislead them.
¹¹⁹ You get rid of all wicked people on earth as if they
      were rubbish.
   That is why I love your written instructions.
¹²⁰ My body shudders in fear of you,
   and I am afraid of your regulations.

¹²¹ I have done what is fair and right.
   Do not leave me at the mercy of those who oppress me.
¹²² Guarantee my well-being.
   Do not let arrogant people oppress me.
¹²³ My eyes are strained from looking for you to save me
   and from looking for the fulfillment of your
      righteous promise.
¹²⁴ Treat me with kindness,
   and teach me your laws.
¹²⁵ I am your servant.
   Help me understand
      so that I may come to know your written instructions.
¹²⁶ It is time for you to act, O Lord.ᵃ
   Even though people have abolished your teachings,

---

ᵃ119:126 One Hebrew manuscript, Latin; other Hebrew manuscripts "It is time to act for the Lord."

¹²⁷ I love your commandments more than gold,
   more than pure gold.
¹²⁸ I follow the straight paths of your guiding principles.
   I hate every pathway that leads to lying.

¹²⁹ Your written instructions are miraculous.
   That is why I obey them.
¹³⁰ Your word is a doorway that lets in light,
   and it helps gullible people understand.
¹³¹ I open my mouth and pant
   because I long for your commandments.
¹³² Turn toward me, and have pity on me
   as you have pledged to do for those who love your name.
¹³³ Make my steps secure through your promise,
   and do not let any sin control me.
¹³⁴ Save me from human oppression
   so that I may obey your guiding principles.
¹³⁵ Smile on me,
   and teach me your laws.
¹³⁶ Streams of tears flow from my eyes
   because others do not follow your teachings.

¹³⁷ You are righteous, O Lord,
   and your regulations are fair.
¹³⁸ You have issued your written instructions.
   They are fair and completely dependable.
¹³⁹ My devotion ⌊for your words⌋ consumes me,
   because my enemies have forgotten your words.
¹⁴⁰ Your promise has been thoroughly tested,
   and I love it.
¹⁴¹ I am unimportant and despised,
   ⌊yet⌋ I never forget your guiding principles.
¹⁴² Your righteousness is an everlasting righteousness,
   and your teachings are reliable.
¹⁴³ Trouble and hardship have found me,
   but your commandments ⌊still⌋ make me happy.
¹⁴⁴ Your written instructions are always right.
   Help me understand ⌊them⌋ so that I will live.

¹⁴⁵ I have called out with all my heart. Answer me, O Lord.
   I want to obey your laws.
¹⁴⁶ I have called out.
   Save me, so that I can obey your written instructions.
¹⁴⁷ I got up before dawn, and I cried out for help.
   My hope is based on your word.

¹⁴⁸ My eyes are wide-open throughout the nighttime hours
   to reflect on your word.
¹⁴⁹ In keeping with your mercy, hear my voice.
   O Lord, give me a new life guided by your regulations.
¹⁵⁰   Those who carry out plots against me are near,
       ⌊yet⌋ they are far away from your teachings.
¹⁵¹   You are near, O Lord,
       and all your commandments are reliable.
¹⁵² Long ago I learned from your written instructions
   that you made them to last forever.

¹⁵³ Look at my misery, and rescue me,
   because I have never forgotten your teachings.
¹⁵⁴ Plead my case ⌊for me⌋, and save me.
   Give me a new life as you promised.
¹⁵⁵ Wicked people are far from being saved,
   because they have not searched for your laws.
¹⁵⁶ Your acts of compassion are many in number, O Lord.
   Give me a new life guided by your regulations.
¹⁵⁷ I have many persecutors and opponents,
   ⌊yet⌋ I have not turned away from your written
       instructions.
¹⁵⁸ I have seen traitors,
   and I am filled with disgust.
       They have not accepted your promise.
¹⁵⁹ See how I have loved your guiding principles!
   O Lord, in keeping with your mercy, give me a new life.
¹⁶⁰ There is nothing but truth in your word,
   and all of your righteous regulations endure forever.

¹⁶¹ Influential people have persecuted me for no reason,
   but it is only your words that fill my heart with terror.
¹⁶² I find joy in your promise
   like someone who finds a priceless treasure.
¹⁶³ I hate lying; I am disgusted with it.
   I love your teachings.
¹⁶⁴ Seven times a day I praise you
   for your righteous regulations.
¹⁶⁵ There is lasting peace for those who love your teachings.
   Nothing can make those people stumble.
¹⁶⁶ I have waited with hope for you to save me, O Lord.
   I have carried out your commandments.
¹⁶⁷ I have obeyed your written instructions.
   I have loved them very much.

¹⁶⁸ I have followed your guiding principles and your
        written instructions,
    because my whole life is in front of you.

¹⁶⁹ Let my cry for help come into your presence, O Lord.
    Help me understand as you promised.
¹⁷⁰ Let my plea for mercy come into your presence.
    Rescue me as you promised.
¹⁷¹ Let my lips pour out praise
    because you teach me your laws.
¹⁷² Let my tongue sing about your promise
    because all your commandments are fair.
¹⁷³ Let your hand help me
    because I have chosen ⌊to follow⌋ your guiding principles.
¹⁷⁴ I have longed for you to save me, O Lord,
    and your teachings make me happy.
¹⁷⁵ Let my soul have new life so that it can praise you.
  Let your regulations help me.
¹⁷⁶ I have wandered away like a lost lamb.
    Search for me,
        because I have never forgotten your commandments.

## Psalm 120

*A song for going up to worship.*

¹ When I was in trouble, I cried out to the Lord,
    and he answered me.
² O Lord, rescue me from lying lips
    and from a deceitful tongue.

³ You deceitful tongue, what can the Lord give you?
    What more can he do for you?
⁴     He will give you a warrior's sharpened arrows and
        red-hot coals.

⁵ How horrible it is to live as a foreigner in Meshech
    or to stay in the tents of Kedar.
⁶     I have lived too long with those who hate peace.
⁷     I am for peace, but when I talk about it,
        they only talk about war.

## Psalm 121
*A song for going up to worship.*

1. I look up toward the mountains.
    Where can I find help?
2. My help comes from the Lord,
    the maker of heaven and earth.
3. He will not let you fall.
    Your guardian will not fall asleep.
4. Indeed, the Guardian of Israel never rests or sleeps.
5. The Lord is your guardian.
   The Lord is the shade over your right hand.
6.   The sun will not beat down on you during the day,
        nor will the moon at night.
7. The Lord guards you from every evil.
    He guards your life.
8. The Lord guards you as you come and go,
    now and forever.

## Psalm 122
*A song by David for going up to worship.*

1. I was glad when they said to me,
    "Let's go to the house of the Lord."
2. Our feet are standing inside your gates, Jerusalem.
3. Jerusalem is built to be a city
    where the people are united.
4. All of the Lord's tribes go to that city
    because it is a law in Israel
        to give thanks to the name of the Lord.
5. The court of justice sits there.
    It consists of ⌞princes who are⌟ David's descendants.

6. Pray for the peace of Jerusalem:
    "May those who love you prosper.
7.   May there be peace inside your walls
        and prosperity in your palaces."
8. For the sake of my relatives and friends, let me say,
    "May it go well for you!"
9. For the sake of the house of the Lord our God,
    I will seek what is good for you.

### Psalm 123

*A song for going up to worship.*

¹ I look up to you,
  to the one who sits enthroned in heaven.
² As servants depend on their masters,
  as a maid depends on her mistress,
    so we depend on the LORD our God
      until he has pity on us.
³ Have pity on us, O LORD.
  Have pity on us
    because we have suffered more than our share
      of contempt.
⁴ We have suffered more than our share of ridicule
    from those who are carefree.
  We have suffered more than our share of contempt
    from those who are arrogant.

### Psalm 124

*A song by David for going up to worship.*

¹ "If the LORD had not been on our side …"
    (Israel should repeat this.)
² "If the LORD had not been on our side when people
      attacked us,
³   then they would have swallowed us alive
      when their anger exploded against us.
⁴   Then the floodwaters would have swept us away.
      An ⌊overflowing⌋ stream would have washed us away.
⁵   Then raging water would have washed us away."

⁶ Thank the LORD, who did not let them sink their teeth
    into us.
⁷ We escaped like a bird caught in a hunter's trap.
    The trap was broken, and we escaped.
⁸ Our help is in the name of the LORD, the maker of heaven
    and earth.

### Psalm 125

*A song for going up to worship.*

¹ Those who trust the LORD are like Mount Zion,
    which can never be shaken.
      It remains firm forever.

² ⌊As⌋ the mountains surround Jerusalem,
   so the LORD surrounds his people now and forever.

³ A wicked ruler will not be allowed to govern
   the land set aside for righteous people.
      That is why righteous people do not use their power
         to do wrong.

⁴ Do good, O LORD, to those who are good,
   to those whose motives are decent.
⁵ But when people become crooked,
   the LORD will lead them away with troublemakers.

Let there be peace in Israel!

## Psalm 126
*A song for going up to worship.*

¹ When the LORD restored the fortunes of Zion,
   it was as if we were dreaming.
² Then our mouths were filled with laughter
   and our tongues with joyful songs.
   Then the nations said,
      "The LORD has done spectacular things for them."

³ The LORD has done spectacular things for us.
   We are overjoyed.
⁴ Restore our fortunes, O LORD,
   as you restore streams ⌊to dry riverbeds⌋ in the Negev.
⁵ Those who cry while they plant
   will joyfully sing while they harvest.
⁶ The person who goes out weeping, carrying his bag of seed,
   will come home singing, carrying his bundles of grain.

## Psalm 127
*A song by Solomon for going up to worship.*

¹ If the LORD does not build the house,
   it is useless for the builders to work on it.
   If the LORD does not protect a city,
   it is useless for the guard to stay alert.
²    It is useless to work hard for the food you eat
         by getting up early and going to bed late.
            The LORD gives ⌊food⌋ to those he loves while
               they sleep.

³ Children are an inheritance from the Lord.
   They are a reward from him.
⁴   The children born to a man when he is young
      are like arrows in the hand of a warrior.
⁵      Blessed is the man who has filled his quiver
         with them.
         He will not be put to shame
            when he speaks with his enemies in the city gate.

## Psalm 128
*A song for going up to worship.*

¹ Blessed are all who fear the Lord
    and live his way.

² You will certainly eat what your own hands
      have provided.
   Blessings to you!
   May things go well for you!
³ Your wife will be like a fruitful vine inside your home.
   Your children will be like young olive trees around
      your table.
⁴   This is how the Lord will bless the person
      who fears him.
⁵   May the Lord bless you from Zion
      so that you may see Jerusalem prospering
         all the days of your life.
⁶   May you live to see your children's children.

Let there be peace in Israel!

## Psalm 129
*A song for going up to worship.*

¹ "From the time I was young, people have attacked me …"
   (Israel should repeat this.)
² "From the time I was young, people have attacked me,
     but they have never overpowered me.
³    They have plowed my back ⌊like farmers plow fields⌋.
     They made long slashes ⌊like furrows⌋."
⁴ The Lord is righteous.
     He has cut me loose
        from the ropes that wicked people tied around me.
⁵ Put to shame all those who hate Zion.
     Force them to retreat.

⁶ Make them be like grass on a roof,
  like grass that dries up before it produces a stalk.
⁷ It will never fill the barns of those who harvest
  or the arms of those who gather bundles.
⁸ Those who pass by will never say ⌊to them⌋,
  "May you be blessed by the Lord"
   or "We bless you in the name of the Lord."

## Psalm 130
*A song for going up to worship.*

¹ O Lord, out of the depths I call to you.
² O Lord, hear my voice.
  Let your ears be open to my pleas for mercy.
³ O Lord, who would be able to stand
  if you kept a record of sins?
⁴ But with you there is forgiveness
  so that you can be feared.
⁵ I wait for the Lord, my soul waits,
  and with hope I wait for his word.
⁶ My soul waits for the Lord
  more than those who watch for the morning,
  more than those who watch for the morning.
⁷ O Israel, put your hope in the Lord,
  because with the Lord there is mercy
   and with him there is unlimited forgiveness.
⁸ He will rescue Israel from all its sins.

## Psalm 131
*A song by David for going up to worship.*

¹ O Lord, my heart is not conceited.
  My eyes do not look down on others.
  I am not involved in things too big or too difficult for me.
² Instead, I have kept my soul calm and quiet.
  My soul is content as a weaned child is content in its
    mother's arms.
³ Israel, put your hope in the Lord now and forever.

## Psalm 132
*A song for going up to worship.*

¹ O Lord, remember David and all the hardships he endured.
² Remember how he swore an oath to the Lord
  and made this vow to the Mighty One of Jacob:

³ "I will not step inside my house,
⁴     get into my bed, shut my eyes, or close my eyelids
⁵     until I find a place for the Lord,
        a dwelling place for the Mighty One of Jacob."

⁶ Now, we have heard about the ark ⌊of the promise⌋ being in Ephrathah.
    We have found it in Jaar.
⁷ Let's go to his dwelling place.
    Let's worship at his footstool.
⁸ O Lord, arise, and come to your resting place
    with the ark of your power.
⁹ Clothe your priests with righteousness.
    Let your godly ones sing with joy.
¹⁰ For the sake of your servant David,
    do not reject your anointed one.
¹¹ The Lord swore an oath to David.
    This is a truth he will not take back:
        "I will set one of your own descendants on your throne.
¹²     If your sons are faithful to my promise*ᵃ*
        and my written instructions that I will teach them,
    then their descendants will also sit on your
        throne forever."

¹³ The Lord has chosen Zion.
    He wants it for his home.
¹⁴ "This will be my resting place forever.
    Here I will sit enthroned because I want Zion.
¹⁵     I will certainly bless all that Zion needs.
    I will satisfy its needy people with food.
¹⁶     I will clothe its priests with salvation.
        Then its godly ones will sing joyfully.
¹⁷ There I will make a horn sprout up for David.
    I will prepare a lamp for my anointed one.
¹⁸     I will clothe his enemies with shame,
    but the crown on my anointed one will shine."

## Psalm 133

*A song by David for going up to worship.*

¹ See how good and pleasant it is
    when brothers and sisters live together in harmony!
²     It is like fine, scented oil on the head,

---
*ᵃ*132:12 Or "covenant."

running down the beard—down Aaron's beard—
   running over the collar of his robes.
3 It is like dew on ⌜Mount⌝ Hermon,
   dew which comes down on Zion's mountains.
      That is where the LORD promised
         the blessing of eternal life.

## Psalm 134
*A song for going up to worship.*

1 Praise the LORD, all you servants of the LORD,
   all who stand in the house of the LORD night after night.
2 Lift your hands toward the holy place, and praise the LORD.
3 May the LORD, the maker of heaven and earth, bless you
      from Zion.

## Psalm 135
1 Hallelujah!

Praise the name of the LORD.
Praise him, you servants of the LORD
2   who are standing in the house of the LORD,
      in the courtyards of the house of our God.
3 Praise the LORD because he is good.
Make music to praise his name because his name
      is beautiful.
4    The LORD chose Jacob to be his own
         and chose Israel to be his own special treasure.

5 I know that the LORD is great,
      that our Lord is greater than all the false gods.
6 The LORD does whatever he wants in heaven or on earth,
      on the seas or in all the depths of the oceans.
7 He is the one who makes the clouds rise from the ends
         of the earth,
      who makes lightning for the thunderstorms,
      and who brings wind out of his storerooms.

8 He is the one who killed every firstborn male in Egypt.
      He killed humans and animals alike.
9 He sent miraculous signs and amazing things into the
         heart of Egypt
      against Pharaoh and all his officials.
10 He is the one who defeated many nations and killed
         mighty kings:

11 King Sihon of the Amorites,
    King Og of Bashan,
        and all the kingdoms in Canaan.
12     He gave their land as an inheritance,
        an inheritance to his people Israel.
13 O Lord, your name endures forever.
    O Lord, you will be remembered throughout every
        generation.
14     The Lord will provide justice for his people
        and have compassion on his servants.

15 The idols of the nations are made of silver and gold.
    They were made by human hands.[a]
16     They have mouths, but they cannot speak.
        They have eyes, but they cannot see.
17     They have ears, but they cannot hear.
        They cannot breathe.
18 Those who make idols end up like them.
    So does everyone who trusts them.

19 Descendants of Israel, praise the Lord.
    Descendants of Aaron, praise the Lord.
20 Descendants of Levi, praise the Lord.
    You people who fear the Lord, praise the Lord.
21     Thank the Lord in Zion.
        Thank the one who lives in Jerusalem.

Hallelujah!

## Psalm 136

1 Give thanks to the Lord because he is good,
                                because his mercy endures forever.
2 Give thanks to the God of gods
                                because his mercy endures forever.
3 Give thanks to the Lord of lords
                                because his mercy endures forever.

4 Give thanks to the only one who does miraculous things—
                                because his mercy endures forever.
5     to the one who made the heavens by his understanding—
                                because his mercy endures forever.
6     to the one who spread out the earth on the water—
                                because his mercy endures forever.

---

[a]135:15 Verses 15-18 are virtually identical in wording to Psalm 115:4-8.

⁷ to the one who made the great lights—
	because his mercy endures forever.
⁸ the sun to rule the day—
	because his mercy endures forever.
⁹ the moon and stars to rule the night—
	because his mercy endures forever.

¹⁰ Give thanks to the one who killed the firstborn males in Egypt—
	because his mercy endures forever.
¹¹ He brought Israel out from among them—
	because his mercy endures forever.
¹² with a mighty hand and a powerful arm—
	because his mercy endures forever.

¹³ Give thanks to one who divided the Red Sea—
	because his mercy endures forever.
¹⁴ He led Israel through the middle of it—
	because his mercy endures forever.
¹⁵ He swept Pharaoh and his army into the Red Sea—
	because his mercy endures forever.

¹⁶ Give thanks to the one who led his people through the desert—
	because his mercy endures forever.

¹⁷ Give thanks to the one who defeated powerful kings—
	because his mercy endures forever.
¹⁸ He killed mighty kings—
	because his mercy endures forever.
¹⁹ King Sihon of the Amorites—
	because his mercy endures forever.
²⁰ and King Og of Bashan—
	because his mercy endures forever.
²¹ He gave their land as an inheritance—
	because his mercy endures forever.
²² as an inheritance for his servant Israel—
	because his mercy endures forever.

²³ He remembered us when we were humiliated—
	because his mercy endures forever.
²⁴ He snatched us from the grasp of our enemies—
	because his mercy endures forever.
²⁵ He gives food to every living creature—
	because his mercy endures forever.

²⁶ Give thanks to the God of heaven
>because his mercy endures forever.

## Psalm 137

¹ By the rivers of Babylon, we sat down and cried
as we remembered Zion.
² We hung our lyres on willow trees.
³ It was there that those who had captured us demanded
that we sing.
Those who guarded us wanted us to entertain them.
⌊They said,⌋ "Sing a song from Zion for us!"

⁴ How could we sing the LORD's song in a foreign land?
⁵ If I forget you, Jerusalem,
let my right hand forget ⌊how to play the lyre⌋.
⁶ Let my tongue stick to the roof of my mouth
if I don't remember you,
if I don't consider Jerusalem my highest joy.

⁷ O LORD, remember the people of Edom.
Remember what they did the day Jerusalem
⌊was captured⌋.
They said, "Tear it down! Tear it down to its
foundation."
⁸ You destructive people of Babylon,
blessed is the one who pays you back
with the same treatment you gave us.
⁹ Blessed is the one who grabs your little children
and smashes them against a rock.

## Psalm 138

*By David.*

¹ I will give thanks to you with all my heart.
I will make music to praise you in front of the false gods.
² I will bow toward your holy temple.
I will give thanks to your name because of your mercy
and truth.
You have made your name and your promise greater
than everything.

³ When I called, you answered me.
You made me bold by strengthening my soul.
⁴ All the kings of the earth will give thanks to you, O LORD,
because they have heard the promises you spoke.

⁵     They will sing this about the ways of the LORD:
       "The LORD's honor is great!"
⁶ Even though the LORD is high above, he sees humble
    people ⌞close up⌟,
  and he recognizes arrogant people from a distance.

⁷ Even though I walk into the middle of trouble,
    you guard my life against the anger of my enemies.
    You stretch out your hand,
    and your right hand saves me.
⁸ The LORD will do everything for me.
O LORD, your mercy endures forever.
Do not let go of what your hands have made.

## Psalm 139

*For the choir director; a psalm by David.*

¹ O LORD, you have examined me, and you know me.
²    You alone know when I sit down and when I get up.
    You read my thoughts from far away.
³    You watch me when I travel and when I rest.
    You are familiar with all my ways.
⁴      Even before there is a ⌞single⌟ word on my tongue,
      you know all about it, LORD.
⁵    You are all around me—in front of me and
      in back of me.
    You lay your hand on me.
⁶      Such knowledge is beyond my grasp.
      It is so high I cannot reach it.

⁷ Where can I go ⌞to get away⌟ from your Spirit?
Where can I run ⌞to get away⌟ from you?
⁸   If I go up to heaven, you are there.
    If I make my bed in hell, you are there.
⁹   If I climb upward on the rays of the morning sun
    ⌞or⌟ land on the most distant shore of the sea where
      the sun sets,
¹⁰     even there your hand would guide me
      and your right hand would hold on to me.
¹¹ If I say, "Let the darkness hide me
    and let the light around me turn into night,"
¹²     even the darkness is not too dark for you.
      Night is as bright as day.
      Darkness and light are the same ⌞to you⌟.

¹³ You alone created my inner being.
   You knitted me together inside my mother.
¹⁴ I will give thanks to you
      because I have been so amazingly and
         miraculously made.
         Your works are miraculous, and my soul is fully
            aware of this.
¹⁵ My bones were not hidden from you
      when I was being made in secret,
      when I was being skillfully woven in an underground
         workshop.
¹⁶ Your eyes saw me when I was still an unborn child.
      Every day ⌊of my life⌋ was recorded in your book
         before one of them had taken place.
¹⁷ How precious are your thoughts concerning me, O God!
   How vast in number they are!
¹⁸   If I try to count them,
        there would be more of them than there are
           grains of sand.
        When I wake up, I am still with you.

¹⁹ I wish that you would kill wicked people, O God,
      and that bloodthirsty people would leave me alone.
²⁰     They say wicked things about you.
   Your enemies misuse your name.
²¹ Shouldn't I hate those who hate you, O Lord?
   Shouldn't I be disgusted with those who attack you?
²²     I hate them with all my heart.
        They have become my enemies.

²³ Examine me, O God, and know my mind.
   Test me, and know my thoughts.
²⁴     See whether I am on an evil path.
        Then lead me on the everlasting path.

## Psalm 140

*For the choir leader; a psalm by David.*

¹ Rescue me from evil people, O Lord.
  Keep me safe from violent people.
²     They plan evil things in their hearts.
   They start fights every day.
³     They make their tongues as sharp as a snake's ⌊fang⌋.
        Their lips hide the venom of poisonous snakes.     *Selah*

⁴ Protect me from the hands of wicked people, O Lord.
  Keep me safe from violent people.
    They try to trip me.
⁵ Arrogant people have laid a trap for me.
  They have spread out a net with ropes.
  They have set traps for me along the road.          *Selah*

⁶ I said to the Lord, "You are my God."
    O Lord, open your ears to hear my plea for pity.
⁷   O Lord Almighty, the strong one who saves me,
      you have covered my head in the day of battle.
⁸   O Lord, do not give wicked people what they want.
    Do not let their evil plans succeed,
      ⌊or⌋ they will become arrogant.                 *Selah*

⁹ Let the heads of those who surround me
    be covered with their own threats.
¹⁰ Let burning coals fall on them.
  Let them be thrown into a pit, never to rise again.
¹¹ Do not let slanderers prosper on earth.
  Let evil hunt down violent people with one blow
        after another.

¹² I know that the Lord will defend the rights of those who
        are oppressed
    and the cause of those who are needy.
¹³    Indeed, righteous people will give thanks to your name.
    Decent people will live in your presence.

## Psalm 141

*A psalm by David.*

¹ O Lord, I cry out to you, "Come quickly."
    Open your ears to me when I cry out to you.
² Let my prayer be accepted
    as sweet-smelling incense in your presence.
  Let the lifting up of my hands in prayer be accepted
    as an evening sacrifice.

³ O Lord, set a guard at my mouth.
    Keep watch over the door of my lips.
⁴ Do not let me be persuaded to do anything evil
    or to become involved with wickedness,
      with people who are troublemakers.
      Do not let me taste their delicacies.

5 A righteous person may strike me or correct me
        out of kindness.
    It is like lotion for my head.
        My head will not refuse it,
            because my prayer is directed against evil deeds.
6 When their judges are thrown off a cliff,
    they will listen to what I have to say.
    It will sound pleasant ˻to them˼.
7 As someone plows and breaks up the ground,
    so our bones will be planted at the mouth of the grave.

8 My eyes look to you, Lord Almighty.
  I have taken refuge in you.
    Do not leave me defenseless.
9   Keep me away from the trap they set for me
        and from the traps set by troublemakers.
10  Let wicked people fall into their own nets,
        while I escape unharmed.

## Psalm 142

*A maskil<sup>a</sup> by David when he was in the cave; a prayer.*

1 Loudly, I cry to the Lord.
  Loudly, I plead with the Lord for mercy.
2   I pour out my complaints in his presence
        and tell him my troubles.
3       When I begin to lose hope,
            you ˻already˼ know what I am experiencing.

    ˻My enemies˼ have hidden a trap for me on the path
        where I walk.
4 Look to my right and see that no one notices me.
    Escape is impossible for me.
        No one cares about me.

5 I call out to you, O Lord.
  I say, "You are my refuge,
        my own inheritance in this world of the living."
6 Pay attention to my cry for help
    because I am very weak.
  Rescue me from those who pursue me
    because they are too strong for me.
7 Release my soul from prison

---
<sup>a</sup>142:1 Unknown musical term.

so that I may give thanks to your name.
    Righteous people will surround me
        because you are good to me.

## Psalm 143
*A psalm by David.*

1 O Lord, listen to my prayer.
    Open your ears to hear my urgent requests.
    Answer me because you are faithful and righteous.
2 Do not take me to court for judgment,
    because there is no one alive
        who is righteous in your presence.

3 The enemy has pursued me.
    He has ground my life into the dirt.
    He has made me live in dark places
        like those who have died long ago.
4   That is why I begin to lose hope
    and my heart is in a state of shock.

5 I remember the days long ago.
I reflect on all that you have done.
I carefully consider what your hands have made.
6 I stretch out my hands to you in prayer.
    Like parched land, my soul thirsts for you.      *Selah*

7 Answer me quickly, O Lord.
    My spirit is worn out.
Do not hide your face from me,
    or I will be like those who go into the pit.
8 Let me hear about your mercy in the morning,
    because I trust you.
Let me know the way that I should go,
    because I long for you.
9 Rescue me from my enemies, O Lord.
    I come to you for protection.

10 Teach me to do your will, because you are my God.
May your good Spirit lead me on level ground.
11 O Lord, keep me alive for the sake of your name.
Because you are righteous, lead me out of trouble.
12 In keeping with your mercy, wipe out my enemies
    and destroy all who torment me,
        because I am your servant.

## Psalm 144
*By David.*

¹ Thank the LORD, my rock,
    who trained my hands to fight
        and my fingers to do battle,
²   my merciful one, my fortress,
    my stronghold, and my savior,
    my shield, the one in whom I take refuge,
        and the one who brings people under my authority.

³ O LORD, what are humans that you should care
        about them?
    What are mere mortals that you should think
        about them?
⁴       Humans are like a breath of air.
        Their life span is like a fleeting shadow.

⁵ O LORD, bend your heaven low, and come down.
    Touch the mountains, and they will smoke.
⁶   Hurl bolts of lightning, and scatter them.
    Shoot your arrows, and throw them into confusion.
⁷   Stretch out your hands from above.
    Snatch me, and rescue me from raging waters
        and from foreigners' hands.
⁸       Their mouths speak lies.
        Their right hands take false pledges.

⁹ O God, I will sing a new song to you.
    I will sing a psalm to you on a ten-stringed harp.
¹⁰ You are the one who gives victory to kings.
    You are the one who snatches your servant David
        away from a deadly sword.
¹¹      Snatch me, and rescue me from foreigners' hands.
            Their mouths speak lies.
            Their right hands take false pledges.

¹² May our sons be like full-grown, young plants.
    May our daughters be like stately columns
        that adorn the corners of a palace.
¹³ May our barns be filled with all kinds of crops.
    May our sheep give birth to thousands of lambs,
        tens of thousands in our fields.
¹⁴ May our cattle have many calves.

May no one break in, and may no one be dragged out.
May there be no cries of distress in our streets.

15 Blessed are the people who have these blessings!
Blessed are the people whose God is the LORD!

## Psalm 145[a]
*A song of praise by David.*

1 I will highly praise you, my God, the king.
I will bless your name forever and ever.
2 I will bless you every day.
I will praise your name forever and ever.

3 The LORD is great, and he should be highly praised.
His greatness is unsearchable.
4 One generation will praise your deeds to the next.
Each generation will talk about your mighty acts.
5 I will think about the glorious honor of your majesty
 and the miraculous things you have done.
6 People will talk about the power of your terrifying deeds,
 and I will tell about your greatness.
7 They will announce what they remember of your
  great goodness,
 and they will joyfully sing about your righteousness.
8 The LORD is merciful, compassionate, patient,
 and always ready to forgive.
9 The LORD is good to everyone
 and has compassion for everything that he has made.
10 Everything that you have made will give thanks to you,
  O LORD,
 and your faithful ones will praise you.
11 Everyone will talk about the glory of your kingdom
 and will tell the descendants of Adam about your might
12   in order to make known your mighty deeds
   and the glorious honor of your kingdom.
13 Your kingdom is an everlasting kingdom.
Your empire endures throughout every generation.

14 The LORD supports everyone who falls.
He straightens ⌊the backs⌋ of those who are bent over.
15 The eyes of all creatures look to you,
 and you give them their food at the proper time.

---
[a] 145:1 Psalm 145 is a poem in Hebrew alphabetical order.

16 You open your hand,
  and you satisfy the desire of every living thing.
17 The Lord is fair in all his ways
  and faithful in everything he does.
18 The Lord is near to everyone who prays to him,
  to every faithful person who prays to him.
19 He fills the needs of those who fear him.
 He hears their cries for help and saves them.
20 The Lord protects everyone who loves him,
  but he will destroy all wicked people.

21 My mouth will speak the praise of the Lord,
  and all living creatures will praise his holy name
   forever and ever.

## Psalm 146

1 Hallelujah!

Praise the Lord, my soul!
2 I want to praise the Lord throughout my life.
 I want to make music to praise my God as long as I live.

3 Do not trust influential people,
  mortals who cannot help you.
4   When they breathe their last breath, they return
    to the ground.
   On that day their plans come to an end.
5 Blessed are those who receive help from the God of Jacob.
  Their hope rests on the Lord their God,
6   who made heaven, earth,
    the sea, and everything in them.
 The Lord remains faithful forever.
7   He brings about justice for those who are oppressed.
  He gives food to those who are hungry.
 The Lord sets prisoners free.
8 The Lord gives sight to blind people.
 The Lord straightens ⌊the backs⌋ of those who are bent over.
 The Lord loves righteous people.
9 The Lord protects foreigners.
 The Lord gives relief to orphans and widows.
  But he keeps wicked people from reaching their goal.
10 The Lord rules as king forever.
 Zion, your God rules throughout every generation.

Hallelujah!

## Psalm 147

1 Hallelujah!

It is good to sing psalms to our God.
It is pleasant to sing ⌊his⌋ praise beautifully.

2 The Lord is the builder of Jerusalem.
    He is the one who gathers the outcasts of Israel together.
3   He is the healer of the brokenhearted.
    He is the one who bandages their wounds.
4   He determines the number of stars.
    He gives each one a name.
5 Our Lord is great, and his power is great.
    There is no limit to his understanding.
6 The Lord gives relief to those who are oppressed.
    He brings wicked people down to the ground.

7 Sing to the Lord a song of thanksgiving.
Make music to our God with a lyre.
8   He covers the sky with clouds.
    He provides rain for the ground.
    He makes grass grow on the mountains.
9   He is the one who gives food to animals
        and to young ravens when they call out.
10  He finds no joy in strong horses,
       nor is he pleased by brave soldiers.
11 The Lord is pleased with those who fear him,
    with those who wait with hope for his mercy.

12 Praise the Lord, Jerusalem!
Praise your God, Zion!
13  He makes the bars across your gates strong.
    He blesses the children within you.
14  He is the one who brings peace to your borders
       and satisfies your ⌊hunger⌋ with the finest wheat.
15  He is the one who sends his promise throughout
       the earth.
    His word travels with great speed.
16  He is the one who sends snow like wool
       and scatters frost like ashes.
17  He is the one who throws his hailstones like
       breadcrumbs.
    Who can withstand his chilling blast?
18  He sends out his word and melts his hailstones.
    He makes wind blow ⌊and⌋ water flow.

¹⁹ He speaks his word to Jacob,
   his laws and judicial decisions to Israel.
²⁰ He has done nothing like this for any other nation.
   The other nations do not know the decisions he has handed down.

Hallelujah!

## Psalm 148

¹ Hallelujah!

Praise the LORD from the heavens.
Praise him in the heights above.
² Praise him, all his angels.
Praise him, his entire heavenly army.
³ Praise him, sun and moon.
Praise him, all shining stars.
⁴ Praise him, you highest heaven
   and the water above the sky.
⁵ Let them praise the name of the LORD
   because they were created by his command.
⁶ He set them in their places forever and ever.
He made it a law that no one can break.

⁷ Praise the LORD from the earth.
Praise him, large sea creatures and all the ocean depths,
⁸   lightning and hail,
   snow and fog,
   strong winds that obey his commands,
⁹   mountains and all hills,
   fruit trees and all cedar trees,
¹⁰  wild animals and all domestic animals,
   crawling animals and birds,
¹¹  kings of the earth and all its people,
   officials and all judges on the earth,
¹²  young men and women,
   old and young together.
¹³ Let them praise the name of the LORD
   because his name is high above all others.
      His glory is above heaven and earth.
¹⁴ He has given his people a strong leader,[a]
   someone praiseworthy for his faithful ones,
      for the people of Israel, the people who are close to him.

---

[a]148:14 Or "given his people strength."

Hallelujah!

## Psalm 149

¹ Hallelujah!

Sing a new song to the LORD.
Sing his praise in the assembly of godly people.
² Let Israel find joy in their creator.
Let the people of Zion rejoice over their king.
³ Let them praise his name with dancing.
Let them make music to him with tambourines and lyres,
⁴ because the LORD takes pleasure in his people.
He crowns those who are oppressed with victory.
⁵ Let godly people triumph in glory.
Let them sing for joy on their beds.
⁶ Let the high praises of God be in their throats
and two-edged swords in their hands
⁷ to take vengeance on the nations,
to punish the people of the world,
⁸ to put their kings in chains
and their leaders in iron shackles,
⁹ to carry out the judgment that is written against them.
This is an honor that belongs to all his godly ones.

Hallelujah!

## Psalm 150

¹ Hallelujah!

Praise God in his holy place.
Praise him in his mighty heavens.
² Praise him for his mighty acts.
Praise him for his immense greatness.
³ Praise him with sounds from horns.
Praise him with harps and lyres.
⁴ Praise him with tambourines and dancing.
Praise him with stringed instruments and flutes.
⁵ Praise him with loud cymbals.
Praise him with crashing cymbals.

⁶ Let everything that breathes praise the LORD!

Hallelujah!

## AUTHOR

*Solomon is thought to have written most of the proverbs in this book. However, he was not the only author; King Lemuel is also credited as a writer of Proverbs 31:1–9, and Agur is credited with chapter 30.*

## DATE

*The date of writing is unknown. Most of the book was written by King Solomon around 950 B.C. Proverbs 25:1 indicates that the material in 25:1–29:27 was put in place after Hezekiah's reign (715–686 B.C.). The final form of the book was not complete until at least 250 years after Solomon.*

## BACKGROUND & PURPOSE

*These proverbs are not merely a collection of wise sayings but are the instructions of the Spirit of God in Solomon. Solomon is credited with 3,000 proverbs and 1,005 songs. His writings cover a broad range of topics, emphasizing correct moral and religious behavior that should be seen in God's people. The first proverb includes the purpose for these writings, "To give insight to gullible people, to give knowledge and foresight to the young" (Proverbs 1:4).*

## MAJOR THEME

*The fear of the LORD as the beginning of knowledge (Proverbs 1:7) is the theme that runs through this book. This knowledge and wisdom are described as the most desirable human possessions. The one who gets wisdom pleases both God and people, lives successfully in this life, and obtains favor from the LORD.*

## OUTLINE

I. The purpose for the Proverbs, 1:1–1:7
II. The search for wisdom, 1:8–9:18
III. Specific proverbs of Solomon, 10:1–24:34
IV. Proverbs of Solomon copied by Hezekiah's men, 25:1–29:27
V. Proverbs of Agur, 30:1–33
VI. Proverbs of King Lemuel, 31:1–9
VII. The virtuous wife, 31:10–31

# PROVERBS

### The Reasons for Proverbs

**1** ¹ The proverbs of Solomon, David's son who was king of Israel, ⌞given⌟
² to grasp wisdom and discipline,
to understand deep thoughts,
³ to acquire the discipline of wise behavior—
righteousness and justice and fairness—
⁴ to give insight to gullible people,
to give knowledge and foresight to the young—
⁵ a wise person will listen and continue to learn,
and an understanding person will gain direction—
⁶ to understand a proverb and a clever saying,
the words of wise people and their riddles.

⁷ The fear of the LORD is the beginning of knowledge.
Stubborn fools despise wisdom and discipline.

### Listen to Wisdom

⁸ My son,
listen to your father's discipline,
and do not neglect your mother's teachings,
⁹ because discipline and teachings
are a graceful garland on your head
and a ⌞golden⌟ chain around your neck.

¹⁰ My son,
if sinners lure you, do not go along.
¹¹ If they say,
"Come with us.
Let's set an ambush to kill someone.
Let's hide to ambush innocent people for fun.
¹² We'll swallow them alive like the grave,
like those in good health who go into the pit.
¹³ We'll find all kinds of valuable possessions.
We'll fill our homes with stolen goods.
¹⁴ Join us.
We'll split the loot equally."

<sup>15</sup> My son,
>    do not follow them in their way.
>    Do not even set foot on their path,
> <sup>16</sup>    because they rush to do evil
>       and hurry to shed blood.
> <sup>17</sup>       It does no good to spread a net
>          within the sight of any bird.
> <sup>18</sup>    But these people set an ambush for their own murder.
>    They go into hiding only to lose their lives.
> <sup>19</sup>    This is what happens to everyone
>       who is greedy for unjust gain.
>          Greed takes away his life.

<sup>20</sup> Wisdom sings her song in the streets.
>    In the public squares she raises her voice.
> <sup>21</sup>    At the corners of noisy streets she calls out.
>    At the entrances to the city she speaks her words,
> <sup>22</sup>       "How long will you gullible people love being
>             so gullible?
>       How long will you mockers find joy in your mocking?
>       How long will you fools hate knowledge?

<sup>23</sup>       "Turn to me when I warn you.
>          I will generously pour out my spirit for you.
>          I will make my words known to you.

<sup>24</sup>       "I called, and you refused to listen.
>          I stretched out my hands to you, and no one
>             paid attention.
> <sup>25</sup>       You ignored all my advice.
>          You did not want me to warn you.
> <sup>26</sup>       I will laugh at your calamity.
>       I will make fun of you
>          when panic strikes you,
> <sup>27</sup>       when panic strikes you like a violent storm,
>          when calamity strikes you like a wind storm,
>          when trouble and anguish come to you.

<sup>28</sup>       "They will call to me at that time, but I will not answer.
>       They will look for me, but they will not find me,
> <sup>29</sup>          because they hated knowledge
>             and did not choose the fear of the L<small>ORD</small>.
> <sup>30</sup>       They refused my advice.
>       They despised my every warning.

³¹ They will eat the fruit of their lifestyle.
   They will be stuffed with their own schemes.

³² "Gullible people kill themselves because of their
      turning away.
   Fools destroy themselves because of their indifference.
³³    But whoever listens to me will live without worry
      and will be free from the dread of disaster."

## The Benefit of Wisdom

**2** ¹My son,
   if you take my words ⌊to heart⌋,
      and treasure my commands within you,
² if you pay close attention to wisdom,
   and let your mind reach for understanding,
³ if indeed you call out for insight,
   if you ask aloud for understanding,
⁴ if you search for wisdom as if it were money
   and hunt for it as if it were hidden treasure,
⁵ then you will understand the fear of the Lord
   and you will find the knowledge of God.
⁶ The Lord gives wisdom.
   From his mouth come knowledge and understanding.
⁷    He has reserved priceless wisdom for decent people.
   He is a shield for those who walk in integrity
⁸ in order to guard those on paths of justice
      and to watch over the way of his godly ones.
⁹    Then you will understand what is right and just
         and fair—
      every good course ⌊in life⌋.

¹⁰ Wisdom will come into your heart.
   Knowledge will be pleasant to your soul.
¹¹ Foresight will protect you.
   Understanding will guard you.

¹² ⌊Wisdom will⌋ save you
      from the way of evil,
      from the person who speaks devious things,
¹³    from those who abandon the paths of righteousness
         to walk the ways of darkness,
¹⁴    from those who enjoy doing evil,
      from those who find joy in the deviousness of evil.
¹⁵       Their paths are crooked.
         Their ways are devious.

16 ⌊Wisdom will⌋ also save you
     from an adulterous woman,
     from a loose woman with her smooth talk,
17    who leaves ⌊her husband,⌋ the closest friend
        of her youth,
        and forgets her marriage vows to her God.
18     Her house sinks down to death.
       Her ways lead to the souls of the dead.
19      None who have sex with her come back.
        Nor do they ever reach the paths of life.

20 So walk in the way of good people
     and stay on the paths of righteous people.
21    Decent people will live in the land.
      People of integrity will remain in it.
22     But wicked people will be cut off from the land
       and treacherous people will be torn<sup>a</sup> from it.

## Using Wisdom

**3** <sup>1</sup> My son,
     do not forget my teachings,
     and keep my commands in mind,
2      because they will bring you
         long life, good years, and peace.

3   Do not let mercy and truth leave you.
    Fasten them around your neck.
    Write them on the tablet of your heart.
4    Then you will find favor and much success
       in the sight of God and humanity.

5   Trust the LORD with all your heart,
      and do not rely on your own understanding.
6    In all your ways acknowledge him,
       and he will make your paths smooth.<sup>b</sup>
7    Do not consider yourself wise.
     Fear the LORD, and turn away from evil.
8     ⌊Then⌋ your body will be healed,
        and your bones will have nourishment.

9    Honor the LORD with your wealth
       and with the first and best part of all your income.<sup>c</sup>

---

<sup>a</sup>2:22 Or "will be swept away."
<sup>b</sup>3:6 Or "straight."
<sup>c</sup>3:9 Or "harvest."

¹⁰     Then your barns will be full,
        and your vats will overflow with fresh wine.

¹¹ Do not reject the discipline of the LORD, my son,
    and do not resent his warning,
¹²     because the LORD warns the one he loves,
        even as a father warns a son with whom
            he is pleased.

¹³ Blessed is the one who finds wisdom
    and the one who obtains understanding.
¹⁴     The profit ⌊gained⌋ from ⌊wisdom⌋ is greater than
        the profit ⌊gained⌋ from silver.
            Its yield is better than fine gold.
¹⁵ ⌊Wisdom⌋ is more precious than jewels,
    and all your desires cannot equal it.
¹⁶     Long life is in ⌊wisdom's⌋ right hand.
        In ⌊wisdom's⌋ left hand are riches and honor.
¹⁷ ⌊Wisdom's⌋ ways are pleasant ways,
    and all its paths lead to peace.
¹⁸ ⌊Wisdom⌋ is a tree of life
    for those who take firm hold of it.
        Those who cling to it are blessed.

¹⁹ By Wisdom the LORD laid the foundation of the earth.
    By understanding he established the heavens.
²⁰ By his knowledge the deep waters were divided,
    and the skies dropped dew.

²¹ My son,
    do not lose sight of these things.
    Use priceless wisdom and foresight.
²²     Then they will mean life for you,
        and they will grace your neck.
²³     Then you will go safely on your way,
        and you will not hurt your foot.
²⁴     When you lie down, you will not be afraid.
        As you lie there, your sleep will be sweet.

²⁵ Do not be afraid of sudden terror
    or of the destruction of wicked people when it comes.
²⁶     The LORD will be your confidence.
        He will keep your foot from getting caught.

⁲⁷ Do not hold back anything good
   from those who are entitled to it
      when you have the power to do so.
²⁸ When you have the good thing with you, do not tell
      your neighbor,
   "Go away!
   Come back tomorrow.
   I'll give you something then."

²⁹ Do not plan to do something wrong to your neighbor
   while he is sitting there with you and
      suspecting nothing.
³⁰ Do not quarrel with a person for no reason
   if he has not harmed you.
³¹ Do not envy a violent person.
   Do not choose any of his ways.
³² The devious person is disgusting to the LORD.
   The LORD's intimate advice is with decent people.

³³ The LORD curses the house of wicked people,
   but he blesses the home of righteous people.
³⁴ When he mocks the mockers,
   he is gracious to humble people.
³⁵ Wise people will inherit honor,
   but fools will bear disgrace.

**Cherish Wisdom**

**4** ¹Sons,
   listen to ⌞your⌟ father's discipline,
      and pay attention in order to gain understanding.
² After all, I have taught you well.
   Do not abandon my teachings.
³ When I was a boy ⌞learning⌟ from my father,
   when I was a tender and only child of my mother,
⁴ they used to teach me and say to me,
      "Cling to my words wholeheartedly.
      Obey my commands so that you may live.
⁵ Acquire wisdom.
   Acquire understanding.
   Do not forget.
   Do not turn away from the words that I have
      spoken.
⁶ Do not abandon wisdom, and it will watch over you.
   Love wisdom, and it will protect you.

7 The beginning of wisdom is to acquire wisdom.
   Acquire understanding with all that you have.
8 Cherish wisdom.
   It will raise you up.
   It will bring you honor when you embrace it.
9 It will give you a graceful garland for your head.
   It will hand you a beautiful crown."

**Stay on the Path of Wisdom**
10 My son,
   listen and accept my words,
      and they will multiply the years of your life.
11 I have taught you the way of wisdom.
   I have guided you along decent paths.
12 When you walk, your stride will not be hampered.
   Even if you run, you will not stumble.

13 Cling to discipline.
   Do not relax your grip on it.
      Keep it because it is your life.
14 Do not stray onto the path of wicked people.
   Do not walk in the way of evil people.
15 Avoid it.
   Do not walk near it.
      Turn away from it,
         and keep on walking.
16 Wicked people cannot sleep
   unless they do wrong,
      and they are robbed of their sleep
         unless they make someone stumble.
17 They eat food obtained through wrongdoing
   and drink wine obtained through violence.

18 But the path of righteous people is like the light of dawn
   that becomes brighter and brighter until it
      reaches midday.
19 The way of wicked people is like deep darkness.
   They do not know what makes them stumble.

**Stay Focused on Wisdom**
20 My son,
   pay attention to my words.
   Open your ears to what I say.
21 Do not lose sight of these things.
   Keep them deep within your heart

²² because they are life to those who find them
  and they heal the whole body.
²³ Guard your heart more than anything else,
  because the source of your life flows from it.
²⁴ Remove dishonesty from your mouth.
  Put deceptive speech far away from your lips.
²⁵ Let your eyes look straight ahead
  and your sight be focused in front of you.
²⁶ Carefully walk a straight path,
  and all your ways will be secure.
²⁷ Do not lean to the right or to the left.
  Walk away from evil.

## Avoid Adultery

**5** ¹My son,
  pay attention to my wisdom.
    Open your ears to my understanding
² so that you may act with foresight
    and speak with insight.

³ The lips of an adulterous woman drip with honey.
  Her kiss is smoother than oil,
⁴ but in the end she is as bitter as wormwood,
    as sharp as a two-edged sword.
⁵ Her feet descend to death.
  Her steps lead straight to hell.
⁶ She doesn't even think about the path of life.
  Her steps wander, and she doesn't realize it.

⁷ But now, sons,
  listen to me,
    and do not turn away from what I say to you.
⁸ Stay far away from her.
  Do not even go near her door.
⁹ Either you will surrender your reputation to others
    and ⌊the rest of⌋ your years to some cruel person,
¹⁰ or strangers will benefit from your strength
    and you will have to work hard in a pagan's house.
¹¹ Then you will groan when your end comes,
    when your body and flesh are consumed.
  You will say,
¹² "Oh, how I hated discipline!
    How my heart despised correction!
¹³ I didn't listen to what my teachers said to me,
    nor did I keep my ear open to my instructors.

<sup>14</sup> I almost reached total ruin
in the assembly and in the congregation."

<sup>15</sup> Drink water out of your own cistern
and running water from your own well.
<sup>16</sup> Why should water flow out of your spring?
Why should your streams flow into the streets?
<sup>17</sup> They should be yours alone,
so do not share them with strangers.
<sup>18</sup> Let your own fountain be blessed,
and enjoy the girl you married when you were young,
<sup>19</sup> a loving doe and a graceful deer.*<sup>a</sup>*
Always let her breasts satisfy you.
Always be intoxicated with her love.
<sup>20</sup> Why should you, my son,
be intoxicated with an adulterous woman
and fondle a loose woman's breast?

<sup>21</sup> Each person's ways are clearly seen by the Lord,
and he surveys all his actions.
<sup>22</sup> A wicked person will be trapped by his own wrongs,
and he will be caught in the ropes of his own sin.
<sup>23</sup> He will die for his lack of discipline
and stumble around because of his great stupidity.

## Avoid Disaster

**6** <sup>1</sup> My son,
if you guarantee a loan for your neighbor
or pledge yourself for a stranger with a handshake,
<sup>2</sup> you are trapped by the words of your own mouth,
caught by your own promise.

<sup>3</sup> Do the following things, my son, so that you may
free yourself,
because you have fallen into your neighbor's hands:
Humble yourself,
and pester your neighbor.
<sup>4</sup> Don't let your eyes rest
or your eyelids close.
<sup>5</sup> Free yourself like a gazelle from the hand of a hunter
and like a bird from the hand of a hunter.

---

*<sup>a</sup>* 5:19 Or "graceful goat."

⁶ Consider the ant, you lazy bum.
 Watch its ways, and become wise.
⁷  Although it has no overseer, officer, or ruler,
⁸   in summertime it stores its food supply.
 At harvest time it gathers its food.

⁹ How long will you lie there, you lazy bum?
 When will you get up from your sleep?
¹⁰  "Just a little sleep,
 just a little slumber,
 just a little nap."
¹¹   Then your poverty will come ⌊to you⌋ like a drifter,
 and your need will come ⌊to you⌋ like a bandit.

¹² A good-for-nothing scoundrel is a person who has a
  dishonest mouth.
¹³  He winks his eye,
 makes a signal with his foot,
 ⌊and⌋ points with his fingers.
¹⁴  He devises evil all the time with a twisted mind.
 He spreads conflict.
¹⁵   That is why disaster will come on him suddenly.
 In a moment he will be crushed beyond recovery.

¹⁶ There are six things that the LORD hates,
 even seven that are disgusting to him:
¹⁷  arrogant eyes,
 a lying tongue,
 hands that kill innocent people,
¹⁸  a mind devising wicked plans,
 feet that are quick to do wrong,
¹⁹  a dishonest witness spitting out lies,
  and a person who spreads conflict among relatives.

**More Advice about Avoiding Adultery**

²⁰ My son,
 obey the command of your father,
  and do not disregard the teachings of your mother.
²¹  Fasten them on your heart forever.
 Hang them around your neck.
²²  When you walk around, they will lead you.
 When you lie down, they will watch over you.
 When you wake up, they will talk to you

<sup>23</sup> because the command is a lamp,
   the teachings are a light,
      and the warnings from discipline are the
         path of life
<sup>24</sup>      to keep you from an evil woman
         and from the smooth talk of a loose woman.

<sup>25</sup> Do not desire her beauty in your heart.
   Do not let her catch you with her eyes.
<sup>26</sup>   A prostitute's price is ⌊only⌋ a loaf of bread,
      but a married woman hunts for ⌊your⌋ life itself.
<sup>27</sup>   Can a man carry fire in his lap
      without burning his clothes?
<sup>28</sup>   Can anyone walk on red-hot coals
      without burning his feet?
<sup>29</sup> So it is with a man who has sex with his neighbor's wife.
   None who touch her will escape punishment.
<sup>30</sup> People do not despise a thief who is hungry
   when he steals to satisfy his appetite,
<sup>31</sup>   but when he is caught,
      he has to repay it seven times.
         He must give up all the possessions in his house.

<sup>32</sup> Whoever commits adultery with a woman has no sense.
   Whoever does this destroys himself.
<sup>33</sup>   An adulterous man will find disease*a* and dishonor,
      and his disgrace will not be blotted out,
<sup>34</sup>      because jealousy arouses a husband's fury.
         The husband will show no mercy when he
            takes revenge.
<sup>35</sup>         No amount of money will change his mind.
            The largest bribe will not satisfy him.

# 7

<sup>1</sup> My son,
   pay attention to my words.
   Treasure my commands that are within you.
<sup>2</sup>   Obey my commands so that you may live.
   Follow my teachings just as you protect the pupil
      of your eye.
<sup>3</sup>   Tie them on your fingers.
   Write them on the tablet of your heart.
<sup>4</sup>   Say to wisdom, "You are my sister."
   Give the name "my relative" to understanding

---

*a* 6:33 Or "wounds."

⁵ in order to guard yourself from an
    adulterous woman,
        from a loose woman with her smooth talk.

⁶ From a window in my house I looked through my screen.
⁷ I was looking at gullible people
    when I saw a young man without much sense
        among youths
⁸ He was crossing a street near her corner
    and walking toward her house
⁹     in the twilight,
    in the evening,
    in the dark hours of the night.

¹⁰ A woman with an ulterior motive meets him.
    She is dressed as a prostitute.
¹¹ She is loud and rebellious.
    Her feet will not stay at home.
¹²     One moment she is out on the street,
        the next she is at the curb,
            on the prowl at every corner.
¹³ She grabs him and kisses him and brazenly says to him,
¹⁴ "I have some sacrificial meat.
    Today I kept my vows.
¹⁵ That's why I came to meet you.
    Eagerly, I looked for you,
        and I've found you.
¹⁶ I've made my bed,
    with colored sheets of Egyptian linen.
¹⁷ I've sprinkled my bed with myrrh, aloes, and cinnamon.
¹⁸ Come, let's drink our fill of love until morning.
    Let's enjoy making love,
¹⁹     because my husband's not home.
        He has gone on a long trip.
²⁰     He took lots of money with him.
        He won't be home for a couple of weeks."

²¹ With all her seductive charms, she persuades him.
    With her smooth lips, she makes him give in.
²²     He immediately follows her
        like a steer on its way to be slaughtered,
        like a ram hobbling into captivity
²³         until an arrow pierces his heart,
        like a bird darting into a trap.
        He does not realize that it will cost him his life.

²⁴ Now, sons,
   listen to me.
   Pay attention to the words from my mouth.
²⁵ Do not let your heart be turned to her ways.
   Do not wander onto her paths,
²⁶ because she has brought down many victims,
   and she has killed all too many.
²⁷ Her home is the way to hell
   and leads to the darkest vaults of death.

## Wisdom's Announcement

**8** ¹ Does not wisdom call out?
Does not understanding raise its voice?
² ⌐Wisdom⌐ takes its stand on high ground,
   by the wayside where the roads meet,
³ near the gates to the city.
   At the entrance ⌐wisdom⌐ sings its song,
⁴ "I am calling to all of you,
   and my appeal is to all people.
⁵ You gullible people, learn how to be sensible.
   You fools, get a heart that has understanding.
⁶ Listen! I am speaking about noble things,
   and my lips will say what is right.
⁷ My mouth expresses the truth,
   and wickedness is disgusting to my lips.
⁸ Everything I say is fair,
   and there is nothing twisted or crooked in it.
⁹ All of it is clear to a person who has understanding
   and right to those who have acquired knowledge.
¹⁰ Take my discipline, not silver,
   and my knowledge rather than fine gold,
¹¹ because wisdom is better than jewels.
   Nothing you desire can equal it.

## Wisdom's Authority

¹² "I, Wisdom, live with insight,
   and I acquire knowledge and foresight.
¹³ To fear the LORD is to hate evil.
   I hate pride, arrogance, evil behavior,
   and twisted speech.
¹⁴ Advice and priceless wisdom are mine.
   I, Understanding, have strength.
¹⁵ Through me kings reign,
   and rulers decree fair laws.

16 Through me princes rule,
    so do nobles and all fair judges.
17 I love those who love me.
    Those eagerly looking for me will find me.
18 I have riches and honor,
    lasting wealth and righteousness.
19 What I produce is better than gold, pure gold.
    What I yield is better than fine silver.
20 I walk in the way of righteousness, on the paths
    of justice,
21     to give an inheritance to those who love me
    and to fill their treasuries.

## Wisdom as Creator

22 "The LORD already possessed me long ago,
    when his way began,
        before any of his works.
23 I was appointed from everlasting
    from the first,
        before the earth began.
24 I was born
    before there were oceans,
    before there were springs filled with water.
25 I was born
    before the mountains were settled in their places
        and before the hills,
26     when he had not yet made land or fields
    or the first dust of the world.

27 "When he set up the heavens, I was there.
    When he traced the horizon on the surface
        of the ocean,
28 when he established the skies above,
    when he determined the currents in the ocean,
29 when he set a limit for the sea
    so the waters would not overstep his command,
    when he traced the foundations of the earth,
30     I was beside him as a master craftsman.
    I made him happy day after day,
        I rejoiced in front of him all the time,
31         found joy in his inhabited world,
        and delighted in the human race.

## Wisdom as Lifegiver

32 "Now, sons, listen to me.

>        Blessed are those who follow my ways.
> 33     Listen to discipline, and become wise.
>        Do not leave my ways.
> 34   Blessed is the person who listens to me,
>        watches at my door day after day,
>        and waits by my doorposts.
> 35   Whoever finds me finds life
>        and obtains favor from the LORD.
> 36   Whoever sins against me harms himself.
>        All those who hate me love death."

## Wisdom Hosts a Banquet

**9** ¹ Wisdom has built her house.
   She has carved out her seven pillars.
² She has prepared her meat.
  She has mixed her wine.
  She has set her table.
³ She has sent out her servant girls.
  She calls from the highest places in the city,
⁴   "Whoever is gullible turn in here!"

She says to a person without sense,
⁵   "Come, eat my bread,
      and drink the wine I have mixed.
⁶ Stop being gullible and live.
  Start traveling the road to understanding."

## Wisdom Prolongs Life

⁷ Whoever corrects a mocker receives abuse.
  Whoever warns a wicked person gets hurt.
⁸  Do not warn a mocker, or he will hate you.
   Warn a wise person, and he will love you.
⁹    Give ⌊advice⌋ to a wise person,
       and he will become even wiser.
     Teach a righteous person,
       and he will learn more.

¹⁰ The fear of the LORD is the beginning of wisdom.
   The knowledge of the Holy One is understanding.

¹¹ You will live longer because of me,
     and years will be added to your life.
¹² If you are wise, your wisdom will help you.
   If you mock, you alone will be held responsible.

### Stupidity Imitates Wisdom's Banquet

¹³ The woman Stupidity is loud, gullible, and ignorant.
¹⁴ She sits at the doorway of her house.
  She is enthroned on the high ground of the city
¹⁵   and calls to those who pass by,
      those minding their own business,
¹⁶    "Whoever is gullible turn in here!"

  She says to a person without sense,
¹⁷   "Stolen waters are sweet,
      and food eaten in secret is tasty."
¹⁸ But he does not know
    that the souls of the dead are there,
    that her guests are in the depths of hell.

# 10
¹The proverbs of Solomon:

### A Wise Son Is Righteous

A wise son makes his father happy,
  but a foolish son brings grief to his mother.

² Treasures gained dishonestly profit no one,
    but righteousness rescues from death.
³ The Lord will not allow a righteous person to starve,
    but he intentionally ignores the desires of a
      wicked person.

⁴ Lazy hands bring poverty,
    but hard-working hands bring riches.
⁵ Whoever gathers in the summer is a wise son.
  Whoever sleeps at harvest time brings shame.

⁶ Blessings cover the head of a righteous person,
    but violence covers the mouths of wicked people.

⁷ The name of a righteous person remains blessed,
    but the names of wicked people will rot away.

### Proverbs Concerning the Mouth

⁸ The one who is truly wise accepts commands,
    but the one who talks foolishly will be thrown
      down headfirst.
⁹ Whoever lives honestly will live securely,
    but whoever lives dishonestly will be found out.
¹⁰ Whoever winks with his eye causes heartache.

The one who talks foolishly will be thrown
>   down headfirst.
11  The mouth of a righteous person is a fountain of life,
>   but the mouths of wicked people conceal violence.
12  Hate starts quarrels,
>   but love covers every wrong.

13  Wisdom is found on the lips of a person who has
>       understanding,
>   but a rod is for the back of one without sense.
14  Those who are wise store up knowledge,
>   but the mouth of a stubborn fool invites ruin.
15  The rich person's wealth is ⌊his⌋ strong city.
>   Poverty ruins the poor.
16  A righteous person's reward is life.
>   A wicked person's harvest is sin.
17  Whoever practices discipline is on the way to life,
>   but whoever ignores a warning strays.

18  Whoever conceals hatred has lying lips.
>   Whoever spreads slander is a fool.
19  Sin is unavoidable when there is much talk,
>   but whoever seals his lips is wise.
20  The tongue of a righteous person is pure silver.
>   The hearts of wicked people are worthless.
21  The lips of a righteous person feed many,
>   but stubborn fools die because they have no sense.

22  It is the LORD's blessing that makes a person rich,
>   and hard work adds nothing to it.
23  Like the laughter of a fool when he carries out an evil plan,
>   so is wisdom to a person who has understanding.

## Righteous People Contrasted to Wicked People

24  That which wicked people dread happens to them,
>   but ⌊the LORD⌋ grants the desire of righteous people.
25  When the storm has passed, the wicked person
>       has vanished,
>   but the righteous person has an everlasting foundation.
26  Like vinegar to the teeth,
>   like smoke to the eyes,
>       so is the lazy person to those who send him
>           ⌊on a mission⌋.
27  The fear of the LORD lengthens ⌊the number of⌋ days,
>   but the years of wicked people are shortened.

²⁸ The hope of righteous people ⌊leads to⌋ joy,
　　but the eager waiting of wicked people comes
　　　　to nothing.
²⁹ The way of the LORD is a fortress for an innocent person
　　but a ruin to those who are troublemakers.
³⁰ A righteous person will never be moved,
　　but wicked people will not continue to live in the land.
³¹ The mouth of a righteous person increases wisdom,
　　but a devious tongue will be cut off.
³² The lips of a righteous person announce good will,
　　but the mouths of wicked people are devious.

### The Value of Righteousness

**11** ¹Dishonest scales are disgusting to the LORD,
　　but accurate weights are pleasing to him.
² Arrogance comes,
　　then comes shame,
　　　　but wisdom remains with humble people.
³ Integrity guides decent people,
　　but hypocrisy leads treacherous people to ruin.

⁴ Riches are of no help on the day of fury,
　　but righteousness saves from death.
⁵ The righteousness of innocent people makes their
　　　　road smooth,
　　but wicked people fall by their own wickedness.
⁶ Decent people are saved by their righteousness,
　　but treacherous people are trapped by their own greed.
⁷　　At the death of a wicked person, hope vanishes.
　　Moreover, his confidence in strength vanishes.

⁸ A righteous person is rescued from trouble,
　　and a wicked person takes his place.
⁹ With his talk a godless person can ruin his neighbor,
　　but righteous people are rescued by knowledge.

¹⁰ When righteous people prosper, a city is glad.
　When wicked people die, there are songs of joy.
¹¹　　With the blessing of decent people a city is raised up,
　　but by the words of wicked people, it is torn down.

¹² A person who despises a neighbor has no sense,
　　but a person who has understanding keeps quiet.
¹³ Whoever gossips gives away secrets,
　　but whoever is trustworthy in spirit can keep a secret.

¹⁴ A nation will fall when there is no direction,
    but with many advisers there is victory.
¹⁵ Whoever guarantees a stranger's loan will get into trouble,
    but whoever hates the closing of a deal remains secure.
¹⁶ A gracious woman wins respect,
    but ruthless men gain riches.
¹⁷ A merciful person helps himself,
    but a cruel person hurts himself.
¹⁸ A wicked person earns dishonest wages,
    but whoever spreads righteousness earns honest pay.
¹⁹ As righteousness leads to life,
    so whoever pursues evil finds his own death.

²⁰ Devious people are disgusting to the LORD,
    but he is delighted with those whose ways are innocent.
²¹ Certainly, an evil person will not go unpunished,
    but the descendants of righteous people will escape.
²² ⌊Like⌋ a gold ring in a pig's snout,
    ⌊so⌋ is a beautiful woman who lacks good taste.
²³ The desire of righteous people ends only in good,
    but the hope of wicked people ends only in fury.

²⁴ One person spends freely and yet grows richer,
    while another holds back what he owes and yet
        grows poorer.
²⁵     A generous person will be made rich,
        and whoever satisfies others will himself
            be satisfied.ᵃ
²⁶ People will curse the one who hoards grain,
    but a blessing will be upon the head of the one
        who sells it.

²⁷ Whoever eagerly seeks good searches for good will,
    but whoever looks for evil finds it.
²⁸ Whoever trusts his riches will fall,
    but righteous people will flourish like a green leaf.
²⁹ Whoever brings trouble upon his family inherits
        ⌊only⌋ wind,
    and that stubborn fool becomes a slave to the wise
        in heart.
³⁰ The fruit of a righteous person is a tree of life,
    and a winner of souls is wise.

---

ᵃ11:25 Or "and whoever gives someone a drink will also get a drink."

⁣³¹ If the righteous person is rewarded on earth,
how much more the wicked person and the sinner!

# 12

¹ Whoever loves discipline loves to learn,
but whoever hates correction is a dumb animal.
² A good person obtains favor from the Lord,
but the Lord condemns everyone who schemes.
³ A person cannot stand firm on a foundation
of wickedness,
and the roots of righteous people cannot be moved.
⁴ A wife with strength of character is the crown of
her husband,
but the wife who disgraces him is like bone cancer.

⁵ The thoughts of righteous people are fair.
The advice of wicked people is treacherous.
⁶ The words of wicked people are a deadly ambush,
but the words*ᵃ* of decent people rescue.
⁷ Overthrow wicked people, and they are no more,
but the families of righteous people continue to stand.

⁸ A person will be praised based on his insight,
but whoever has a twisted mind will be despised.
⁹ Better to be unimportant and have a slave
than to act important and have nothing to eat.
¹⁰ A righteous person cares ⌊even⌋ about the life of
his animals,
but the compassion of wicked people is ⌊nothing
but⌋ cruelty.
¹¹ Whoever works his land will have plenty to eat,
but the one who chases unrealistic dreams has no sense.
¹² A wicked person delights in setting a trap for ⌊other⌋
evil people,
but the roots of righteous people produce ⌊fruit⌋.
¹³ An evil person is trapped by his own sinful talk,
but a righteous person escapes from trouble.
¹⁴ One person enjoys good things as a result of his
speaking ability.
Another is paid according to what his hands have
accomplished.

¹⁵ A stubborn fool considers his own way the right one,
but a person who listens to advice is wise.

---

*ᵃ*12:6 Or "mouths."

¹⁶ When a stubborn fool is irritated, he shows it immediately,
   but a sensible person hides the insult.

¹⁷ A truthful witness speaks honestly,
   but a lying witness speaks deceitfully.
¹⁸ Careless words stab like a sword,
   but the words of wise people bring healing.
¹⁹ The word of truth lasts forever,
   but lies last only a moment.
²⁰ Deceit is in the heart of those who plan evil,
   but joy belongs to those who advise peace.

²¹ No ⌞lasting⌟ harm comes to a righteous person,
   but wicked people have lots of trouble.
²² Lips that lie are disgusting to the LORD,
   but honest people are his delight.
²³ A sensible person ⌞discreetly⌟ hides knowledge,
   but foolish minds preach stupidity.
²⁴ Hard-working hands gain control,
   but lazy hands do slave labor.
²⁵ A person's anxiety will weigh him down,
   but an encouraging word makes him joyful.
²⁶ A righteous person looks out for his neighbor,
   but the path of wicked people leads others astray.
²⁷ A lazy hunter does not catch his prey,
   but a hard-working person becomes wealthy.
²⁸ Everlasting life is on the way of righteousness.
   Eternal death is not along its path.

## A Wise Son Lives Righteously

**13** ¹ A wise son listens to his father's discipline,
   but a mocker does not listen to reprimands.
² A person eats well as a result of his speaking ability,
   but the appetite of treacherous people ⌞craves⌟ violence.
³ Whoever controls his mouth protects his own life.
   Whoever has a big mouth comes to ruin.
⁴ A lazy person craves food and there is none,
   but the appetite of hard-working people is satisfied.
⁵ A righteous person hates lying,
   but a wicked person behaves with shame and disgrace.
⁶ Righteousness protects the honest way of life,
   but wickedness ruins a sacrifice for sin.

⁷ One person pretends to be rich but has nothing.
   Another pretends to be poor but has great wealth.

⁸ A person's riches are the ransom for his life,
  but the poor person does not pay attention to threats.
⁹ The light of righteous people beams brightly,
  but the lamp of wicked people will be snuffed out.
¹⁰ Arrogance produces only quarreling,
  but those who take advice gain wisdom.
¹¹ Wealth ⌞gained⌟ through injustice dwindles away,
  but whoever gathers little by little has plenty.
¹² Delayed hope makes one sick at heart,
  but a fulfilled longing is a tree of life.
¹³ Whoever despises ⌞God's⌟ words will pay the penalty,
  but the one who fears ⌞God's⌟ commands will
    be rewarded.

¹⁴ The teachings of a wise person are a fountain of life
  to turn ⌞one⌟ away from the grasp of death.
¹⁵ Good sense brings favor,
  but the way of treacherous people is always the same.ᵃ
¹⁶ Any sensible person acts with knowledge,
  but a fool displays stupidity.
¹⁷ An undependable messenger gets into trouble,
  but a dependable envoy brings healing.
¹⁸ Poverty and shame come to a person who ignores
    discipline,
  but whoever pays attention to constructive criticism
    will be honored.

¹⁹ A fulfilled desire is sweet to the soul,
  but turning from evil is disgusting to fools.
²⁰ Whoever walks with wise people will be wise,
  but whoever associates with fools will suffer.
²¹ Disaster hunts down sinners,
  but righteous people are rewarded with good.
²² Good people leave an inheritance to their grandchildren,
  but the wealth of sinners is stored away for a
    righteous person.

²³ When poor people are able to plow, there is much food,
  but a person is swept away where there is no justice.
²⁴ Whoever refuses to spank his son hates him,
  but whoever loves his son disciplines him from early on.
²⁵ A righteous person eats to satisfy his appetite,
  but the bellies of wicked people are always empty.

---

ᵃ 13:15 Masoretic Text; Greek "is their disaster."

## Wise People Live Righteously

**14** ¹The wisest of women builds up her home,
   but a stupid one tears it down with her own hands.
² Whoever lives right fears the LORD,
   but a person who is devious in his ways despises him.
³ Because of a stubborn fool's words a whip is lifted against him,
   but wise people are protected by their speech.

⁴ Where there are no cattle, the feeding trough is empty,
   but the strength of an ox produces plentiful harvests.
⁵ A trustworthy witness does not lie,
   but a dishonest witness breathes lies.
⁶ A mocker searches for wisdom without finding it,
   but knowledge comes easily to a person who has understanding.

⁷ Stay away from a fool,
   because you will not receive knowledge from his lips.
⁸ The wisdom of a sensible person guides his way of life,
   but the stupidity of fools misleads them.
⁹ Stubborn fools make fun of guilt,
   but there is forgiveness among decent people.

¹⁰ The heart knows its own bitterness,
   and no stranger can share its joy.
¹¹ The houses of wicked people will be destroyed,
   but the tents of decent people will continue to expand.
¹² There is a way that seems right to a person,
   but eventually it ends in death.
¹³ Even while laughing a heart can ache,
   and joy can end in grief.

¹⁴ A heart that turns ⌊from God⌋ becomes bored with its own ways,
   but a good person is satisfied with God's ways.
¹⁵ A gullible person believes anything,
   but a sensible person watches his step.
¹⁶ A wise person is cautious and turns away from evil,
   but a fool is careless and overconfident.
¹⁷ A short-tempered person acts stupidly,
   and a person who plots evil is hated.
¹⁸ Gullible people are gifted with stupidity,
   but sensible people are crowned with knowledge.

¹⁹ Evil people will bow to good people.
　　Wicked people will bow at the gates of a righteous person.

²⁰ A poor person is hated even by his neighbor,
　　but a rich person is loved by many.
²¹ Whoever despises his neighbor sins,
　　but blessed is the one who is kind to humble people.

²² Don't those who stray plan what is evil,
　　　while those who are merciful and faithful plan what is good?
²³ 　In hard work there is always something gained,
　　but idle talk leads only to poverty.
²⁴ The crown of wise people is their wealth.
　　The stupidity of fools is just that—stupidity!
²⁵ 　An honest witness saves lives,
　　but one who tells lies is dangerous.
²⁶ In the fear of the LORD there is strong confidence,
　　and his children will have a place of refuge.
²⁷ The fear of the LORD is a fountain of life
　　to turn ⌞one⌟ away from the grasp of death.
²⁸ A large population is an honor for a king,
　　but without people a ruler is ruined.

²⁹ A person of great understanding is patient,
　　but a short temper is the height of stupidity.
³⁰ A tranquil heart makes for a healthy body,
　　but jealousy is ⌞like⌟ bone cancer.
³¹ Whoever oppresses the poor insults his maker,
　　but whoever is kind to the needy honors him.
³² A wicked person is thrown down by his own wrongdoing,
　　but even in his death a righteous person has a refuge.
³³ Wisdom finds rest in the heart of an understanding person.
　　Even fools recognize this.

## Wise Ways to Live

³⁴ Righteousness lifts up a nation,
　　but sin is a disgrace in any society.
³⁵ A king is delighted with a servant who acts wisely,
　　but he is furious with one who acts shamefully.

**15** ¹ A gentle answer turns away rage,
　　but a harsh word stirs up anger.
² The tongues of wise people give good expression to knowledge,
　　but the mouths of fools pour out a flood of stupidity.

³ The eyes of the Lord are everywhere.
  They watch evil people and good people.
⁴ A soothing tongue is a tree of life,
  but a deceitful tongue breaks the spirit.
⁵ A stubborn fool despises his father's discipline,
  but whoever appreciates a warning shows good sense.
⁶ Great treasure is in the house of a righteous person,
  but trouble comes along with the income of a
     wicked person.
⁷ The lips of wise people spread knowledge,
  but a foolish attitude does not.

⁸ A sacrifice brought by wicked people is disgusting
     to the Lord,
  but the prayers of decent people please him.
⁹ The way of wicked people is disgusting to the Lord,
  but he loves those who pursue righteousness.

¹⁰ Discipline is a terrible ⌊burden⌋ to anyone who leaves
     the ⌊right⌋ path.
   Anyone who hates a warning will die.
¹¹ If Sheol and Abaddon lie open in front of the Lord
   how much more the human heart!
¹² A mocker does not appreciate a warning.
   He will not go to wise people.

¹³ A joyful heart makes a cheerful face,
   but with a heartache comes depression.
¹⁴ The mind of a person who has understanding searches
      for knowledge,
   but the mouths of fools feed on stupidity.
¹⁵ Every day is a terrible day for a miserable person,
   but a cheerful heart has a continual feast.

¹⁶ Better to have a little with the fear of the Lord
      than great treasure and turmoil.
¹⁷ Better to have a dish of vegetables where there is love
      than juicy steaks where there is hate.

¹⁸ A hothead stirs up a fight,
   but one who holds his temper calms disputes.
¹⁹ The path of lazy people is like a thorny hedge,
   but the road of decent people is an ⌊open⌋ highway.

### A Wise Son Brings Blessings to Others

<sup>20</sup> A wise son makes his father happy,
>   but a foolish child despises its mother.

<sup>21</sup> Stupidity is fun to the one without much sense,
>   but a person who has understanding forges straight ahead.
<sup>22</sup> Without advice plans go wrong,
>   but with many advisers they succeed.
<sup>23</sup> A person is delighted to hear an answer from his own mouth,
>   and a timely word—oh, how good!

<sup>24</sup> The path of life for a wise person leads upward
>   in order to turn him away from hell below.
<sup>25</sup> The LORD tears down the house of an arrogant person,
>   but he protects the property of widows.
<sup>26</sup> The thoughts of evil people are disgusting to the LORD,
>   but pleasant words are pure to him.
<sup>27</sup> Whoever is greedy for unjust gain brings trouble to his family,
>   but whoever hates bribes will live.

<sup>28</sup> The heart of a righteous person carefully considers how to answer,
>   but the mouths of wicked people pour out a flood of evil things.
<sup>29</sup> The LORD is far from wicked people,
>   but he hears the prayers of righteous people.

<sup>30</sup> A twinkle in the eye delights the heart.
>   Good news refreshes the body.
<sup>31</sup> The ear that listens to a life-giving warning
>   will be at home among wise people.

<sup>32</sup> Whoever ignores discipline despises himself,
>   but the person who listens to warning gains understanding.
<sup>33</sup> The fear of the LORD is discipline ⌊leading to⌋ wisdom,
>   and humility comes before honor.

### Wisdom's Blessings Come from the LORD

**16** <sup>1</sup> The plans of the heart belong to humans,
>   but an answer on the tongue comes from the LORD.
<sup>2</sup> A person thinks all his ways are pure,

but the LORD weighs motives.
³ Entrust your efforts to the LORD,
 and your plans will succeed.
⁴ The LORD has made everything for his own purpose,
 even wicked people for the day of trouble.
⁵ Everyone with a conceited heart is disgusting to the LORD.
 Certainly, ⌊such a person⌋ will not go unpunished.

⁶ By mercy and faithfulness, peace is made with the LORD.
 By the fear of the LORD, evil is avoided.
⁷ When a person's ways are pleasing to the LORD,
 he makes even his enemies to be at peace with him.
⁸ Better a few ⌊possessions⌋ gained honestly
 than many gained through injustice.
⁹ A person may plan his own journey,
 but the LORD directs his steps.

¹⁰ When a divine revelation is on a king's lips,
 he cannot voice a wrong judgment.
¹¹ Honest balances and scales belong to the LORD.
 He made the entire set of weights.
¹² Wrongdoing is disgusting to kings
 because a throne is established through righteousness.
¹³ Kings are happy with honest words,
 and whoever speaks what is right is loved.
¹⁴ A king's anger announces death,
 but a wise man makes peace with him.
¹⁵ When the king is cheerful, there is life,
 and his favor is like a cloud bringing spring rain.

¹⁶ How much better it is to gain wisdom than gold,
 and the gaining of understanding should be chosen
  over silver.
¹⁷ The highway of decent people turns away from evil.
 Whoever watches his way preserves his own life.

¹⁸ Pride precedes a disaster,
 and an arrogant attitude precedes a fall.
¹⁹ Better to be humble with lowly people
 than to share stolen goods with arrogant people.

²⁰ Whoever gives attention to the LORD's word prospers,
 and blessed is the person who trusts the LORD.
²¹ The person who is truly wise is called understanding,
 and speaking sweetly helps others learn.

²² Understanding is a fountain of life to the one who has it,
    but stubborn fools punish themselves with
        their stupidity.
²³ A wise person's heart controls his speech,
    and what he says helps others learn.
²⁴ Pleasant words are ⌊like⌋ honey from a honeycomb—
    sweet to the spirit and healthy for the body.

## Words of Advice to a Wise Son

²⁵ There is a way that seems right to a person,
    but eventually it ends in death.
²⁶ A laborer's appetite works to his advantage,
    because his hunger drives him on.
²⁷ A worthless person plots trouble,
    and his speech is like a burning fire.
²⁸ A devious person spreads quarrels.
   A gossip separates the closest of friends.
²⁹ A violent person misleads his neighbor
    and leads him on a path that is not good.
³⁰ Whoever winks his eye is plotting something devious.
   Whoever bites his lips has finished his evil work.

³¹ Silver hair is a beautiful crown found in a righteous life.
³²   Better to get angry slowly than to be a hero.
   Better to be even-tempered than to capture a city.
³³ The dice are thrown,
    but the LORD determines every outcome.

**17** ¹Better a bite of dry bread ⌊eaten⌋ in peace
    than a family feast filled with strife.
² A wise slave will become master over a son who
    acts shamefully,
   and he will share the inheritance with the brothers.
³ The crucible is for refining silver and the smelter for gold,
    but the one who purifies hearts ⌊by fire⌋ is the LORD.
⁴ An evildoer pays attention to wicked lips.
   A liar opens his ears to a slanderous tongue.
⁵   Whoever makes fun of a poor person insults his maker.
    Whoever is happy ⌊to see someone's⌋ distress will not
        escape punishment.
⁶ Grandchildren are the crown of grandparents,
    and parents are the glory of their children.

## The Consequences of Being a Fool

⁷ Refined speech is not fitting for a godless fool.
    How much less does lying fit a noble person!

⁸ A bribe seems ⌐like⌐ a jewel to the one who gives it.ᵃ
　Wherever he turns, he prospers.
⁹ Whoever forgives an offense seeks love,
　but whoever keeps bringing up the issue separates the closest of friends.

¹⁰ A reprimand impresses a person who has understanding
　more than a hundred lashes impress a fool.
¹¹ A rebel looks for nothing but evil.
　Therefore, a cruel messenger will be sent ⌐to punish⌐ him.
¹² Better to meet a bear robbed of its cubs
　than a fool ⌐carried away⌐ with his stupidity.
¹³ Whoever pays back evil for good—
　evil will never leave his home.
¹⁴ Starting a quarrel is ⌐like⌐ opening a floodgate,
　so stop before the argument gets out of control.
¹⁵ Whoever approves of wicked people
　and whoever condemns righteous people
　　is disgusting to the LORD.

¹⁶ Why should a fool have money in his hand to buy wisdom
　when he doesn't have a mind to grasp anything?
¹⁷ A friend always loves,
　and a brother is born to share trouble.
¹⁸ A person without good sense closes a deal with a handshake.
　He guarantees a loan in the presence of his friend.
¹⁹ Whoever loves sin loves a quarrel.
　Whoever builds his city gate high invites destruction.
²⁰ 　A twisted mind never finds happiness,
　　and one with a devious tongue ⌐repeatedly⌐ gets into trouble.
²¹ The parent of a fool has grief,
　and the father of a godless fool has no joy.
²² A joyful heart is good medicine,
　but depression drains one's strength.
²³ A wicked person secretly accepts a bribe to corrupt the ways of justice.
²⁴ Wisdom is directly in front of an understanding person,
　but the eyes of a fool ⌐are looking around⌐ all over the world.

---

ᵃ17:8 Or "who receives it."

### How Fools Live

²⁵ A foolish son is a heartache to his father
  and bitter grief to his mother.

²⁶ To punish an innocent person is not good.
  To strike down noble people is not right.
²⁷   Whoever has knowledge controls his words,
    and a person who has understanding is
      even-tempered.

²⁸ Even a stubborn fool is thought to be wise if he keeps silent.
  He is considered intelligent if he keeps his lips sealed.

**18** ¹ A loner is out to get what he wants for himself.
  He opposes all sound reasoning.
² A fool does not find joy in understanding
  but only in expressing his own opinion.

³ When wickedness comes, contempt also comes,
    and insult comes along with disgrace.
⁴ The words of a person's mouth are like deep waters.
  The fountain of wisdom is an overflowing stream.
⁵ It is not good to be partial toward a wicked person,
    thereby depriving an innocent person of justice.

⁶ By talking, a fool gets into an argument,
    and his mouth invites a beating.
⁷ A fool's mouth is his ruin.
  His lips are a trap to his soul.
⁸ The words of a gossip are swallowed greedily,
    and they go down into a person's innermost being.

### How to Avoid Fools and Foolishness

⁹ Whoever is lazy in his work is related to a vandal.
¹⁰ The name of the LORD is a strong tower.
    A righteous person runs to it and is safe.
¹¹ A rich person's wealth is his strong city
  and is like a high wall in his imagination.

¹² Before destruction a person's heart is arrogant,
    but humility comes before honor.
¹³ Whoever gives an answer before he listens is stupid
    and shameful.
¹⁴ A person's spirit can endure sickness,
  but who can bear a broken spirit?

¹⁵ The mind of a person who has understanding acquires
    knowledge.
  The ears of wise people seek knowledge.
¹⁶ A gift opens doors for the one who gives it
    and brings him into the presence of great people.

¹⁷ The first to state his case seems right
    ⌊until⌋ his neighbor comes to cross-examine him.
¹⁸ Flipping a coin ends quarrels
    and settles ⌊issues⌋ between powerful people.
¹⁹ An offended brother is more ⌊resistant⌋ than a strong city,
    and disputes are like the locked gate of a castle tower.

²⁰ A person's speaking ability provides for his stomach.
  His talking provides him a living.
²¹ The tongue has the power of life and death,
    and those who love to talk will have to eat their
      own words.

²² Whoever finds a wife finds something good
    and has obtained favor from the LORD.
²³ A poor person is timid when begging,
    but a rich person is blunt when replying.
²⁴ Friends can destroy one another,ᵃ
    but a loving friend can stick closer than family.

# 19

¹ Better to be a poor person who lives innocently
    than to be one who talks dishonestly and is a fool.
² A person without knowledge is no good.
  A person in a hurry makes mistakes.
³ The stupidity of a person turns his life upside down,
    and his heart rages against the LORD.
⁴ Wealth adds many friends,
    but a poor person is separated from his friend.
⁵ A lying witness will not go unpunished.
  One who tells lies will not escape.
⁶  Many try to win the kindness of a generous person,
    and everyone is a friend to a person who gives gifts.
⁷  The entire family of a poor person hates him.
    How much more do his friends keep their distance
      from him!
    When he chases them with words, they are gone.

---

ᵃ18:24 Or "A person has friends as companions."

⁸ A person who gains sense loves himself.
  One who guards understanding finds something good.
⁹ A lying witness will not go unpunished.
  One who tells lies will die.

¹⁰ Luxury does not fit a fool,
   much less a slave ruling princes.
¹¹ A person with good sense is patient,
   and it is to his credit that he overlooks an offense.
¹² The rage of a king is like the roar of a lion,
   but his favor is like dew on the grass.

## A Foolish Son Brings Ruin to Others

¹³ A foolish son ruins his father,
   and a quarreling woman is like constantly
     dripping water.
¹⁴ Home and wealth are inherited from fathers,
   but a sensible wife comes from the Lord.

¹⁵ Laziness throws one into a deep sleep,
   and an idle person will go hungry.
¹⁶ Whoever obeys the law preserves his life,
   ⌊but⌋ whoever despises the Lord's ways will be
     put to death.

¹⁷ Whoever has pity on the poor lends to the Lord,
   and he will repay him for his good deed.
¹⁸ Discipline your son while there is still hope.
   Do not be the one responsible for his death.
¹⁹ A person who has a hot temper will pay for it.
   If you rescue him, you will have to do it over and over.
²⁰ Listen to advice and accept discipline
   so that you may be wise the rest of your life.
²¹ Many plans are in the human heart,
   but the advice of the Lord will endure.
²² Loyalty is desirable in a person,
   and it is better to be poor than a liar.

²³ The fear of the Lord leads to life,
   and such a person will rest easy without suffering harm.
²⁴ A lazy person puts his fork in his food.
   He doesn't even bring it back to his mouth.
²⁵ Strike a mocker, and a gullible person may learn a lesson.
   Warn an understanding person, and he will gain
     more knowledge.

## Foolproof Instructions

²⁶ A son who assaults his father ⌊and⌋ who drives away
   his mother
      brings shame and disgrace.
²⁷ If you stop listening to instruction, my son,
      you will stray from the words of knowledge.

²⁸ A worthless witness mocks justice,
      and the mouths of wicked people swallow up trouble.
²⁹ Punishments are set for mockers
      and beatings for the backs of fools.

**20** ¹ Wine ⌊makes people⌋ mock,
      liquor ⌊makes them⌋ noisy,
         and everyone under their influence is unwise.
² The rage of a king is like the roar of a lion.
      Whoever makes him angry forfeits his life.
³ Avoiding a quarrel is honorable.
      After all, any stubborn fool can start a fight.

⁴ A lazy person does not plow in the fall.[a]
      He looks for something in the harvest but finds nothing.
⁵ A motive in the human heart is like deep water,
      and a person who has understanding draws it out.
⁶ Many people declare themselves loyal,
      but who can find someone who is ⌊really⌋ trustworthy?
⁷ A righteous person lives on the basis of his integrity.
      Blessed are his children after he is gone.
⁸ A king who sits on his throne to judge sifts out every evil
      with his eyes.

⁹ Who can say,
      "I've made my heart pure.
      I'm cleansed from my sin"?
¹⁰ A double standard of weights and measures—
      both are disgusting to the LORD.
¹¹ Even a child makes himself known by his actions,
      whether his deeds are pure or right.
¹² The ear that hears,
      the eye that sees—
         the LORD made them both.
¹³ Do not love sleep or you will end up poor.
      Keep your eyes open, and you will have plenty to eat.

---

[a] 20:4 Fall was the start of the planting season in Palestine.

¹⁴ "Bad! Bad!" says the buyer.
   Then, as he goes away, he brags ⌞about his bargain⌟.
¹⁵ There are gold and plenty of jewels,
   but the lips of knowledge are precious gems.
¹⁶ Hold on to the garment of one who guarantees a
       stranger's loan,
   and hold responsible the person who makes a loan
       on behalf of a foreigner.
¹⁷ Food gained dishonestly tastes sweet to a person,
   but afterwards his mouth will be filled with gravel.
¹⁸ Plans are confirmed by getting advice,
   and with guidance one wages war.
¹⁹ Whoever goes around as a gossip tells secrets.
   Do not associate with a person whose mouth
       is always open.

²⁰ The lamp of the person who curses his father and mother
   will be snuffed out in total darkness.[a]
²¹ An inheritance quickly obtained in the beginning
   will never be blessed in the end.
²² Do not say, "I'll get even with you!"
   Wait for the Lord, and he will save you.
²³ A double standard of weights is disgusting to the Lord,
   and dishonest scales are no good.
²⁴ The Lord is the one who directs a person's steps.
   How then can anyone understand his own way?
²⁵ It is a trap for a person to say impulsively, "This is a
       holy offering!"
   and later to have second thoughts about those vows.

²⁶ A wise king scatters the wicked
   and then runs them over.
²⁷ A person's soul is the Lord's lamp.
   It searches his entire innermost being.
²⁸ Mercy and truth protect a king,
   and with mercy he maintains his throne.
²⁹ While the glory of young men is their strength,
   the splendor of older people is their silver hair.
³⁰ Brutal beatings cleanse away wickedness.
   Such beatings cleanse the innermost being.

---

[a] 20:20 Or "snuffed out as darkness approaches."

## The LORD Controls Wise and Foolish People

**21** ¹ The king's heart is like streams of water.
　　Both are under the LORD's control.
　　　He turns them in any direction he chooses.
² A person thinks everything he does is right,
　　but the LORD weighs hearts.
³ Doing what is right and fair
　　is more acceptable to the LORD than offering a sacrifice.
⁴ A conceited look and an arrogant attitude,
　　which are the lamps of wicked people, are sins.

⁵ The plans of a hard-working person lead to prosperity,
　　but everyone who is ⌜always⌝ in a hurry ends up
　　　in poverty.
⁶ Those who gather wealth by lying are wasting time.
　　They are looking for death.
⁷ The violence of wicked people will drag them away
　　since they refuse to do what is just.
⁸ The way of a guilty person is crooked,
　　but the behavior of those who are pure is moral.

⁹ Better to live on a corner of a roof
　　than to share a home with a quarreling woman.
¹⁰ The mind of a wicked person desires evil
　　and has no consideration for his neighbor.
¹¹ When a mocker is punished, a gullible person
　　　becomes wise,
　　and when a wise person is instructed, he gains
　　　knowledge.
¹² A righteous person wisely considers the house of a
　　　wicked person.
　　He throws wicked people into disasters.

¹³ Whoever shuts his ear to the cry of the poor will call and
　　　not be answered.
¹⁴ A gift ⌜given⌝ in secret calms anger,
　　and a secret bribe calms great fury.
¹⁵ When justice is done, a righteous person is delighted,
　　but troublemakers are terrified.
¹⁶ A person who wanders from the way of wise behavior
　　will rest in the assembly of the dead.

¹⁷ Whoever loves pleasure will become poor.
　Whoever loves wine and expensive food will not
　　　become rich.

¹⁸ Wicked people become a ransom for righteous people,
  and treacherous people will take the place of
    decent people.
¹⁹ Better to live in a desert
  than with a quarreling and angry woman.
²⁰ Costly treasure and wealth are in the home of a
    wise person,
  but a fool devours them.
²¹ Whoever pursues righteousness and mercy
  will find life, righteousness, and honor.

²² A wise man attacks a city of warriors
  and pulls down the strong defenses in which they trust.
²³ Whoever guards his mouth and his tongue keeps himself
    out of trouble.
²⁴ An arrogant, conceited person is called a mocker.
  His arrogance knows no limits.

²⁵ The desire of a lazy person will kill him
  because his hands refuse to work.
²⁶    All day long he feels greedy,
    but a righteous person gives and does not hold back.

²⁷ The sacrifice of wicked people is disgusting,
  especially if they bring it with evil intent.
²⁸ A lying witness will die,
  but a person who listens to advice will continue to speak.
²⁹ A wicked person puts up a bold front,
  but a decent person's way of life is his own security.

³⁰ No wisdom, no understanding, and no advice
  ⌊can stand up⌋ against the Lord.
³¹ The horse is made ready for the day of battle,
  but the victory belongs to the Lord.

# 22

¹ A good name is more desirable than great wealth.
  Respect is better than silver or gold.
² The rich and the poor have this in common:
  the Lord is the maker of them all.
³ Sensible people foresee trouble and hide ⌊from it⌋,
  but gullible people go ahead and suffer ⌊the
    consequence⌋.
⁴ On the heels of humility (the fear of the Lord)
  are riches and honor and life.

⁵ A devious person has thorns and traps ahead of him.
　　Whoever guards himself will stay far away from them.
⁶ Train a child in the way he should go,
　　and even when he is old he will not turn away from it.
⁷ A rich person rules poor people,
　　and a borrower is a slave to a lender.
⁸ Whoever plants injustice will harvest trouble,
　　and this weapon of his own fury will be destroyed.
⁹ Whoever is generous will be blessed
　　because he has shared his food with the poor.

¹⁰ Drive out a mocker, and conflict will leave.
　　Quarreling and abuse will stop.
¹¹ Whoever loves a pure heart and whoever speaks graciously
　　has a king as his friend.
¹² The LORD's eyes watch over knowledge,
　　but he overturns the words of a treacherous person.

¹³ A lazy person says,
　　"There's a lion outside!
　　　I'll be murdered in the streets!"
¹⁴ The mouth of an adulterous woman is a deep pit.
　　The one who is cursed by the LORD will fall into it.
¹⁵ Foolishness is firmly attached to a child's heart.
　　Spanking will remove it far from him.
¹⁶ Oppressing the poor for profit
　　⌊or⌋ giving to the rich
　　　certainly leads to poverty.

## Listen to My Advice

¹⁷ Open your ears, and hear the words of wise people,
　　and set your mind on the knowledge I give you.
¹⁸ 　　It is pleasant if you keep them in mind
　　　　⌊so that⌋ they will be on the tip of your tongue,
¹⁹ 　　so that your trust may be in the LORD.
　Today I have made them known to you, especially to you.
²⁰ Didn't I write to you previously with advice and knowledge
²¹ 　　in order to teach you the words of truth
　　　　so that you can give an accurate report to those who
　　　　　send you?

## Living with Your Neighbor

²² Do not rob the poor because they are poor
　　or trample on the rights of an oppressed person at the
　　　city gate,

²³ because the LORD will plead their case
   and will take the lives of those who rob them.
²⁴ Do not be a friend of one who has a bad temper,
   and never keep company with a hothead,
²⁵ or you will learn his ways
   and set a trap for yourself.

²⁶ Do not be ⌊found⌋ among those who make deals with
      a handshake,
   among those who guarantee other people's loans.
²⁷ If you have no money to pay back a loan,
   why should your bed be repossessed?
²⁸ Do not move an ancient boundary marker
   that your ancestors set in place.
²⁹ Do you see a person who is efficient in his work?
   He will serve kings.
   He will not serve unknown people.

# 23

¹ When you sit down to eat with a ruler,
   pay close attention to what is in front of you,
² and put a knife to your throat if you have a big appetite.
³ Do not crave his delicacies,
   because this is food that deceives you.

⁴ Do not wear yourself out getting rich.
   Be smart enough to stop.
⁵ Will you catch only a fleeting glimpse of wealth before
      it is gone?
   It makes wings for itself like an eagle flying into the sky.

⁶ Do not eat the food of one who is stingy,
   and do not crave his delicacies.
⁷ As he calculates the cost to himself, this is what
      he does:
   He tells you, "Eat and drink,"
   but he doesn't really mean it.
⁸ You will vomit the little bit you have eaten
   and spoil your pleasant conversation.

⁹ Do not talk directly to a fool,
   because he will despise the wisdom of your words.
¹⁰ Do not move an ancient boundary marker
   or enter fields that belong to orphans,
¹¹ because the one who is responsible for them is strong.
   He will plead their case against you.

## Learning from Your Father

¹² Live a more disciplined life,
   and listen carefully to words of knowledge.
¹³ Do not hesitate to discipline a child.
   If you spank him, he will not die.
¹⁴   Spank him yourself,
       and you will save his soul from hell.

¹⁵ My son,
   if you have a wise heart,
     my heart will rejoice as well.
¹⁶   My heart rejoices when you speak what is right.

¹⁷ Do not envy sinners in your heart.
   Instead, continue to fear the LORD.
¹⁸   There is indeed a future,
       and your hope will never be cut off.

¹⁹ My son,
   listen, be wise,
     and keep your mind going in the right direction.
²⁰ Do not associate with those who drink too much wine,
   with those who eat too much meat,
²¹   because both a drunk and a glutton will become poor.
       Drowsiness will dress a person in rags.

²² Listen to your father since you are his son,
     and do not despise your mother because she is old.
²³ Buy truth (and do not sell it),
     ⌞that is,⌟ buy wisdom, discipline, and understanding.
²⁴ A righteous person's father will certainly rejoice.
   Someone who has a wise son will enjoy him.
²⁵   May your father and your mother be glad.
     May she who gave birth to you rejoice.

²⁶ My son,
   give me your heart.
   Let your eyes find happiness in my ways.
²⁷   A prostitute is a deep pit.
     A loose woman is a narrow well.
²⁸   She is like a robber, lying in ambush.
     She spreads unfaithfulness throughout society.

²⁹ Who has trouble?
   Who has misery?

Who has quarrels?
Who has a complaint?
Who has wounds for no reason?
Who has bloodshot eyes?
<sup>30</sup> Those who drink glass after glass of wine
and mix it with everything.
<sup>31</sup> Do not look at wine
because it is red,
because it sparkles in the cup,
because it goes down smoothly.
<sup>32</sup> Later it bites like a snake
and strikes like a poisonous snake.
<sup>33</sup> Your eyes will see strange sights,
and your mouth will say embarrassing things.
<sup>34</sup> You will be like someone lying down in the middle
of the sea
or like someone lying down on top of a ship's mast,
saying,
<sup>35</sup> "They strike me, but I feel no pain.
They beat me, but I'm not aware of it.
Whenever I wake up, I'm going to look for
another drink."

# 24

<sup>1</sup> Do not envy evil people
or wish you were with them,
<sup>2</sup> because their minds plot violence,
and their lips talk trouble.

<sup>3</sup> With wisdom a house is built.
With understanding it is established.
<sup>4</sup> With knowledge its rooms are filled
with every kind of riches, both precious and pleasant.

<sup>5</sup> A strong man knows how to use his strength,
but a person with knowledge is even more powerful.
<sup>6</sup> After all, with the right strategy you can wage war,
and with many advisers there is victory.

<sup>7</sup> Matters of wisdom are beyond the grasp of a stubborn fool.
At the city gate he does not open his mouth.
<sup>8</sup> Whoever plans to do evil will be known as a schemer.
<sup>9</sup> Foolish scheming is sinful,
and a mocker is disgusting to everyone.

<sup>10</sup> If you faint in a crisis, you are weak.

¹¹ Rescue captives condemned to death,
   and spare those staggering toward their slaughter.
¹² When you say, "We didn't know this,"
   won't the one who weighs hearts take note of it?
   Won't the one who guards your soul know it?
   Won't he pay back people for what they do?

¹³ Eat honey, my son, because it is good.
   Honey that flows from the honeycomb tastes sweet.
¹⁴    The knowledge of wisdom is like that for your soul.
      If you find it, then there is a future,
         and your hope will never be cut off.

¹⁵ You wicked one,
   do not lie in ambush at the home of a righteous person.
   Do not rob his house.
¹⁶    A righteous person may fall seven times, but he gets
         up again.
      However, in a disaster wicked people fall.

¹⁷ Do not be happy when your enemy falls,
   and do not feel glad when he stumbles.
¹⁸    The LORD will see it, he won't like it,
      and he will turn his anger away from that person.

¹⁹ Do not get overly upset with evildoers.
   Do not envy wicked people,
²⁰    because an evil person has no future,
      and the lamps of wicked people will be snuffed out.

²¹ Fear the LORD, my son.
   Fear the king as well.
      Do not associate with those who always insist
         upon change,
²²    because disaster will come to them suddenly.
      Who knows what misery both may bring?

## Learning from Wise People
²³ These also are the sayings of wise people:

Showing partiality as a judge is not good.
²⁴    Whoever says to a guilty person, "You are innocent,"
         will be cursed by people and condemned by nations.
²⁵    But people will be pleased with those who convict a
         guilty person,

and a great blessing will come to them.
²⁶ Giving a straight answer is ⌊like⌋ a kiss on the lips.

²⁷ Prepare your work outside,
  and get things ready for yourself in the field.
    Afterwards, build your house.

²⁸ Do not testify against your neighbor without a reason,
  and do not deceive with your lips.
²⁹ Do not say,
  "I'll treat him as he treated me.
  I'll pay him back for what he has done to me."

³⁰ I passed by a lazy person's field,
  the vineyard belonging to a person without sense.
³¹ I saw that it was all overgrown with thistles.
  The ground was covered with weeds,
    and its stone fence was torn down.
³² When I observed ⌊this⌋, I took it to heart.
  I saw it and learned my lesson.
³³   "Just a little sleep,
    just a little slumber,
    just a little nap."
³⁴     Then your poverty will come like a drifter,
      and your need will come like a bandit.

# 25

¹These also are Solomon's proverbs that were copied by the men of King Hezekiah of Judah.

## Advice for Kings

² It is the glory of God to hide things
  but the glory of kings to investigate them.
³ ⌊Like⌋ the high heavens and the deep earth,
  so the mind of kings is unsearchable.
⁴ Take the impurities out of silver,
  and a vessel is ready for the silversmith to mold.
⁵ Take a wicked person away from the presence of a king,
  and justice will make his throne secure.

⁶ Do not brag about yourself in front of a king
  or stand in the spot that belongs to notable people,
⁷    because it is better to be told, "Come up here,"
    than to be put down in front of a prince
      whom your eyes have seen.

⁸ Do not be in a hurry to go to court.
　　What will you do in the end if your neighbor
　　　　disgraces you?
⁹ 　Present your argument to your neighbor,
　　　but do not reveal another person's secret.
¹⁰ 　　Otherwise, when he hears about it, he will
　　　　humiliate you,
　　　and his evil report about you will never
　　　　disappear.

¹¹ ⌊Like⌋ golden apples in silver settings,
　　⌊so⌋ is a word spoken at the right time.
¹² ⌊Like⌋ a gold ring and a fine gold ornament,
　　⌊so⌋ is constructive criticism to the ear of one who listens.
¹³ Like the coolness of snow on a harvest day,
　　⌊so⌋ is a trustworthy messenger to those who send him:
　　He refreshes his masters.
¹⁴ ⌊Like⌋ a dense fog or a dust storm,
　　⌊so⌋ is a person who brags about a gift that he does
　　　　not give.

¹⁵ With patience you can persuade a ruler,
　　and a soft tongue can break bones.
¹⁶ When you find honey, eat only as much as you need.
　　Otherwise, you will have too much and vomit.
¹⁷ Do not set foot in your neighbor's house too often.
　　Otherwise, he will see too much of you and hate you.

¹⁸ ⌊Like⌋ a club and a sword and a sharp arrow,
　　⌊so⌋ is a person who gives false testimony against
　　　　his neighbor.
¹⁹ ⌊Like⌋ a broken tooth and a lame foot,
　　⌊so⌋ is confidence in an unfaithful person in a ⌊time
　　　　of⌋ crisis.
²⁰ ⌊Like⌋ taking off a coat on a cold day
　　or pouring vinegar on baking soda,
　　　so is singing songs to one who has an evil heart.

²¹ If your enemy is hungry, give him some food to eat,
　　and if he is thirsty, give him some water to drink.
²² 　⌊In this way⌋ you will make him feel guilty and
　　　　ashamed,
　　　and the LORD will reward you.

²³ ⌊As⌋ the north wind brings rain,
   so a whispering tongue brings angry looks.
²⁴ Better to live on a corner of a roof
   than to share a home with a quarreling woman.
²⁵ ⌊Like⌋ cold water to a thirsty soul,
   so is good news from far away.
²⁶ ⌊Like⌋ a muddied spring and a polluted well,
   ⌊so⌋ is a righteous person who gives in to a wicked person.

²⁷ Eating too much honey is not good,
   and searching for honor is not honorable.

²⁸ ⌊Like⌋ a city broken into ⌊and⌋ left without a wall,
   ⌊so⌋ is a person who lacks self-control.

**All about Fools**

**26** ¹ Like snow in summertime and rain at harvest time,
   so honor is not right for a fool.
² Like a fluttering sparrow,
  like a darting swallow,
   so a hastily spoken curse does not come to rest.
³ A whip is for the horse,
   a bridle is for the donkey,
      and a rod is for the backs of fools.

⁴ Do not answer a fool with his own stupidity,
   or you will be like him.
⁵ Answer a fool with his own stupidity,
   or he will think he is wise.
⁶ Whoever uses a fool to send a message
   cuts off his own feet and brings violence upon himself.

⁷ ⌊Like⌋ a lame person's limp legs,
   so is a proverb in the mouths of fools.
⁸ Like tying a stone to a sling,
   so is giving honor to a fool.
⁹ ⌊Like⌋ a thorn stuck in a drunk's hand,
   so is a proverb in the mouths of fools.
¹⁰ ⌊Like⌋ many people who destroy everything,
   so is one who hires fools or drifters.
¹¹ As a dog goes back to its vomit,
   ⌊so⌋ a fool repeats his stupidity.
¹² Have you met a person who thinks he is wise?
   There is more hope for a fool than for him.

¹³ A lazy person says,
   "There's a ferocious lion out on the road!
   There's a lion loose in the streets!"
¹⁴ ⌊As⌋ a door turns on its hinges,
   so the lazy person turns on his bed.
¹⁵ A lazy person puts his fork in his food.
   He wears himself out as he brings it back to his mouth.
¹⁶ A lazy person thinks he is wiser than seven people who
      give a sensible answer.

¹⁷ ⌊Like⌋ grabbing a dog by the ears,
   ⌊so⌋ is a bystander who gets involved in someone
      else's quarrel.
¹⁸ Like a madman who shoots flaming arrows, arrows,
      and death,
¹⁹ so is the person who tricks his neighbor and says,
      "I was only joking!"

²⁰ Without wood a fire goes out,
   and without gossip a quarrel dies down.
²¹    ⌊As⌋ charcoal fuels burning coals and wood fuels fire,
      so a quarrelsome person fuels a dispute.
²²    The words of a gossip are swallowed greedily,
      and they go down into a person's innermost being.

²³ ⌊Like⌋ a clay pot covered with cheap silver,
   ⌊so⌋ is smooth talk that covers up an evil heart.
²⁴ Whoever is filled with hate disguises it with his speech,
   but inside he holds on to deceit.
²⁵    When he talks charmingly, do not trust him
         because of the seven disgusting things in his heart.
²⁶    His hatred is deceitfully hidden,
         but his wickedness will be revealed to the
            community.

²⁷ Whoever digs a pit will fall into it.
   Whoever rolls a stone will have it roll back on him.
²⁸    A lying tongue hates its victims,
      and a flattering mouth causes ruin.

## All about Life

**27** ¹Do not brag about tomorrow,
      because you do not know what another day
         may bring.

² Praise should come from another person
    and not from your own mouth,
  from a stranger and not from your own lips.
³ A stone is heavy, and sand weighs a lot,
    but annoyance caused by a stubborn fool is heavier
        than both.
⁴ Anger is cruel, and fury is overwhelming,
    but who can survive jealousy?

⁵ Open criticism is better than unexpressed love.
⁶ Wounds made by a friend are intended to help,
    but an enemy's kisses are too much to bear.
⁷ One who is full despises honey,
    but to one who is hungry,
        even bitter food tastes sweet.
⁸ Like a bird wandering from its nest,
    so is a husband wandering from his home.

⁹ Perfume and incense make the heart glad,
    but the sweetness of a friend is a fragrant forest.ᵃ
¹⁰ Do not abandon your friend or your father's friend.
  Do not go to a relative's home when you are in trouble.
    A neighbor living nearby is better than a relative far away.

¹¹ Be wise, my son, and make my heart glad
    so that I can answer anyone who criticizes me.
¹² Sensible people foresee trouble and hide.
  Gullible people go ahead ⌊and⌋ suffer.
¹³    Hold on to the garment of one who guarantees
            a stranger's loan,
        and hold responsible the person
            who makes a loan in behalf of a foreigner.
¹⁴ Whoever blesses his friend early in the morning with
        a loud voice—
  his blessing is considered a curse.

¹⁵ Constantly dripping water on a rainy day is like
        a quarreling woman.
¹⁶    Whoever can control her can control the wind.
        He can even pick up olive oil with his right hand.

¹⁷ ⌊As⌋ iron sharpens iron,
    so one person sharpens the wits of another.

---
ᵃ 27:9 Or "is sincere advice."

¹⁸ Whoever takes care of a fig tree can eat its fruit,
    and whoever protects his master is honored.
¹⁹ As a face is reflected in water,
    so a person is reflected by his heart.
²⁰ Hell and decay are never satisfied,
    and a person's eyes are never satisfied.

²¹ The crucible is for refining silver and the smelter for gold,
    but a person ⌊is tested⌋ by the praise given to him.
²² If you crush a stubborn fool in a mortar with a pestle
        along with grain,
    ⌊even then⌋ his stupidity will not leave him.
²³ Be fully aware of the condition of your flock,
    and pay close attention to your herds.
²⁴     Wealth is not forever.
        Nor does a crown last from one generation
            to the next.

²⁵ ⌊When⌋ grass is cut short, the tender growth appears,
    and vegetables are gathered on the hills.
²⁶     Lambs ⌊will provide⌋ you with clothing,
        and the money from the male goats will buy a field.
²⁷         There will be enough goat milk to feed you,
            to feed your family,
                and to keep your servant girls alive.

# 28

¹ A wicked person flees when no one is chasing him,
    but righteous people are as bold as lions.
² When a country is in revolt, it has many rulers,
    but only with a person who has understanding
        and knowledge
    will it last a long time.
³ A poor person who oppresses poorer people
    is like a driving rain that leaves no food.
⁴ Those who abandon ⌊God's⌋ teachings praise
        wicked people,
    but those who follow ⌊God's⌋ teachings oppose
        wicked people.
⁵ Evil people do not understand justice,
    but those who seek the Lord understand everything.
⁶ Better to be a poor person who has integrity
    than to be rich and double-dealing.

⁷ Whoever follows ⌊God's⌋ teachings is a wise son.
    Whoever associates with gluttons disgraces his father.

⁸ Whoever becomes wealthy through ⌞unfair⌟ loans
     and interest
  collects them for the one who is kind to the poor.
⁹ Surely the prayer of someone who refuses
     to listen to ⌞God's⌟ teachings is disgusting.
¹⁰ Whoever leads decent people into evil will fall into
     his own pit,
  but innocent people will inherit good things.

¹¹ A rich person is wise in his own eyes,
  but a poor person with understanding sees right
     through him.
¹² When righteous people triumph, there is great glory,
  but when wicked people rise, people hide themselves.
¹³ Whoever covers over his sins does not prosper.
  Whoever confesses and abandons them receives
     compassion.
¹⁴ Blessed is the one who is always fearful ⌞of sin⌟,
  but whoever is hard-hearted falls into disaster.

¹⁵ ⌞Like⌟ a roaring lion and a charging bear,
     ⌞so⌟ a wicked ruler is a threat to poor people.
¹⁶ A leader without understanding taxes ⌞his
     people⌟ heavily,
  but those who hate unjust gain will live longer.
¹⁷ A person burdened with the guilt of murder
     will be a fugitive down to his grave.
       No one will help him.

¹⁸ Whoever lives honestly will be safe.
  Whoever lives dishonestly will fall all at once.
¹⁹ Whoever works his land will have plenty to eat.
  Whoever chases unrealistic dreams will have plenty
     of nothing.

²⁰ A trustworthy person has many blessings,
  but anyone in a hurry to get rich will not escape
     punishment.
²¹ Showing partiality is not good,
  because some people will turn on you even for a piece
     of bread.
²² A stingy person is in a hurry to get rich,
  not realizing that poverty is about to overtake him.

²³ Whoever criticizes people will be more highly regarded
     in the future
   than the one who flatters with his tongue.
²⁴ The one who robs his father or his mother
   and says, "It isn't wrong!" is a companion to a vandal.
²⁵ A greedy person stirs up a fight,
   but whoever trusts the LORD prospers.

²⁶ Whoever trusts his own heart is a fool.
   Whoever walks in wisdom will survive.
²⁷ Whoever gives to the poor lacks nothing.
   Whoever ignores the poor receives many curses.

²⁸ When wicked people rise, people hide.
   When they die, righteous people increase.

# 29

¹ A person who will not bend after many warnings
   will suddenly be broken beyond repair.
² When righteous people increase, the people
     ⌞of God⌟ rejoice,
   but when a wicked person rules, everybody groans.
³ A person who loves wisdom makes his father happy,
   but one who pays prostitutes wastes his wealth.
⁴ By means of justice, a king builds up a country,
   but a person who confiscates religious contributions
     tears it down.

⁵ A person who flatters his neighbor
   is spreading a net for him to step into.
⁶ To an evil person sin is bait in a trap,
   but a righteous person runs away from it and is glad.
⁷ A righteous person knows the just cause of the poor.
   A wicked person does not understand this.
⁸ Mockers create an uproar in a city,
   but wise people turn away anger.

⁹ When a wise person goes to court with a stubborn fool,
   he may rant and rave,
     but there is no peace and quiet.
¹⁰ Bloodthirsty people hate an innocent person,
   but decent people seek ⌞to protect⌟ his life.
¹¹ A fool expresses all his emotions,
   but a wise person controls them.
¹² If a ruler pays attention to lies,
   all his servants become wicked.

¹³ A poor person and an oppressor have this in common:
   The Lord gives both of them sight.
¹⁴ When a king judges the poor with honesty,
   his throne will always be secure.

¹⁵ A spanking and a warning produce wisdom,
   but an undisciplined child disgraces his mother.
¹⁶ When wicked people increase, crime increases,
   but righteous people will witness their downfall.
¹⁷ Correct your son, and he will give you peace of mind.
   He will bring delight to your soul.

¹⁸ Without prophetic vision people run wild,
   but blessed are those who follow ⌊God's⌋ teachings.
¹⁹ A slave cannot be disciplined with words.
   He will not respond, though he may understand.
²⁰ Have you met a person who is quick to answer?
   There is more hope for a fool than for him.
²¹ Pamper a slave from childhood,
   and later he will be ungrateful.

²² An angry person stirs up a fight,
   and a hothead does much wrong.
²³ A person's pride will humiliate him,
   but a humble spirit gains honor.
²⁴ Whoever is a thief's partner hates his own life.
   He will not testify under oath.
²⁵ A person's fear sets a trap ⌊for him⌋,
   but one who trusts the Lord is safe.
²⁶ Many seek an audience with a ruler,
   but justice for humanity comes from the Lord.
²⁷ An unjust person is disgusting to righteous people.
   A decent person is disgusting to wicked people.

# 30
¹The words of Agur, son of Jakeh. Agur's prophetic revelation.

**Agur Speaks about God**
[TO GOD]
   This man's declaration:
      "I'm weary, O God.
      I'm weary and worn out, O God.
²     I'm more ⌊like⌋ a dumb animal than a human being.
      I don't ⌊even⌋ have human understanding.

³ I haven't learned wisdom.
  I don't have knowledge of the Holy One.ᵃ

[TO THE AUDIENCE]
⁴ "Who has gone up to heaven and come down?
  Who has gathered the wind in the palm of his hand?
  Who has wrapped water in a garment?
  Who has set up the earth from one end to the other?
  What is his name or the name of his son?
    Certainly, you must know!

⁵ "All of God's word has proven to be true.
    He is a shield to those who come to him for protection.
⁶ Do not add to his words,
    or he will reprimand you, and you will be found
      to be a liar.

## A Prayer
[TO GOD]
⁷ "I've asked you for two things.
  Don't keep them from me before I die:
⁸   Keep vanity and lies far away from me.
  Don't give me either poverty or riches.
    Feed me ⌊only⌋ the food I need,
⁹     or I may feel satisfied and deny you
        and say, 'Who is the LORD?'
      or I may become poor and steal
        and give the name of my God a bad reputation.

## Against Slander
[TO THE AUDIENCE]
¹⁰ "Do not slander a slave to his master.
    The slave will curse you,
      and you will be found guilty."

## Four Kinds of People
¹¹ A certain kind of person curses his father
    and does not bless his mother.
¹² A certain kind of person thinks he is pure
    but is not washed from his own feces.ᵇ
¹³ A certain kind of person looks around arrogantly
    and is conceited.

---
ᵃ 30:3 Or "holy ones."
ᵇ 30:12 Blunt Hebrew term but not considered vulgar.

¹⁴ A certain kind of person,
   whose teeth are like swords
      and whose jaws are ⌊like⌋ knives,
         devours oppressed people from the earth
            and people from among humanity.

### Human Bloodsuckers
¹⁵ The bloodsucking leech has two daughters—"Give!"
      and "Give!"

### Four Things That Are Never Satisfied
   Three things are never satisfied.
   Four never say, "Enough!":
¹⁶   the grave,
      a barren womb,
      a land that never gets enough water,
      a fire that does not say, "Enough!"

### Disrespectful Children—Their Punishment
¹⁷ The eye that makes fun of a father and hates to obey
         a mother
      will be plucked out by ravens in the valley and eaten
         by young vultures.

### Four Things of Intrigue
¹⁸ Three things are too amazing to me,
   even four that I cannot understand:
¹⁹   an eagle making its way through the sky,
      a snake making its way over a rock,
      a ship making its way through high seas,
      a man making his way with a virgin.

### About the Woman Who Commits Adultery
²⁰ This is the way of a woman who commits adultery:
   She eats, wipes her mouth,
      and says, "I haven't done anything wrong!"

### Four Things That Are Intolerable
²¹ Three things cause the earth to tremble,
   even four it cannot bear up under:
²²   a slave when he becomes king,
      a godless fool when he is filled with food,
²³   a woman who is unloved when she gets married,
      a maid when she replaces her mistress.

### Four Things That Are Small—Yet Smart and Strong

²⁴ Four things on earth are small,
yet they are very wise:
²⁵    Ants are not a strong species,
      yet they store their food in summer.
²⁶    Rock badgers are not a mighty species,
      yet they make their home in the rocks.
²⁷    Locusts have no king,
      yet all of them divide into swarms by instinct.
²⁸    A lizard you can hold in your hands,
      yet it can even be found in royal palaces.

### Four Things That Move with Dignity

²⁹ There are three things that walk with dignity,
even four that march with dignity:
³⁰    a lion, mightiest among animals, which turns away
        from nothing,
³¹    a strutting rooster,
   a male goat,
   a king at the head of his army.

### Keep Calm and Quiet

³² If you are such a godless fool as to honor yourself,
   or if you scheme,
      you had better put your hand over your mouth.
³³      As churning milk produces butter
        and punching a nose produces blood,
           so stirring up anger*ᵃ* produces a fight.

# 31

¹The sayings of King Lemuel, a prophetic revelation, used by his mother to discipline him.

### Advice to a Prince

² "What, my son?
What, son to whom I gave birth?
What, son of my prayers?
³    Don't give your strength to women
      or your power to those who ruin kings.

⁴ "It is not for kings, Lemuel.
It is not for kings to drink wine or for rulers to crave liquor.

---

*ᵃ 30:33* In Hebrew there is a play on words in verse 33 where the same verb is used to express all three actions.

⁵ Otherwise, they drink and forget what they have decreed
   and change the standard of justice for all oppressed people.
⁶ Give liquor to a person who is dying
   and wine to one who feels resentful.
⁷ Such a person drinks
   and forgets his poverty
   and does not remember his trouble anymore.

⁸ "Speak out for the one who cannot speak,
   for the rights of those who are doomed.
⁹ Speak out,
   judge fairly,
   and defend the rights of oppressed and needy people."

**A Poem in Hebrew Alphabetical Order**
¹⁰ "Who can find a wife with a strong character?
   She is worth far more than jewels.
¹¹ Her husband trusts her with ⌊all⌋ his heart,
   and he does not lack anything good.
¹² She helps him and never harms him all the days of her life.

¹³ "She seeks out wool and linen ⌊with care⌋
   and works with willing hands.
¹⁴ She is like merchant ships.
   She brings her food from far away.
¹⁵ She wakes up while it is still dark
   and gives food to her family
   and portions of food to her female slaves.

¹⁶ "She picks out a field and buys it.
   She plants a vineyard from the profits she has earned.
¹⁷ She puts on strength like a belt
   and goes to work with energy.
¹⁸ She sees that she is making a good profit.
   Her lamp burns late at night.

¹⁹ "She puts her hands on the distaff,
   and her fingers hold a spindle.
²⁰ She opens her hands to oppressed people
   and stretches them out to needy people.

²¹ She does not fear for her family when it snows
   because her whole family
      has a double layer of clothing.
²² She makes quilts for herself.
   Her clothes are ⌊made of⌋ linen and purple cloth.

²³ "Her husband is known at the city gates
   when he sits with the leaders of the land.

²⁴ "She makes linen garments and sells them
   and delivers belts to the merchants.
²⁵ She dresses with strength and nobility,
   and she smiles at the future.

²⁶ "She speaks with wisdom,
   and on her tongue there is tender instruction.
²⁷ She keeps a close eye on the conduct of her family,
   and she does not eat the bread of idleness.
²⁸ Her children and her husband
   stand up and bless her.
In addition, he sings her praises, by saying,
²⁹    'Many women have done noble work,
   but you have surpassed them all!'

³⁰ "Charm is deceptive, and beauty evaporates,
   ⌊but⌋ a woman who has the fear of the Lord should
      be praised.
³¹ Reward her for what she has done,
   and let her achievements praise her at the city gates."

# THE TRANSLATION PROCESS OF GOD'S WORD

GOD'S WORD® Translation (GW), produced by God's Word to the Nations Mission Society, fills a need that has remained unmet by English Bibles: to translate the Bible from the Hebrew, Aramaic, and Greek texts to their closest natural English equivalent.

GW consciously combines scholarly fidelity with natural English. Because it was translated by a committee of biblical scholars, GW is an accurate, trustworthy translation. Because of the involvement of English reviewers at every stage of the translation process, GW reads like contemporary literature.

## Closest Natural Equivalence

Like many Bibles published before it, GW has been translated directly from the Hebrew, Aramaic, and Greek texts. Unlike many Bibles before it, however, GW used a translation theory that reflects the advancement of translation theory and practice.

Closest natural equivalent (CNE) translation provides readers with a meaning in the target language that is equivalent to that of the source language. It seeks to express that meaning naturally, in a way that a native English speaker would speak or write. Finally, it expresses the meaning with a style that preserves many of the characteristics of the source text.

However, CNE does not attempt to make all books or passages function on the same level. The more difficult books of the Bible are translated to the same level of difficulty as the original languages. In addition, abstract concepts in Greek and Hebrew are translated into abstract concepts in English, and concrete concepts remain concrete in translation.

This translation theory is designed to avoid the awkwardness and inaccuracy associated with formal-equivalent translations, and to avoid the loss of meaning and oversimplification associated with functional-equivalent translations.

## Translation Process

The first consideration for the translators of GW was to find equivalent English ways of expressing the meaning of the original text, ensuring that the translation is faithful to the meaning of the source text. The next consideration was readability; the meaning is expressed in natural English by using common English punctuation, capitalization, grammar, and vocabulary. The third consideration was to choose the natural equivalent that most closely reflects the style of the Hebrew, Aramaic, or Greek text. At the core of this effort was a full-time translation team composed of biblical scholars who served as translators, English experts who actively reviewed English style with scholars at every stage of the translation process, and professional production personnel who oversaw the work. The basic process is outlined below.

### TRANSLATION

In the first step of this process, a biblical scholar used the principles of closest natural equivalence to produce an initial translation of one of the books of the Bible. During this time, the translator was able to consult with the rest of the translation team as needed.

### ENGLISH REVIEW

With the initial draft of a book completed, an expert in English style reviewed the translator's text and suggested changes. The English reviewer was concerned primarily with a natural English rendering.

Additionally, the English reviewer electronically searched the entire translation to ensure that any proposed revisions would not destroy the translation's consistency.

The translator and the English reviewer then worked together to produce a second draft that improved both the naturalness and accuracy of the translation. Upon completion of the second draft, the translator and English reviewer served as resources for the rest of the editorial process.

**PEER REVIEW**
After the English review process, the second draft was circulated to the other full-time translators and English reviewers for comments. This peer review stage allowed the other members of the translation team to compare the draft with their own work, offer suggestions for further improvement, and maintain consistency from one book of the Bible to another.

**TECHNICAL REVIEW**
The translator and English reviewer incorporated all appropriate suggestions offered in the peer review stage to produce a third draft. This draft was then submitted to a number of scholarly technical reviewers, who submitted written suggestions for improvements in the translation.

**REVIEW BY BOOK EDITORIAL COMMITTEE**
The next step in the process produced a fourth draft of the text. Taking into account the comments of the technical reviewers, a book editorial committee met to read and discuss the text for each book of the Bible.

The final step for the book editorial committee was reading the text aloud. Since the Bible is read not only silently but also aloud in worship and instructional settings, having a Bible translation that can be immediately grasped by the listener or reader and understood without the benefit of rereading was an important consideration.

**REVIEW BY CONSULTATIVE COMMITTEE**
After the members of the book editorial committee finished their work, they passed the fourth draft to the members of the consultative committee. This group of more than fifty Christian leaders from various denominations submitted comments and suggestions.

**REVIEW BY OLD TESTAMENT, NEW TESTAMENT, AND BIBLE EDITORIAL COMMITTEES**
The final editorial changes were made when all the books of the Bible had been completed or were near completion. Old and New Testament committees and, finally, a Bible editorial committee approved the accuracy and readability of the text.

## Features of *GOD'S WORD*
**LAYOUT**
The features that distinguish GW from other Bible translations are designed to aid readers. The most obvious of these is the open, single-column format. This invites readers into the page.

In prose, GW looks like other works of literature. It contains frequent paragraphing. Whenever a different speaker's words are quoted, a new paragraph begins. Lists, genealogies, and long prayers are formatted to help readers recognize the thought pattern of the text. The prose style of GW favors concise, clear sentences. While avoiding very long, complicated sentences, which characterize many English Bible translations, GW strives to vary the word arrangement in a natural way. Doing this enhances readability and brings the Scriptures to life.

The books that are primarily poetry in GW are instantly recognized by their format. The single-column format enables readers to recognize parallel thoughts in parallel lines of poetry. In a single-column, across-the-page layout, a variety of indentations are possible. The translators have used indentation to indicate the relationship of one line to others in the same context. This enables a person reading the Bible in English to appreciate the Bible's poetry in much the same way as a person reading the Bible in the original languages of Hebrew, Aramaic, or Greek.

**PUNCTUATION AND CAPITALIZATION**
In English, meaning is conveyed not only by words but also by punctuation. However, no punctuation existed in ancient Hebrew and Greek writing, and words were used where English would use punctuation marks. GW strives to use standard English punctuation wherever possible. At times this means that a punctuation mark or paragraph break represents the meaning that could only be expressed in words in Hebrew or Greek.

Italics are also used as they would be in other printed English texts: for foreign words or to indicate that a word is used as a word. (GW never uses italics to indicate emphasis.)

Wherever possible, GW has supplied information in headings or half-brackets to identify the speaker in quoted material. To minimize the confusion produced by quotations within quotations, quotation marks are used sparingly. For instance, they are not used after formulaic statements such as "This is what the Lord says: ..."

Contractions can fit comfortably into many English sentences. Certainly, "Don't you care that we're going to die" is more natural than, "Do you not care that we are going to die?" GW achieves a warmer style by using contractions where appropriate. But uncontracted words are used in contexts that require special emphasis.

GW capitalizes the first letter in proper nouns and sentences and all the letters in the word Lord when it represents *Yahweh*, the name of God in the Old Testament. Some religious literature chooses to capitalize pronouns that refer to the deity. As in the original languages, GW does not capitalize any pronouns (unless they begin sentences). In some cases scholars are uncertain whether pronouns in the original texts refer to God or someone else. In these cases the presence of capitalized pronouns would be misleading. Additionally, in some cases Hebrew or Greek pronouns are not ambiguous but an English pronoun would be. In those cases, GW uses the appropriate proper noun in its place.

**GENDER REFERENCES**
The Scriptures contain many passages that apply to all people. Therefore, GW strives to use gender-inclusive language in these passages so that all readers will apply these passages to themselves. For example, traditionally, Psalm 1:1 has been translated, "Blessed is the man who does not follow the advice of the wicked...." As a result, many readers will understand this verse to mean that only adult males, not women or children, can receive a blessing. In GW the first Psalm begins "Blessed is the person who does not follow the advice of the wicked...."

If a passage focuses upon an individual, however, GW does not use plural nouns and pronouns to avoid the gender-specific pronouns *he*, *him*, and *his*. In these cases the translators considered the text's focus upon an individual more important than an artificial use of plural pronouns. For example, Psalm 1:2 has been translated "Rather, he delights in the teachings of the Lord...." In addition, gender-accurate language is preserved in passages that apply specifically to men or specifically to women.

**WORD CHOICE**
The translation team chose words that were natural in context and that were as easily understood as possible without losing accuracy and faithfulness to the Hebrew and Greek texts of the Bible.

One of the challenges faced by the translators of GW was finding words that accurately communicate the meaning

# The Translation Process of God's Word

of important theological concepts in the Bible. Many of these concepts have traditionally been translated by words that no longer communicate to most English speakers. Examples of these theological terms include *covenant, grace, justify, repent,* and *righteousness*. While these words continue to be used by theologians and even by many Christians, the meanings that readers assign to them in everyday use do not equate to the meanings of the Hebrew or Greek words they are intended to translate. GW avoids using these terms and substitutes words that carry the same meaning in clear, natural English. In some cases traditional theological words are contained in footnotes the first time they occur in a chapter.

## Living, Active, and Life-Changing

While all these features make GW an accurate and readable Bible, the ultimate goal of the God's Word to the Nations Mission Society is to bring the readers of GW into a new or closer relationship with Jesus. The translation team and support staff of the Mission Society pray that your reading of GW makes the living, active, and life-changing words of our great God and Savior clear and meaningful.

For more details on the translation process and the unique features that enable GW to accurately and clearly communicate God's saving, life-changing message, visit godsword.org.

## Notes on the Text of *GOD'S WORD*

### BRACKETS

Proper names or foreign words whose meaning is significant for understanding a particular Bible passage are translated in brackets ( [ ] ) following the name or phrase. When reading aloud a bracketed word may be treated as "that is."

Half-brackets ( ⌊ ⌋ ) enclose words that the translation team supplied because the context contains meaning that is not explicitly stated in the original language.

### FOOTNOTES

Three types of footnotes are used in GW:

**1.** Explanatory footnotes clarify historical, cultural, and geographical details from the ancient world to make the text more understandable to modern readers. These footnotes also identify word play in Hebrew or Greek that would otherwise be lost to the English reader.

**2.** Alternate translation footnotes offer other plausible translations. They are introduced by the word *or*.

**3.** Textual footnotes are included wherever GW translates the meaning of some text other than the Masoretic Text printed in *Biblia Hebraica Stuttgartensia* or its footnotes (Old Testament) or the Greek text printed in the twenty-seventh edition of *Novum Testamentum Graece* (New Testament).

## Terms Used in Footnotes

- Aramaic: one of the languages of the Old Testament, related to Hebrew
- Dead Sea Scrolls: one or more of the Qumran manuscripts
- Egyptian: one or more of the ancient translations of the Bible into the ancient Egyptian or Ethiopic languages
- Greek: in the Old Testament: one or more of the ancient Greek translations of the Old Testament; in the New Testament: the Greek language, the language of the New Testament
- Hebrew: the primary language of the Old Testament
- Latin: one or more of the ancient Latin translations of the Bible
- Masoretic Text: the traditional Hebrew text of the Old Testament
- Manuscript: an ancient, handwritten copy of a text
- Samaritan Pentateuch: Samaritan Hebrew version of the first five books of the Bible
- Syriac: the ancient Syriac translation of the Bible
- Targum: one of the ancient Aramaic translations of the Old Testament

# ABOUT GOD'S WORD TO THE NATIONS

**Our Identity**
God's Word to the Nations is a mission society—a mission resource for God's people.

**Our Mission**
To identify and empower individuals to take GOD'S WORD® to the English-speaking people of the world, focusing especially upon those who do not know Jesus as their Savior.

**Our Promise to Our Partners**
Our Society will equip you with materials that may be used by the Holy Spirit to comfort and strengthen you and others, as well as promote and support a movement among God's people to be active participants in his mission *"to seek and to save people who are lost"* (Luke 19:10). To this end we promote the biblical outreach strategy: **Become a Seed Planter and Change Lives.**™

Our mission society managed and funded the translation of *GOD'S WORD.*® This translation is faithful to the original meaning of the Hebrew, Aramaic, and Greek languages through which God spoke to his people in earlier days and speaks in clear, natural English to his people today.

For more information, or to purchase a variety of *GOD'S WORD*® ministry resources:
- Write to us at God's Word to the Nations Mission Society, P.O. Box 400, Orange Park, FL 32067-0400
- Visit godsword.org
- Call us at 1-877-GODSWORD (1-877-463-7967)

**MISSION SOCIETY**

www.ingramcontent.com/pod-product-compliance
Lightning Source LLC
Chambersburg PA
CBHW070422010526
44118CB00014B/1864